University Press of Florida
Gainesville · Tallahassee · Tampa · Boca Raton
Pensacola · Orlando · Miami · Jacksonville · Ft. Myers

Wild Orchids of
Florida

with References to the Atlantic and Gulf Coastal Plains

Paul Martin Brown

Drawings by Stan Folsom

07 06 05 04 03 02   6 5 4 3 2 1

LIBRARY OF CONGRESS CATALOGING-IN-PUBLICATION DATA
Brown, Paul Martin.
Wild orchids of Florida : with references to the Atlantic and Gulf
Coastal Plains / Paul Martin Brown; drawings by Stan Folsom.
p. cm.
Includes bibliographical references and index (p.).
ISBN 0-8130-2438-2 (c. : alk. paper)
ISBN 0-8130-2439-0 (p. : alk. paper)
1. Orchids—Florida—Identification. 2. Orchids—Florida—
Pictorial works. I. Title.
QK495.O64 B73 2002
584'.4'09759—dc21   2001043716

The University Press of Florida is the scholarly publishing agency
for the State University System of Florida, comprising Florida A&M
University, Florida Atlantic University, Florida Gulf Coast University,
Florida International University, Florida State University, University
of Central Florida, University of Florida, University of North Florida,
University of South Florida, and University of West Florida.

University Press of Florida
15 Northwest 15th Street
Gainesville, FL 32611–2079
http://www.upf.com

To Carlyle A. Luer, M.D.

In appreciation for the endless hours he has spent searching for the native orchids of Florida. His inspiration and generosity in sharing those results have been the foundation of this field guide.

Contents

Foreword

The first floras restricted to orchids were written in Europe in the nineteenth century. The first of note in the Americas was *The Native Orchids of New England,* a popular treatise by Henry Baldwin, published in 1884. *Our Native Orchids,* a superb effort by William Hamilton Gibson, appeared posthumously in 1905. Others followed, but my favorite remains *Our Wild Orchids,* published in 1929 by Frank Morris and Edward A. Eames. By this time, the invention of "modern" transportation and photography had displaced the use of horses and pen and ink drawings. The trials and tribulations Morris and Eames faced in capturing each species on a photographic plate are described in fascinating detail.

Donovan S. Correll's scholarly masterpiece *Native Orchids of North America,* published in 1950, was my indispensable companion during the years of collecting material for *The Native Orchids of Florida.* I wore out two copies. The resulting work was published in 1972 by the New York Botanical Garden as the first flora to treat only the orchids of Florida. Advanced technologies had produced rapid, convenient travel and photography in full color, both of which added new dimensions to the work. About twelve years were required to find and photograph every species known to occur in the state at that time. Now, some thirty years later, Paul Martin Brown has prepared a sequel, *Wild Orchids of Florida,* in a mere three years of enthusiasm plus an astounding forty-five thousand miles of travel.

A native of Massachusetts and interested in botany since childhood, Paul earned his master's degree from the University of Massachusetts. He has taught for several institutions, specializing in contract courses and field trips. In 1995 he founded the North American Native Orchid Alliance and the quarterly *North American Native Orchid Journal.* In 1997 he and his partner Stan Folsom published *Wild Orchids of the Northeastern United States: A Field Guide,* a comprehensive treatise on the orchid flora of that area. The same year, they retired to Florida and immediately set to work to do the same for Florida. *Wild Orchids of Florida* is intended to be used as a field guide, but it is actually a lot more than that. This comprehensive work includes not only descriptions, drawings by Stan Folsom, numerous photographs in color, historical notes, and discussions of ecology and conservation, but also maps with distribution by county. Interesting and informative innovations such as checklists and discussion of geographical regions increase the value of the work. Not only are new discoveries included, but so are numerous nomenclatural changes that have been made since *The Native Orchids of Florida.* This new work brings present knowledge of the orchids of Florida to a high level of completeness for the beginning of the second millennium. It will be interesting to follow the progression during the years to come.

Carlyle A. Luer

Preface and Acknowledgments

The state of Florida has 118 species and varieties of orchids growing within its borders, of which 106 are truly native, five are naturalized, and seven are garden escapes, introduced plants, or waifs. In addition to the 118 species and varieties, six named hybrids and 26 color and growth forms are found. This constitutes about half of the known species to be found in the United States and Canada. In 1997, with the cooperation of the Herbarium, Florida Museum of Natural History at the University of Florida, I commenced the Florida Native Orchid Project with the goal of documenting the extant sites for all the orchids occurring in the state. During the first three years of the project I have been able to add 331 new county records, based either on existing herbarium specimens or on new collections. Four species and one variety were added to the existing list for Florida. I have also described from Florida four species new to science, revalidated two species and one variety, and described 19 new forms. All of this information is presented in this volume in a format that enables both experienced botanists and novice orchid enthusiasts to search for and identify all the orchids within Florida and the southeastern Atlantic and Gulf coastal plains.

Many new names have been applied to familiar species, much of this based upon recent DNA analyses as well as literature research. Do not be put off by all the new names; view these as an opportunity to be part of a better way of looking at our orchids. The project is by no means finished, but is at a point where a field guide is a practical answer to the needs of the orchid-loving public.

Much of this work could never have been undertaken without a great deal of help from many sources, beginning with Norris H. Williams, keeper of the Herbarium, Florida Museum of Natural History at the University of Florida, and his staff: Mark Whitten, senior biological scientist; Kent Perkins, manager of the Herbarium; Trudy Lindler, program assistant; and Robert L. Dressler and Wendy Zomlefer, research associates. Major financial support was gratefully received from George and Jeanne Schudel, who have been endlessly encouraging and supportive for the past three years, and from Peter and Elinor Burgher for work done specifically in south Florida. The following organizations contributed varying amounts as grants and speakers' fees to assist in the project:

Oak Run Garden Club, Ocala
Floral City Garden Club
Middleburg Garden Club
Brevard County Orchid Society
Greater Orlando Orchid Society
Greater Tampa Orchid Society
Jacksonville Orchid Society
Ocala Orchid Society
Orchid Society of the Palm Beaches
Sanibel–Captiva Orchid Society
Southwest Florida Orchid Society
Spring Hill Orchid Society
Tallahassee Orchid Society
Tropical Orchid Society, West Palm Beach
Massachusetts Orchid Society
New Hampshire Orchid Society
Twin States Orchid Society
Marion County Audubon Society
Paynes Prairie Chapter, Florida Native Plant Society
Hernando Chapter, Florida Native Plant Society
West Pasco Chapter, Florida Native Plant Society

The work could not have happened smoothly without the help, advice, and assistance of many others in locating plants, watching plants to minimize my traveling, gathering permissions, and doing some of the legwork. Those who have helped in a considerable way include Carlyle A. Luer, Chuck Sheviak, Paul M. Catling, Roger Hammer, Chuck McCartney, Cliff Pelchat, Russ Clusman, John Beckner, Rita and Jim Lassiter, Mark Larocque, Chuck Wilson, Marv Ragan, Larry Zettler, Jim Ackerman, Mark Nir, Brenda Herring, Dan Ward, John Tobe, Dave McDonald, John Hicks, Nancy Coile at the Division of Plant Industry, Linda Chafin at Florida Natural Areas Inventory, Pete Landry at the Rayonier Corporation, Guido Braem, Sid Taylor, Greg Allikas for information on *Spathoglottis plicata,* and especially Mr. and Mrs. Wayne Frizzell for permissions.

Visiting different herbaria always resulted in finding new and interesting records as well as allowing research for describing the new species. The following herbaria and their staffs all were of great help: Gustavo Romero, Orchid Herbarium of Oakes Ames; Emily Wood, Judy Warnament, and K. Gandhi, Harvard University Herbaria; G. F. Guala and Lynka Woodbury, Fairchild Tropical Garden; Dick Wunderlin and Bruce Hansen, University of South Florida; Loren Anderson, Florida State University; John Atwood and John Beckner, Marie Selby Tropical Garden; Dan Austin, Florida Atlantic University; Patricia Holmgren and Ken Cameron, New York Botanical Garden; and Dick Reimus, Tony Pernas, and Sonny Bass, Everglades National Park.

My forays into the many Florida state parks were greatly assisted by Mark Latch and his staff in Tallahassee as well as the park personnel, especially Mike Owen and Bobby Hattaway of Fakahatchee Strand State Preserve.

Stan Folsom, Philip Keenan, Larry Zettler, Chuck Sheviak, Hal Horwitz, Cliff Pelchat, and Ann Malmquist made many helpful suggestions and corrections to the manuscript. Ken Scott, director of the University Press of Florida, has expressed a personal interest in the project for many months.

Last but far from least is my partner Stan Folsom, who so laboriously did all the drawings for the field guide. His endless hours accompanying me in the field, often spotting plants that I had passed by, and then further hours chained to the drawing table, have resulted in illustrations that give a far clearer picture of the orchids than any photograph can do.

Abbreviations and Symbols

ca. = about or approximately, in reference to measurements

cf. = confer or compare to; comparable to the usage of "?" in front of a name, at the end of a name, and in between the generic name and specific epithet, indicating doubtful affinity with that species

cm = centimeter

f. = *filius;* son of, or the younger

m = meter

mm = millimeter

subsp. = subspecies

var. = variety

× between names or preceding a name denotes a hybrid or hybrid combination

* = naturalized

≠ = misapplied name

Publications

FNA = *Flora of North America*

NANOJ = *North American Native Orchid Journal*

1 ℘

Orchids and Florida

Searching for orchids in Florida has a long and colorful history. Because so much of the state was not developed until the 1920s, many wild areas have persisted. Outside Alaska, Florida has proportionately more protected land than any other state. The abundance of local, county, state, federal, and private lands that are protected assures the continuance of good orchid habitat.

The first significant publication about orchids in the state was *A Contribution to Our Knowledge of the Orchid Flora of Southern Florida* by Oakes Ames in 1904. This detailed the results of a two-year orchid expedition to southern Florida by A. A. Eaton. Working with J. K. Small and James Layne while he was there, Eaton documented several species new to science as well as species new for the United States. Although other authors—among them J. K. Small, A. W. Chapman, and D. S. Correll—included the orchids within their greater works, no publication was completely devoted to the orchids of Florida until Luer's monumental *Native Orchids of Florida* in 1972. However, given its design and size, that was not a field guide. It was curious that a readily usable field guide was never published for a state containing nearly half of the species of orchids to be found in the United States and Canada and for an area so popular with both professional and amateur botanists.

Some of the many names that are part of the orchid history of Florida include (in loosely chronological order) William Bartram, Mark Catesby,

John Torrey, A. P. Garber, Alvan Wentworth Chapman, George Nash, Allen Hiram Curtis, J. J. Carter, John Kunkel Small, C. A. Mosier, Oakes and Blanche Ames, Alva Augustus Eaton, James E. Layne, Fred Fuchs, Sr. and Jr., Donovan and Helen Correll, Walter Buswell, Roy Woodbury, Frank Craighead, George Avery, Ruben Sauleda, John Beckner, Carlyle A. Luer, Roger Hammer, and Chuck McCartney. The last four remain active in orchid research at the time of writing.

An Introduction to Orchids

Orchids hold a special fascination for many people, perhaps because of their perceived extreme beauty, rarity, and mystery. They constitute the largest family of flowering plants on earth with nearly 30,000 species. Although many have exceedingly beautiful flowers, many more have flowers that are small and green, barely 2 or 3 mm across. There is hardly any place on this planet, other than the Antarctic, that does not have some species of orchid growing within its native flora. Even the oases within the great deserts of the world harbor a few species. In the more northerly climes orchids can be found well within the Arctic Circle. At elevations above 5,000 meters and even within the highly developed urban areas of the globe, orchids persist. An acquaintance who was climbing a glacier in Switzerland found an orchid growing through the ice!

In Florida orchids abound in all 67 counties, and although the southern four counties hold more than half of the species in the state, some of the state's rarest species are to be found in the northern counties. Because of its geographic position in North America, Florida contains the southernmost locales for several northern species and the northernmost locales for many southern species. The state also has three species that are endemic, found nowhere else on earth. A graduate student was once asked by an examining professor how, if he were out walking, the professor would know that the subject of the student's thesis was an orchid (the thesis involved several species of *Spiranthes*, the ladies'-tresses). After a brief moment of thought, realizing that not all orchids are readily recognizable as such at first glance, the student replied, "You wouldn't." The professor signed off on the thesis. Because of the sheer number of orchids in the world, there is an enormous

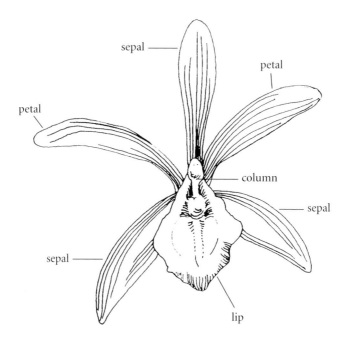

sepal ——

petal

petal

—— column

—— sepal

sepal ——

lip

amount of morphological diversity. Although orchids all possess a certain number of qualifying characters, their general morphology can be as variable as the imagination. But viewed closely under a lens, even the tiniest of orchids has the distinctive characters that make it an orchid.

Characteristics of the family Orchidaceae are quite simple, despite the diversity within the family. First, they are monocotyledons or monocots—a major class of the plant kingdom having a single emerging leaflike structure when the seed germinates (as opposed to dicotyledons or dicots, which have two leaflike structures when emerging). Grasses, lilies, and palms are also monocots. Second, orchids have three sepals, two petals, and a third petal that is modified into a lip. This prominent structure is actually a guide for the pollinator—a kind of landing platform that guides the insect toward the nectary, where it passes by the column and, in doing so, effects pollination. Again because of the size of the family, there are many agents of pollination, not just insects. Orchids have been documented to be pollinated by the usual bees, butterflies, wasps, and flies but also by hummingbirds, and a few are even assisted by rain in their pollination. Many orchids emit a fragrance at a particular time of day or night to attract a specific pollinator. Third, the stamens and pistil are united into a column, a structure unique to the orchids.

Because of the number of genera and species, occasionally there are what appear to be exceptions. A few genera have monoecious or dioecious flowers—male and female flowers on separate inflorescences or plants. In others the petals or lip may be so modified as to be barely recognizable. And in yet others, the flowers never open—they are cleistogamous and are self-fertilized in the bud. These exceptions aside, however, the vast majority of orchid flowers do look like orchids.

In Florida we have both terrestrial and epiphytic orchids. The terrestrials grow with their roots in the ground and take in water and nutrients through root hairs and/or swollen stems that are tuber-, bulb-, or corm-like. Epiphytic orchids live within trees, their roots covered with a hard coating called a velamen layer, and the tips are often green and soft so as to absorb water and nutrients. Many epiphytes also have pseudobulbs, swollen stems that act as water storage organs. On occasion a genus that is typically epiphytic, such as *Oncidium*, includes a species that meets all the criteria for an epiphyte except that it grows terrestrially, such as the **Florida oncidium**, *Oncidium floridanum*. Although this is not typical of any of Florida's orchids, there are also some species that are lithophytic—growing on rock strata.

In nature, all orchids consume fungi as a food (carbon) source, prompting seed germination and seedling development. At maturity when an orchid is capable of photosynthesis, these fungi continue to be consumed within orchid roots. Wild orchids are extremely difficult to transplant, apparently because the fungus association is disrupted. Consequently, transplanted orchids usually die within a few years of their removal from their native habitat. Surprisingly little is known about orchid mycorrhizal associations, but it is believed that all orchids grow with a fungal association. The various fungi, referred to as mycorrhiza, are present to aid in germination and growth of the orchids. Different fungi may function at different levels during the life of the orchid. Although difficult to see with the unaided eye, these fungi are most critical in the development of the plants.

The leaves of orchids are nearly as diverse as their flowers. As is characteristic of all monocots, orchid leaves have parallel veins. The leaves may be long and slender, grasslike, round and fat, hard and leathery, or soft and hairy—just about any configuration. If you are a novice, take a few moments to look through the photographs and drawings in this book to develop an eye for the floral parts that typify what an orchid is to help you when you go out to find them.

Which Orchid Is It?

A key is a written means for identification of an unknown species. The principles involved in keying are simple. The user needs to provide a positive or negative response to a series of questions. Couplets are used to ask these questions. Be sure to read both halves of the couplet before deciding on your answer. As you progress through the key, the illustrations should help you in making your determinations. Terms are illustrated within the key or can be found in the glossary at the back of the book.

Choose carefully the specimen you wish to identify. Look for a typical, average plant—neither the largest nor the smallest. This key is designed to be used without the need to pick any of the orchids. Only for a few similar species are detailed examinations necessary. The use of measurements has been kept to a minimum, as has the use of color. Be aware that white-flowered forms exist in many species, usually occurring with the typical color form.

Before you start to use the key, you should always mentally note the following:

1. placement and quantity of leaves—basal vs. cauline (see glossary); opposite vs. alternate; 1, 2, or more
2. placement and quantity of flowers—terminal vs. axillary; single vs. multiple
3. geographic location and habitat

Some concepts that will help in your understanding of the key are:

terrestrial—growing with the roots in the ground
epiphytic—growing with the roots in the air, usually on tree bark

lithophytic—growing on rocks

twig epiphyte—tiny plants typically found on the tips of twigs

pseudobulb—the swollen storage organ at the base of the leaves, primarily on epiphytes, occasionally on terrestrials

bract—a small, reduced leaf that usually is found on the flowering stem

Other terms are illustrated within the key or can be found in the glossary.

Using the Key

If you are using the key for the first time, start with a species with which you are familiar—perhaps the **Florida butterfly orchid**, *Encyclia tampensis*. Following is a trial run through the key to identify this orchid, starting with couplet 1 of the Key to the Genera:

    1a   plants terrestrial . . . 2

    1b   plants epiphytic . . . 47

which takes us to couplet 47

    47a   plants leafy . . . 48

    47b   plants leafless . . . 68

which takes us to couplet 48

    48a   plants with pseudobulbs . . . 49

    48b   plants without pseudobulbs . . . 61

which takes us to couplet 49

    49a   inflorescence terminal from the tip of the pseudobulb . . . 50

    49b   inflorescence arising from the base or side of the pseudobulb . . . 56

which takes us to couplet 50

    50a   inflorescence a spike, with numerous small flowers . . . 51

    50b   inflorescence otherwise . . . 52

which takes us to couplet 52

52a inflorescence pendant . . . *Macradenia*, p. 150
52b inflorescence erect or clustered . . . 53
which takes us to couplet 53

53a lip uppermost . . . *Prosthechea*, p. 221
53b lip lowermost . . . 54
which takes us to couplet 54

54a petal and sepals striped and barred with brown . . . *Prosthechea*, p. 221
54b petals and sepals otherwise . . . 55
which takes us to couplet 55

55a pseudobulbs flattened and wrinkled . . . *Laelia*, p. 316
55b pseudobulbs rounded . . . *Encyclia*, p. 85
     and we note that the pseudobulbs are rounded, not flattened,
which takes us to couplet 55b . . . *Encyclia*, p. 85

To continue to species, use the species key for *Encyclia* on page 85 and follow the same procedure.

The keys in this book are constructed for use in the field or with live specimens and are based on characters that are readily seen. They are not technical keys in the strictest sense but are simply intended to aid in field identification. Keys are not difficult if you take your time, learn the vocabulary, and hone your observational skills. As with any skills, the more you use them, the easier the exercise becomes.

Key to the Genera

Plants Terrestrial

1a plants terrestrial (rarely lithophytic) . . . 2
1b plants epiphytic . . . 47

2a leaves present . . . 3
2b leaves absent . . . 38

3a   leaves in a basal rosette . . . 31
3b   leaves variously arranged but not in a distinct basal rosette . . . 4

4a   flowering stem with leaves . . . 5
4b   flowering stem lacking leaves;
      bracts may be present . . . 22

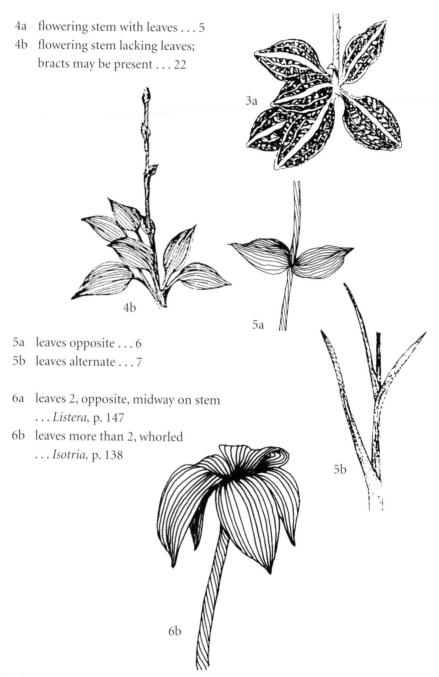

3a

4b

5a

5a   leaves opposite . . . 6
5b   leaves alternate . . . 7

6a   leaves 2, opposite, midway on stem
      . . . *Listera*, p. 147
6b   leaves more than 2, whorled
      . . . *Isotria*, p. 138

5b

6b

7a plants vinelike or appearing so . . . 8
7b plants otherwise . . . 9

8a plants a true vine with twining stems . . . *Vanilla*, p. 301
8b plant growth a scandent terrestrial appearing to be vinelike
    . . . *Tolumnia*, p. 277

9a inflorescence a few-flowered (1–12) spike or raceme . . . 10
9b inflorescence a many-flowered spike or raceme . . . 15

10a plants with 1 stem leaf and 1 leafy floral bract . . . 11
10b plants with leaves otherwise . . . 12

11a petals clasping lip . . . *Cleistes*, p. 53
11b petals spreading and distinct from lip . . . *Pogonia*, p. 207

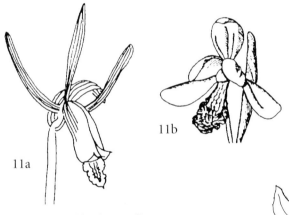

12a leaves grasslike, linear; lip uppermost
     (nonresupinate) . . . *Calopogon*, p. 39
12b leaves otherwise . . . 13

13a leaves small and oval or scalelike . . . *Triphora*, p. 287
13b leaves otherwise . . . *Bletilla*, p. 314

Inflorescence a Many-Flowered Spike or Raceme

14a   leaves 1 or 2 . . . 15
14b   leaves more than 2 . . . 16

15a   leaves forming a sheath at the base with spike arising from within
        the sheath . . . *Govenia,* p. 115
15b   leaves otherwise . . . *Malaxis,* p. 153

16a   stem leafy; leaves scattered along the stem, often decreasing
        in size . . . 17
16b   leaves primarily clustered near the base of
        the flowering stem . . . 20

17a   lip entire (margin may be fringed or erose) . . . 18
17b   lip divided . . . *Habenaria,* p. 119

18a   lip with a distinct yellow portion . . . *Zeuxine,* p. 310
18b   lip otherwise . . . 19

19a   individual flowers less than 5 mm . . . *Platythelys,* p. 199
19b   individual flowers greater than 5 mm . . . *Platanthera,* p. 179

20a   flowers in a dense cluster or raceme . . . *Tropidia,* p. 298
20b   flowers arranged in a spike . . . 21

21a   flowers purple . . . *Liparis,* p. 143
21b   flowers white or cream . . . *Spiranthes,* p. 240

Flowering Stem Lacking Leaves, Although Bracts May Be Evident

22a   leaves with prominent white markings . . . 23
22b   leaves entirely green . . . 24

23a   leaves ovate, spattered with white markings
        . . . *Pelexia,* p. 172
23b   leaves oblong, with white horizontal bands and markings
        Oeceoclades, p. 166

24a   lip with a fringed margin, leaves long-petioled
     ... *Eltroplectris*, p. 82

24b   lip without a fringed margin ... 25

24a

25a   plants with pseudobulbs ... 26

25b   plants without pseudobulbs, although surficial corms
     may be present ... 27

26a   flowers yellow in branching sprays ... *Oncidium*, p. 169

26b   flowers white, bronze, and pink in a terminal raceme
     ... *Phaius*, p. 175

27a   inflorescence a panicle, or branched raceme ... 28

27b   inflorescence a spike ... 30

28a   plants leafy, tall, usually over 50 cm ... 29

28b   plants short with a single leaf, flowers usually cleistogamous
     ... *Basiphyllaea*, p. 26

29a   lip with prominent ridges, flowers occasionally cleistogamous
     ... *Bletia*, p. 31

29b   lip strongly 3-lobed with a narrow isthmus
     ... *Spathoglottis*, p. 238

30a lip with a prominent crest . . . *Eulophia*, p. 108
30b lip lacking a crest . . . *Pteroglossaspis*, p. 228

Leaves in a Basal Rosette

31a flowers white or cream . . . 33
31b flowers colored otherwise (although the lip may be white) . . . 32

32a lip white . . . *Cyclopogon*, p. 67
32b lip copper colored . . . *Mesadenus*, p. 164

33a inflorescence a spike or raceme with individual white flowers held
     horizontally to the axis . . . *Ponthieva*, p. 213
33b inflorescence a dense spike of small flowers . . . 34

34a leaves of basal rosette marked with white
     reticulations . . . *Goodyera*, p. 112
34b leaves unmarked . . . 35

35a

35a margin of lip with a delicate fringe . . . *Spiranthes*, p. 240
35b margin of lip otherwise . . . 36

36a lip lowermost . . . *Beloglottis*, p. 28
36b lip uppermost . . . 37

37a lip spotted with green . . . *Cranichis*, p. 64
37b lip unspotted . . . *Prescottia*, p. 218

Leaves Absent

38a chlorophyll present; stem, bracts, or ovaries green . . . 39
38b chlorophyll lacking; green not present . . . 46

39a flowers in a raceme or cluster or few-flowered (1–12) spike . . . 40
39b flowers in a many-flowered spike . . . 45

40a plants vining . . . *Vanilla*, p. 301
40b plants not vining . . . 41

41a   flowers asymmetrical, with a long tapered spur
      . . . *Tipularia,* p. 273

41b   flowers otherwise . . . 42

42a   flower white, nonresupinate . . . *Ponthieva,* p. 213
42b   flowers other than white, usually shades of pink and green . . . 43

43a   flowers in a cyme, greenish white . . . *Triphora,* p. 287
43b   flowers in a raceme . . . 44

44a   flowers cleistogamous . . . *Basiphyllaea,* p. 26
44b   flowers fully open . . . *Galeandra,* p. 110

45a   flowers red, green, or gold, over 1.5 cm long
      . . . *Sacoila,* p. 231
45b   flowers white or cream, less than 1.5 cm long
      . . . *Spiranthes,* p. 240

46a   flowers less than 5 mm, often cleistogamous
      . . . *Corallorhiza,* p. 59
46b   flowers greater than 5 mm . . . *Hexalectris,* p. 133

Plants Epiphytic

47a   plants leafy . . . 48
47b   plants leafless . . . 68

48a   plants with pseudobulbs . . . 49
48b   plants without pseudobulbs . . . 61

Plants with Pseudobulbs

49a   inflorescence terminal from the
      tip of the pseudobulb . . . 50
49b   inflorescence arising from the base
      or side of the pseudobulb . . . 56

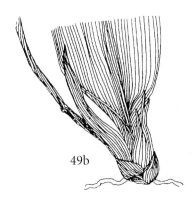

50a inflorescence a spike with numerous small flowers . . . 51
50b inflorescence otherwise . . . 52

51a inflorescence a spike (usually multiple spikes) of small yellow helmet-shaped flowers . . . *Polystachya*, p. 210
51b inflorescence a slender pendant spike . . . *Bulbophyllum*, p. 36

52a inflorescence pendant . . . *Macradenia*, p. 150
52b inflorescence erect or clustered . . . 53

53a lip uppermost . . . *Prosthechea*, p. 221
53b lip lowermost . . . 54

54a petal and sepals striped and barred with brown . . . *Prosthechea*, p. 221
54b petals and sepals otherwise . . . 55

55a pseudobulbs flattened and wrinkled . . . *Laelia*, p. 316
55b pseudobulbs rounded . . . *Encyclia*, p. 85

Inflorescence Arising from Base or Side of Pseudobulb

56a flowers spiderlike with long, slender sepals . . . *Brassia*, p. 34
56b flowers otherwise . . . 57

57a pseudobulb hidden within the bases of the sheathing leaves . . . 58
57b pseudobulb otherwise . . . 60

58a flowers single or in dense clusters . . . *Maxillaria*, p. 159
58b flowers in a panicle, or branched raceme . . . 59

59a plants scandent and often vinelike . . . *Tolumnia*, p. 277
59b plant a twig epiphyte . . . *Ionopsis*, p. 136

60a   inflorescence from previous year's growth, new growth leafy
       . . . *Cyrtopodium,* p. 73
60b   plants with mature leaves at time of flowering
       . . . *Trichocentrum,* p. 281

Plants without Pseudobulbs

61a   inflorescence a many-flowered spike . . . 62
61b   inflorescence a few- to many-flowered cluster or raceme . . . 63

62a   leaves shorter than 5 cm, flowers crimson
       . . . *Lepanthopsis,* p. 140
62b   leaves 5 cm, usually 15 cm or more, flowers silvery white
       . . . *Pleurothallis,* p. 204

63a   plant vining . . . 64
63b   growth habit otherwise . . . 65

64a   plant a true vine . . . *Vanilla,* p. 301
64b   growth a scandent terrestrial with fanlike leaves at intervals,
       appearing to be climbing (pseudobulbs minute and hidden
       within the sheathing bases of the leaves) . . . *Tolumnia,* p. 277

65a   flowers individual or in a dense cluster hidden at the leaf bases
       (pseudobulbs minute and hidden within the sheathing bases of
       the leaves) . . . *Maxillaria,* p. 159
65b   inflorescence a few- to many-flowered umbel or raceme . . . 66

66a   plant a twig epiphyte (pseudobulbs minute and hidden within
       the sheathing bases of the leaves) . . . *Ionopsis,* p. 136
66b   plant otherwise . . . 67

67a   growth a scandent terrestrial appearing to be epiphytic
       (pseudobulbs minute and hidden within the sheathing bases of
       the leaves) . . . *Tolumnia,* p. 277
67b   growth otherwise . . . *Epidendrum,* p. 91

Plants Leafless

    68a   plant vining ... *Vanilla*, p. 301
    68b   plant habit otherwise ... 69

    69a   plants with large, slender pseudobulbs ... *Cyrtopodium*, p. 73
    69b   plants a mass of leafless roots clearly adherent to the host ... 70

    70a   roots flattened, flowers apricot, in a dense spike
           ... *Campylocentrum*, p. 50
    70b   roots terete ... 71

    71a   roots with white dashes, flowers white, large, spectacular
           (froglike) ... *Dendrophylax*, p. 79
    71b   roots minute, lacking white dashes, flowers yellow, very small,
           old fruit usually persistent and hanging like bells
           ... *Harrisella*, p. 130

Some Important Notes about Plant Names

The Latin names used consist of a genus name and a species epithet. The genus is the broader group to which the plant belongs, and the species is the specific plant being treated. After the two Latin names comes the name of the person or people who described the plant. An example would be the **spurred neottia**, *Eltroplectris calcarata* (Swartz) Garay & Sweet. Swartz was the first person to name this species, therefore his name comes first; because he assigned the plant to a different genus, his name is in parentheses. Garay & Sweet transferred the species to the genus *Eltroplectris* and therefore their names follow.

Other ranks may occur, such as subspecies, variety, and forma. Subspecies and variety usually designate a variation that has a significant difference from the species and a definite geographic range—as in *Prosthechea cochleata* (Linnaeus) W. E. Higgins var. *triandra* (Ames) W. E. Higgins. The variety *triandra* has three stamens instead of two and is self-fertilizing. It also occurs primarily in Florida, and perhaps in Cuba, hence it is a variety. Varieties and subspecies should always breed true. The matter of whether a plant is a variety or subspecies and which term is better used is often open to disagreement. Color variations that occur throughout the range of the species are best treated as forma, as in *Pteroglossaspis ecristata* (Fernald) Rolfe forma *flava* P. M. Brown—the yellow-flowered form. They can, and do, occur randomly and rarely breed true. Only forma known from Florida are listed. Literature references and synonyms for each species are given in part 3.

Common Names

Common names are never as consistent throughout the range of the plants as we would like. The most frequently used common names are listed here, as are some regional names. On the question of whether to use *orchid* or *orchis*—for common names either may be used, but traditionally *orchis* has been applied to certain genera, and that tradition is maintained here.

Size

Average height of the plants, floral size, and number of flowers are given, with extremes in parentheses. The relative scale within each line drawing is for an average plant and is based upon the flower size.

Color

Color of the flowers as it normally occurs is given. Remember to check to see if color variants such as white-flowered forms occur. In some genera the overall color of the petals and sepals—the perianth—is given and the lip color follows.

Flowering Periods

Flowering periods are not as easy to isolate in Florida as they are in many other states. Although seasonal weather patterns greatly affect flowering times for most species, there are also those that flower sporadically year-round. Autumn flowering species tend to flower earlier in the north and later southward. A good example would be the **fragrant ladies'-tresses**, *Spiranthes odorata*, which flowers regularly in October in north Florida but in southern Florida is at its best in late November and even into January. The **common grass-pink**, *Calopogon tuberosus*, a spring flowering species, on the other hand, starts in the Everglades of south Florida in late December and early January but does not flower until May in north Florida. Flowering periods given for each species are intended to indicate the time of year that is most typical. For nearly all of Florida's orchids, it would not be surprising to find extreme records at both ends of the flowering times given.

Range Maps

Solid circles represent a vouchered, or verifiable, record for the species within a given county. These records are normally specimens housed in herbaria at botanical gardens, colleges, and universities. On rare occasions a verifiable report is allowed. This would be a photograph from a reliable source, documented with date and place. Literature reports (L) are just that: a report in any one of a number of publications that cannot be backed up by either a specimen or verifiable record. On the range maps there is no attempt to differentiate between extant and extirpated populations, nor are there indications of how many populations are known from a given county. An open circle (o) indicates a documented introduced population. For more detail on the evolution of Florida counties, please refer to Plant Records and County Lines in part 3.

2 ❧

Wild Orchids of Florida:
Native and Naturalized

The arrangement of native and naturalized genera and species that follows is alphabetical to make locating a given species easier. Following these on page 313 are those genera and species that are considered to be non-native—introduced, escaped, or waifs. Each genus and species treated follows a similar arrangement. General information is given for each genus and is followed by a full page on each species. That page contains both all of the written information as well as a line drawing and distribution map. On the facing page are several color photographs that illustrate most aspects of the species including the various color and growth forms.

All the references for individual species are to be found in Recent Literature References for New Taxa, Combinations, and Additions to the Orchid Flora of Florida. The Selected Bibliography contains additional references of a more general and historical nature. Users should always consult the Recent References section first as it is arranged by species.

❧ Native and Naturalized Species

Basiphyllaea

Basiphyllaea is a small genus of three species found in the Bahamas and West Indies as well as Florida. The diminutive plants are often exceedingly difficult to find as they hide among the grasses in the coral-rock pinelands. We have only one species in Florida, **Carter's orchid**, *B. corallicola,* and it is extremely rare and local in the southern counties. The genus is closely related to *Bletia.*

Basiphyllaea corallicola (Small) Ames

Carter's orchid

Florida; the Bahamas, West Indies
Florida: known only from Miami-Dade and Monroe Counties, where it has rarely been seen; endangered
Plant: terrestrial, 10–40 cm tall
Leaves: 1 or 2, 12 × 5 cm
Flowers: 3–10; incompletely opening, sepals and petals yellow-green; lip suffused with crimson; individual flower size 0.8–1 cm
Habitat: coral-rock pinelands
Flowering period: late September–November
This is one of the most elusive orchids to be found in Florida. It is confined to the rocky pinelands, and the tiny, partially opened flowers combined with a slender habit make detection very difficult. Only a few additional sightings of this species have been made since its discovery in 1903. To complicate things further, plants do not appear with regularity every year.

Beloglottis

This is the first, within this field guide, of several genera that are segregates from the genus *Spiranthes*. Many of these spiranthoid orchids have a similar growth habit with a small rosette of ovate leaves and a slender spike of tiny flowers, often held on one side of the stem. *Beloglottis,* in the strictest sense, has seven species in the neosubtropics and neotropics. We have only one, the **Costa Rican ladies'-tresses**, *B. costaricensis,* in Florida.

Beloglottis costaricensis (Reichenbach *f.*) Schlechter

Costa Rican ladies'-tresses

Florida; the Bahamas, West Indies
Florida: known only from scattered sites in Everglades National Park in Miami-Dade County; endangered
Plant: terrestrial, spike to 30 cm tall
Leaves: 4–5 in a basal rosette 3–8 × 1–3 cm, withering at flowering time
Flowers: 8–40; white with green striping; individual flower size 3–4 mm
Habitat: hardwood hammocks
Flowering period: late January–April
A recent addition (1953) to the orchid flora of both the United States and Florida, this diminutive spiranthoid species appears to be spreading itself around within Long Pine Key in Everglades National Park. In 2000, several small colonies were located. The distinctive white and green striped flowers make identification easy for those fortunate enough to encounter plants in flower. The basal rosettes, however, are very similar to those of other spiranthoid species.

Bletia

A showy genus of about 40 neotropical species, *Bletia* is widespread in south Florida, occurring in almost every country in the region. We have only one native, the **pine-pink**, *Bletia purpurea,* in Florida, but two other species have been found as escapes or waifs (for details, see Introduced, Escaped, and Waifs at the end of part 2). Occasionally orchid enthusiasts mistake *Bletia* for *Calopogon* or vice versa. The difference is easy to see as in *Calopogon* the lip is uppermost, or nonresupinate, and in *Bletia* it is lowermost, or resupinate. *Bletia* also branches freely, which *Calopogon* does not normally do.

1a   lip clearly longer than the undulate petals
      . . . *Bletia patula,* p. 314
1b   lip equal to or shorter than the nonundulate petals . . . 2
2a   lip with 5 yellow crests; only the 3 central ones extending onto
      the midlobe . . . *Bletia florida,* p. 313
2b   lip with 5–7 yellow crests, all extending onto the midlobe
      . . . *Bletia purpurea,* p. 32

Bletia purpurea (Lamark) de Candolle

pine-pink

Florida; West Indies, Central America, northern South America
    forma *alba* (Ariza-Julia & J. Jiménez Alm.) P. M. Brown, white-flowered form
Florida: known primarily from the southern four counties, where it can be locally abundant; threatened
Plant: terrestrial, occasionally semi-epiphytic on floating logs, plant to 1.5 m tall
Leaves: 3–5, light green, linear-lanceolate, up to 100 × 5 cm
Flowers: 3–80; pink to purple or, in the forma *alba*, white; lip with golden crests; individual flower size 1.5–4 cm
Habitat: open wet pinelands and wooded swamps
Flowering period: primarily December–March in the Everglades to April–May in the Fakahatchee Swamp; may flower at any time of year

Among the showiest features of the open pinelands and glades of southern Florida are the brilliant pink flowers of the pine-pink. Although many plants are cleistogamous, finding large clumps of fully opened flowers is not difficult. Unlike most species, which produce both cleistogamous and chasmogomous flowering plants, *Bletia* may have both types of flowers on the same plant, and plants vary from year to year. In Everglades National Park the plants are found in open habitats, whereas in the Fakahatchee Swamp they often grow on floating logs and at the bases of old stumps in denser shade.

forma *alba*

Brassia

One of the truly tropical genera that just brushes into southernmost Florida, *Brassia* is a showy, distinctive genus of about 25 species. The flowers are often typified by their long, slender sepals, giving rise to the common name of spider orchids. We have, or had, but one species in Florida, the **spider orchid**, *B. caudata*, perhaps the showiest of all of the species in the genus.

Brassia caudata (Linnaeus) Lindley

spider orchid

Florida; West Indies, Central America, northern South America
Florida: known only from Miami-Dade County; endangered
Plant: epiphytic, pseudobulb ovoid to 12 × 2.7 cm; spike arching to 40 cm long
Leaves: 2, glossy green, 30 × 5 cm
Flowers: up to 15; sepals yellow-green, barred and blotched with brown, petals and lip similar in color; lateral sepals to 15 cm long; individual flower size 15–25 cm
Habitat: hardwood hammocks in Everglades National Park
Flowering period: May–June
One of the several "lost orchids" of south Florida, the spider orchid was last seen prior to the freeze and fires in the late 1960s. Extensive searches have been made nearly every year for surviving plants, so far with no success. In flower, the species is most distinctive, but when not in bloom the plants can resemble several other orchids.

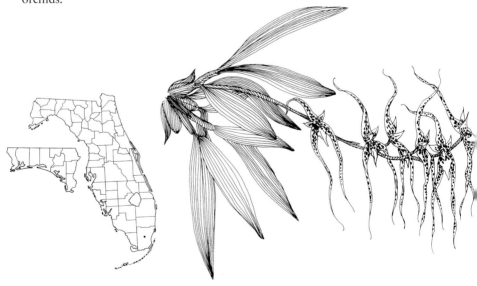

Bulbophyllum

This is an enormous genus of about 1,000 species, primarily in Africa and Asia, with about 15 species in the New World. Although we have only one species in Florida, the **rat-tail orchid**, *Bulbophyllum pachyrhachis*, it is by far one of the less dramatic species in the genus. Elsewhere, many of the species have exotic hinged lips that sway about or produce dozens of showy and colorful flowers. Our Florida representative is a lesson in not judging a genus by one species.

Bulbophyllum pachyrhachis (A. Richard) Grisebach

rat-tail orchid

Florida; West Indies, Central America, South America
Florida: known only from the Fakahatchee Swamp in Collier County; endangered
Plant: epiphytic, pseudobulb ovoid, 3–5 angled, 5 × 2 cm; spike pendant to 24 cm long and 8 mm thick
Leaves: 2, glossy green, keeled, up to 15 × 2 cm
Flowers: up to 30; sepals and petals greenish brown spotted with purple, lip red; individual flower size 5–8 mm
Habitat: hardwood hammocks in Fakahatchee Swamp
Flowering period: November

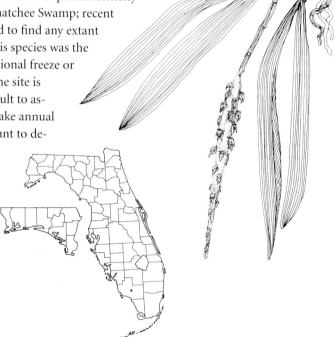

This was one of the choicest species formerly found in the Fakahatchee Swamp; recent searches have failed to find any extant plants. Whether this species was the victim of the occasional freeze or overcollecting or the site is simply lost is difficult to assess. Those who make annual searches are reluctant to declare it extirpated.

Calopogon

The genus *Calopogon* is a New World genus consisting of five species, only one of which occurs outside the United States and Canada. Four of these species, and one variety, are found in Florida. The nonresupinate lip is distinctive and easily identifies the genus.

1a   the vast majority of the flowers open simultaneously . . . 2

1b   1–4 flowers open at a time, plants flowering over several weeks . . . 3

2a   petals widest below the middle . . . *Calopogon barbatus,* p. 40

2b   petals widest above the middle . . . *Calopogon multiflorus,* p. 42

3a   petals narrow and strongly ascending . . . *Calopogon pallidus,* p. 44

3b   petals broad and spreading . . . 4

4a   leaves flat, about 1 cm wide, apex of lip not whitened (except in forma *albiflorus*) . . . *Calopogon tuberosus* var. *tuberosus,* p. 46

4b   leaves very narrow (actually inrolled), appearing about 2–3 mm wide; apex of lip whitened; plants of southern Florida marls and pinelands . . . *Calopogon tuberosus* var. *simpsonii,* p. 48

Calopogon barbatus (Walter) Ames

bearded grass-pink

North Carolina south to Florida and west to Louisiana
Florida: widely distributed throughout the central and northern counties and rare in the southern counties
Plant: terrestrial, 5–20 cm tall
Leaves: 1 or 2; slender, to 20 × 0.5–1 cm
Flowers: 3–7, most of which are open simultaneously; bright magenta pink; individual flower size 2–2.5 cm
Habitat: wet meadows, pine flatwoods, and sphagnous roadsides
Flowering period: late March–late April

This is the earliest of the grass-pinks to flower and is similar to the many-flowered grass-pink, *C. multiflorus*, but it grows in a much wider variety of habitats and can be separated from *C. multiflorus* by the shape of the petals. The petals are wider below the middle on *C. barbatus;* it usually flowers earlier than the common grass-pink, *C. tuberosus,* and is a much smaller plant. The bearded grass-pink is often found in the company of a variety of carnivorous plants—pitcherplants, *Sarracenia* spp.; sundews, *Drosera* spp.; and butterworts, *Pinguicula* spp.

unusual pale form

Calopogon multiflorus Lindley

many-flowered grass-pink

Georgia to Florida west to Mississippi
Florida: widely distributed throughout the central and northern counties and rare in the southern counties; endangered
Plant: terrestrial, 15–30 cm tall
Leaves: 1 or 2; slender, 10 × 3 mm and less than the height of the plant
Flowers: 5–15, nonresupinate, most of which are open simultaneously; bright magenta pink with a golden crest on the lip; individual flower size 2–2.5 cm
Habitat: damp meadows, pine flatwoods
Flowering period: (March) April (July)
This is the rarest of the grass-pinks to be found in Florida and the United States. This species has declined dramatically over the last 25 years. It is primarily a fire-respondent species and often does not flower until a few weeks following a spring burn. Most populations consist of only a few plants, although at the Disney Wilderness Preserve near Kissimmee the many-flowered grass-pink is widespread and several hundred plants can be seen in flower in a good year. Hybrids with *C. pallidus* have been reported by Goldman (2000).

possible hybrid with C. pallidus

Calopogon pallidus Chapman

pale grass-pink

Virginia south to Florida west to Louisiana
   forma *albiflorus* P. M. Brown, white-flowered form
Florida: widely distributed throughout the central and
northern counties and less frequently in the southern
counties
Plant: terrestrial, 15–50 cm tall
Leaves: 1 or 2; slender, ribbed, 10–20 × 5 mm and less
than the height of the plant
Flowers: 5–12, nonresupinate, opening in slow succession;
typically pale magenta pink with a golden crest on the lip;
or, in the forma *albiflorus,* white; individual flower size
2–3.5 cm
Habitat: wet meadows, pine flatwoods, and sphagnous roadsides
Flowering period: March–July

Second in abundance to the common grass-pink, this species
is widespread through most of Florida and the southeastern
United States. It often grows in habitats with other species of
grass-pinks, and the distinctive upward-curved sepals make it
easy to separate from those species. Despite its specific epithet,
the flower color is not always pale and can vary from white to a
rich, deep magenta. Hybrids with *C. multiflorus* have been reported by Goldman (2000).

forma *albiflorus*

Calopogon tuberosus (Linnaeus) Britton, Sterns & Poggenberg var. *tuberosus*

common grass-pink

Minnesota east to Newfoundland, south to Florida, and west to Texas
forma *albiflorus* Britton, white-flowered form
Florida: widely distributed throughout the central and northern counties and less frequently in the southern counties, where it is replaced by the var. *simpsonii*
Plant: terrestrial, 25–75 cm tall
Leaves: 1–5; slender, ribbed, 50 × 4 cm and less than the height of the plant
Flowers: 3–17, nonresupinate, opening in slow succession; deep to pale pink with a golden crest on the lip; or, in the forma *albiflorus,* white; individual flower size 2.5–3.5 cm
Habitat: wet meadows, pine flatwoods, and sphagnous roadsides
Flowering period: March–August

One of the orchids most frequently encountered in the eastern and central United States and Canada, this brilliant, showy plant prefers open, wet, sandy roadsides and prairies in Florida. Plants flower over an extended period of time, with only a few flowers open at once.

As in other grass-pinks, the flowers have the lip uppermost, nonresupinate, and this feature easily separates the genus from any other with a similar morphology.

forma
albiflorus

forma
albiflorus

Calopogon tuberosus (Linnaeus) Britton, Sterns & Poggenberg var. *simpsonii* (Small) Magrath

Simpson's grass-pink

Florida; the Bahamas, Cuba
>   forma *niveus* P. M. Brown, white-flowered form

Florida: confined to the southern counties
Plant: terrestrial, 50–120 cm tall
Leaves: 1–5; slender, inrolled, 50 × 0.5 cm and usually less than the height of the plant
Flowers: 5–25, nonresupinate, opening in slow succession; typically pale magenta pink, with the golden crest on the lip lacking or less evident and the broadened apex white; or, in the forma *niveus,* the entire flower white; individual flower size 2–3.5 cm
Habitat: the open marls and rocky prairies
Flowering period: late December–June

Growing much taller than the common grass-pink and with a very slender leaf, Simpson's grass-pink is confined to the rocky marls and glades of southernmost Florida. The narrow leaf is actually inrolled to form a slender tube, and the larger corms are often wedged in the marly limestone. In Everglades National Park (Miami-Dade and Monroe Counties), plants of this variety start to flower in late December and continue through early May. Else-where, especially in Big Cypress National Preserve (Monroe and Collier Counties) flowers are seen primarily from late April through early June. The lip on var. *simpsonii* has a slightly different shape (less pronouncedly triangular) than that of var. *tuberosus,* and the beard is pink to white or very slightly yellowed, with the broadened apex of the lip white. Another interesting feature of var. *simpsonii* is that it occasion-ally produces an axillary side branch of flowers as the primary raceme concludes flowering. A speci-men from Palm Beach County appears to be this taxon, but the location is a great distance from the typical distribution.

forma *niveus*

branching plant

Campylocentrum

The first of three genera with leafless, epiphytic plants, *Campylocentrum* is a small genus of about 30 neotropical species, not all of which are leafless. Of the seven leafless members of the genus in the greater West Indies area, only one, the **crooked-spur** or **ribbon orchid**, *C. pachyrrhizum,* is found in Florida. Some authors also place the genus *Harrisella* within *Campylocentrum*. At one time it was thought that perhaps a second species in the genus, *C. filiforme* (synonyms: *C. monteverdi, C. uniflora*), might also be found in the Fakahatchee Swamp in Collier County, but it was never verified.

Campylocentrum pachyrrhizum (Reichenbach *f.*) Rolfe

crooked-spur orchid; ribbon orchid

Florida; West Indies, northern South America
Florida: known only from the Fakahatchee Swamp in Collier County; endangered
Plant: epiphytic, leafless, roots gray-green to bronze, flattened, 4–5 mm wide radiating from a central growth
Flowers: up to 30; arranged in two ranks along a somewhat pendant stem; sepals pale yellowish brown to peach and petals and lip white with a pink overlay; individual flower size 3–5 mm
Habitat: hardwood hammocks, tramways, and sloughs in the Fakahatchee Swamp, usually on royal palms, pond apple, pop ash
Flowering period: September–November

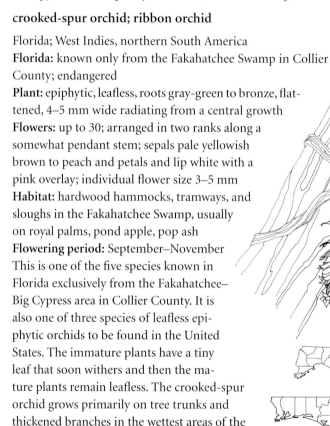

This is one of the five species known in Florida exclusively from the Fakahatchee–Big Cypress area in Collier County. It is also one of three species of leafless epiphytic orchids to be found in the United States. The immature plants have a tiny leaf that soon withers and then the mature plants remain leafless. The crooked-spur orchid grows primarily on tree trunks and thickened branches in the wettest areas of the swamps. The flowers are in crowded spikes and are a distinctive apricot-orange in color.

Cleistes

The genus *Cleistes* includes about 25 species in the Western Hemisphere, many of which grow in wet savannas in northern South America. Most of the species have, at one time, been classified as *Pogonia*, a closely related genus, and some current authors treat them that way today. Based on recent DNA analyses, the two species in the United States may properly belong in a new genus.

1a column 13–19 mm long; lip 26 mm long; leaf and bract broadly lanceolate . . . *Cleistes bifaria,* p. 54

1b column 21–25 mm long; lip 34–56 mm long; leaf and bract narrowly lanceolate . . . *Cleistes divaricata,* p. 56

Note: Because of the nomenclatural confusion within the two species, many reports exist for *C. divaricata* in the panhandle. All specimens and extant plants examined west of Baker County have proven to be *C. bifaria.* This is consistent with the finding of Catling and Gregg (1992).

Cleistes bifaria (Fernald) Catling & Gregg

upland spreading pogonia

West Virginia south to Florida and west to eastern Louisiana
Florida: widespread and scattered throughout most of the panhandle and northern counties; proposed threatened
Plant: terrestrial, 20–50 cm tall
Leaves: 1, broadly lanceolate, glaucous, 15 × 3 cm; a smaller floral bract, 6.5 × 1.5 cm and resembling a leaf, subtends the flower
Flowers: 1, rarely 2; sepals bronzy green, petals pale pink to blush; lip whitish veined in darker pink with a yellow crest; lip to 26 mm long, individual flower size 5 × 5 cm
Habitat: open pine flatwoods, shaded prairies, seepy meadows
Flowering period: April–May

Both species of *Cleistes* are among the showiest orchids in the southeastern United States. Although range overlap is minimal, they can both be found in the same site in at least two places in Florida. Size, coloration, and flowering time are all helpful criteria in determining identification. *Cleistes bifaria* seems to prefer a wetter habitat than *C. divaricata*, flowers earlier, and is generally paler in color. The only absolute criteria are those in the key and require measurements. After a few seasons of experience it becomes quite easy to tell them apart at a glance. *Cleistes bifaria* does not seem to be as fire-dependent as *C. divaricata*.

Cleistes divaricata (Linnaeus) Ames

large spreading pogonia

New Jersey south to Florida, primarily along the coastal plain
  forma *leucantha* P. M. Brown, white-flowered form
Florida: local and scattered in the northeastern counties; proposed endangered
Plant: terrestrial, 30–70 cm tall
Leaves: 1, narrowly lanceolate, glaucous, 20 × 2.5 cm; a smaller floral bract, 8 × 1.5 cm, resembling a leaf, subtends the flower
Flowers: 1, rarely 2; sepals purple, petals deep pink; lip pink veined in darker pink with a yellow crest; or, in the forma *leucantha,* apple green and white; lip to 34–56 mm long, individual flower size 7 × 7 cm
Habitat: open pine flatwoods, shaded prairies, damp meadows;
usually in recently burned areas
Flowering period: April–May

The large spreading pogonia is unquestionably one of the most highly sought after native orchids found on the southeastern coastal plain. The large, showy, rosy pink flowers hold their heads high among the vegetation. Plants seem to flower best in Florida in the two to three years following a burn. Subsequently the competition becomes too dense and only sterile leaves can be found. This is currently one of the rarest species in Florida, confined to a few sites in the northeastern portion of the state, all of which are areas that are occasionally burned.

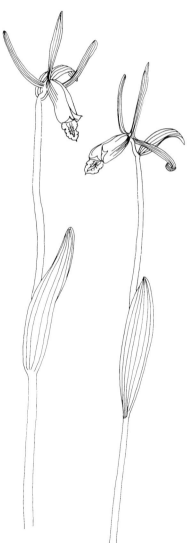

forma *leucantha*

Corallorhiza

The genus *Corallorhiza* has about 13 species throughout North America, Mexico, and Hispanola. One species, *C. trifida,* is widespread across Eurasia. The plants are entirely mycotrophic and some are thought to be saprophytes. They arise from a coralloid rhizome, hence the name. The entire genus is easily recognizable by its leafless stems, although they may be variously colored, and by small flowers.

1a   flowers usually cleistogamous; lip narrow; plants autumn flowering
    . . . *Corallorhiza odontorhiza,* p. 60

1b   flowers chasmogomous, lip broad and prominent, white with maroon spotting; winter–spring flowering . . . *Corallorhiza wisteriana,* p. 62

Corallorhiza odontorhiza (Willdenow) Poiret var. *odontorhiza*

autumn coralroot

South Dakota east to Maine, south to Oklahoma and northern Florida
Florida: very rare and known from only a single site in Columbia County; endangered
Plant: terrestrial, mycotrophic, 5–10 cm tall; stems bronzy green
Leaves: lacking
Flowers: 5–12; cleistogamous; sepals green suffused with purple, covering the petals; lip white spotted with purple, rarely evident in our variety; individual flower size 3–4 mm
Habitat: rich, calcareous woodlands
Flowering period: September–October

The fact that this inconspicuous little orchid has rarely been found in Florida may be attributable to its size and habit and not necessarily to its rarity. The species is never common anywhere and is usually found by accident. The short stems often flower among fallen leaves in the autumn months and the bronzy stem color, lacking chlorophyll, makes them even harder to see. Known only from a single collection in 1946 until its rediscovery in 1999, this ranks as one of the rarest orchids in Florida.

Corallorhiza wisteriana Conrad

Wister's coralroot

Montana east to New Jersey, south to Arizona and Florida; Mexico
   forma *albolabia* P. M. Brown, white-lipped, yellow-stemmed form
   forma *rubra* P. M. Brown, red-stemmed form
Florida: common and widespread in north-central Florida, becoming rarer southward
Plant: terrestrial, mycotrophic, 5–30 cm tall, stem brownish yellow
Leaves: lacking
Flowers: 5–25; sepals green to yellow suffused and mottled with purple; lip white spotted with purple; or, in the forma *albolabia,* yellow-stemmed with a pure white lip; or, in the forma *rubra,* red-stemmed with flowers marked red; individual flower size 5–7 mm
Habitat: rich, calcareous woodlands, pine flatwoods, occasionally in lawns and foundation plantings
Flowering period: late December–April

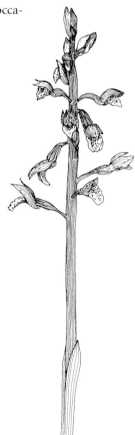

The first truly native orchid to flower in the new year in central and northern Florida is Wister's coralroot. The pale brown stems and small spotted white flowers can often be seen in early January and on into March or early April in scattered locations in open woods and even at homesites. Although the plants are often found as individuals, some sites have several thousand in large clustered colonies. The two color forms are exceedingly rare and known from only one site each in Florida.

forma *albolabia*

forma *rubra*

Cranichis

Although closely related to the spiranthoid orchids, the genus *Cranichis* was never one of the segregate genera. It differs from the spiranthoid genera in several characters, including the inflorescence and flower position. With about 30 species in the tropics and subtropics, several of which have recently been described, the genus reaches its northern limit of distribution in Florida. We have but one species here, the **moss-loving cranichis**, *C. muscosa,* and although it was a relatively early discovery in the orchid history of Florida, it has remained one of the most elusive species in the state.

Cranichis muscosa Swartz

moss-loving cranichis

Florida; West Indies, Central America, northern South America
Florida: very rare and known from two collections in 1903 from southern Florida; endangered
Plant: terrestrial, 5–35 cm tall
Leaves: 4 or 5 in a basal rosette, elliptic, 2–9 × 1–4 cm with petioles up to 4 cm long, reduced on the stem to 4 or 5 prominent, sheathing bracts
Flowers: 12–40; nonresupinate; sepals and petals white; lip white with green flecks; individual flower size 6 mm
Habitat: mossy sinkholes, cypress knees, and rich hammocks
Flowering period: January–February
This Caribbean species has rarely been seen in Florida in the past 100 years. It was first discovered in 1903 in what was then Lee County, but in all probability in the Fakahatchee Swamp region that is now in Collier County, and then later that same year in Miami-Dade County, A report in 1991, and a plant that was suspect and was subsequently stolen from Everglades National Park in 2000, are the only other indications of it known at this time. Although the leaves are similar to those on young plants of *Eltroplectris,* the inflorescence is so distinctive that identification is relatively easy.

Cyclopogon

The genus *Cyclopogon* is one of several segregate genera from the genus *Spiranthes*. While most of the species in the segregate genera were at one time treated as *Spiranthes*, many were originally described in those segregate genera and later merged into *Spiranthes*. *Cyclopogon*, in the strictest sense, has about 54 species in the neotropics. The vast majority of those species have also been treated in the genus *Beadlea*. The two *Cyclopogon* species in Florida represent the northern limit for the genus.

1a   petals and sepals divergent . . . *Cyclopogon cranichoides*, p. 68
1b   petals and sepals appressed . . . *Cyclopogon elatus*, p. 70

Cyclopogon cranichoides (Grisebach) Schlechter

speckled ladies'-tresses

Florida; the Bahamas, West Indies, Central America, South America
   forma *albolabium* (Brown & McCartney) P. M. Brown, white-lipped form
Florida: rare and local but widespread; colonies are susceptible to eradication by feral hogs; proposed endangered
Plant: terrestrial, 5–40 cm tall; the green stem mottled or speckled with brown and purple
Leaves: 4–6 in a basal rosette, ovate, green suffused with purple, 2–8 × 1–4 cm with petioles up to 2 cm long, withering at or just after flowering
Flowers: 10–30; sepals and petals greenish brown, lip white suffused with pink; or, in the forma *albolabia,* the petals and sepals green and the lip pure white; individual flower size 5–8 mm
Habitat: damp, shady forests and moist oak woodlands
Flowering period: late February–late April
Although there are several records for this species from scattered areas within Florida, only a few extant sites can now be found. The slender brown and white flowers rise above dark olive green leaves and often hide among the foliage on the forest floor. In wet areas plants can easily reach 30–40 cm in height, but in the drier live oak forests they are usually no more than 5 cm tall.

forma *albolabia*

Cyclopogon elatus (Swartz) Schlechter

tall neottia

Florida; West Indies, Mexico, Central America, northern South America
Florida: exceedingly rare and known from only a few collections, the original in Hernando (now Citrus) County, others in southern Florida; not recently seen; endangered
Plant: terrestrial, 20–55 cm tall
Leaves: 4–6 in an erect basal rosette withering at or just after flowering, elliptic, green, 5–15 × 1–4 cm with petioles up to 2 cm long
Flowers: 10–30; sepals and petals greenish brown, lip white marked with tan; the sepals appressed; individual flower size 5 mm
Habitat: damp, shady forests in hardwood hammocks
Flowering period: March

This species was originally found in 1881 in what is now Citrus County, probably in the Lecanto area; all subsequent sightings have been in southern Florida, primarily near Homestead. It appears that the species has never been abundant. When not in flower, its basal rosette is similar to that of *Cyclopogon cranichoides*. Too many orchid enthusiasts ignore some of these less-than-attractive spiranthoid species and this is one that should be actively searched for.

Cyrtopodium

The genus *Cyrtopodium* is a neotropical and subtropical genus of about 15 species, one of which is native and one naturalized in Florida. They are all typified by their large, fusiform pseudobulbs, long, plicate leaves, and showy flowers. Because of their size and attractive flowers they have long been popular with collectors.

1a   flowers pure yellow . . . *Cyrtopodium polyphyllum,* p. 74
1b   flowers heavily spotted . . . *Cyrtopodium punctatum,* p. 76

Cyrtopodium polyphyllum (Vell) Pabst *ex* F. Barrios*

yellow cowhorn orchid

Florida; South America
Florida: known only from a few scattered areas
in Miami-Dade County, where it has naturalized
Plant: terrestrial, pseudobulbs fusiform up to 60 cm long;
an erect panicle up to 75 cm in length
Leaves: 10–12, plicate to 50 × 3–6 cm
Flowers: 30–50; sepals and petals
clear bright yellow; individual flower
size 2.5–4 cm
Habitat: vacant lots and pinelands
Flowering period: April–June
This rather spectacular terrestrial
member of a genus that is otherwise
epiphytic in Florida has become
naturalized in several places in Miami-
Dade County. The nomenclature has
had a somewhat checkered history.
Luer cited these plants as *C. andersonii* and subsequently Roger Hammer determined that they were *C.
paranaense*. More recently Gustavo
Romero has determined that *C.
polyphyllum* is the correct name
and *C. paranaense* is a synonym.
For full details of the history of this
plant in Florida, see Hammer
(2001).

Cyrtopodium punctatum (Linnaeus) Lindley

cowhorn orchid, cigar orchid

Florida; Mexico, Central America, West Indies, South America

Florida: formerly abundant in the southern counties; however, because of gross overcollecting, remaining plants are scattered; endangered

Plant: epiphytic, pseudobulb fusiform, up to 30 cm long with a broad flowering panicle often up to 1 m in length

Leaves: 10–12, plicate to 70 × 5 cm

Flowers: 30–50; sepals pale yellow-green spotted and marked with purple, petals brighter yellow with fewer, smaller markings, lip reddish brown with orange markings in the center; individual flower size 4–6 cm

Habitat: hardwood hammocks, open swamps on a variety of trees

Flowering period: March–May

With plants measuring up to 1.5 meters across and sometimes bearing more than 500 flowers, this is one of the largest and most dramatic orchids to be found in Florida. Because of heavy collecting over the years it is becoming more difficult to find substantial plants in the wild. The plants are so distinctive both in and out of flower that identification is never a problem. They are always epiphytic and generally at a low elevation on the trees. An exception is a massive plant high in a cypress above the boardwalk at Corkscrew Swamp.

Dendrophylax

The genus *Dendrophylax* was created in 1864 and now consists of eight species in the West Indies and Florida, of which only one, *D. lindenii,* occurs in Florida (Nir 2000). In the past this species was treated within the genus *Polyrrhiza* (1910), and in 1969 L. A. Garay created the genus *Polyradicion* for those two species with bifurcate lips. Recent cladistic analyses of morphological (Nir, unpubl.) and molecular (M. Whitten, unpubl.) data indicate that *Polyradicion* and *Polyrrhiza* are nested within *Dendrophylax* and should not be maintained as distinct genera.

Dendrophylax lindenii (Lindley) Bentham *ex* Rolfe

ghost orchid; frog orchid

Florida; Cuba

Florida: very local in the Fakahatchee–Big Cypress areas of Collier and Hendry Counties; endangered

Plant: epiphytic, leafless, roots gray-green with short white markings, 3–5 mm wide to over 50 cm long

Flowers: 1, rarely 2; sepals and petals similar, lanceolate; lip 3-lobed, the central lobe triangular and tapering to 2 elongated twisting lobes; the spur slender and elongated to 15 cm long; perianth white; individual flower size to 12 cm, excluding the spur

Habitat: on trees in hardwood hammocks, tramways and sloughs, cypress domes; trees include pop ash, maple, oak, pond apple, bald cypress, and reported from royal palm

Flowering period: May–August, although individuals have been found in flower at other months

Certainly one of the most sought after orchids in North America, the ghost orchid has in recent years been the subject of a rather scandalous book as well as numerous media articles (*The Orchid Thief,* S. Orlean. 1998. Random House). Although confined to the Big Cypress and Fakahatchee Strand State Preserve and adjacent areas, it is widespread and many healthy plants can be found. Unfortunately only a small percentage of those plants flower well. Anyone who has seen the ghost orchid in flower will clearly recount that first encounter with this spectacular and endearing plant. Often it requires several years of watching nonflowering plants to catch one finally in flower. Although the plant is leafless, first-year seedlings do possess a small leaf that soon withers as the root mass grows. This is also seen in the other two leafless species we have in Florida. The report from Miami-Dade County is of a plant that was moved there.

Eltroplectris

Closely related to *Spiranthes* but not one of the many segregates from that genus, *Eltroplectris* consists of only 10 or so species, all in the neosubtropics and neotropics. The long-petioled leaves are not unlike those of *Pelexia*, and the young plants are reminiscent of *Cranichis*. We have only one species in Florida, the **spurred neottia**, *E. calcarata*, but that is more than enough. It is without question one of the most beautiful of all the native orchids in the state, and although it is a rarity, time spent searching for it is well worthwhile.

Eltroplectris calcarata (Swartz) Garay & Sweet

spurred neottia

Florida; the Bahamas, West Indies, northern South America
Florida: known from a few hardwood hammocks within Everglades National Park and Miami-Dade parks as well as historically from Highlands Hammock State Park in Highlands County; endangered
Plant: terrestrial, to 50 cm tall
Leaves: 1 or 2, blue-green, elliptic, 18 × 6 cm on long reddish petioles to 10 cm
Flowers: 3–17; sepals white, greenish toward the base; petals tan, greenish toward the base; lip white, delicately fringed and recurved; 4–6 cm
Habitat: hardwood hammocks
Flowering period: January–March

This is one of the most beautiful and striking flowering plants that we have in Florida. The majestic scape rises to nearly 50 cm in height and bears several "egrets-in-flight" over many weeks. The colony at Highlands Hammock State Park in Highlands County appears to have been completely destroyed by feral hogs. Plants are still widely scattered through southern Miami-Dade County in a variety of public and private hammocks.

Encyclia

The genus *Encyclia* is a large genus of about 100 species found in the tropics and subtropics of the New World. It is one of several genera in the *Epidendrum* alliance, and most species have been placed in that genus at one time.

1a   flowers dingy yellow–reddish brown; lip entire, oblong . . . *Encyclia rufa*, p. 86

1b   flowers yellow, white, and brown; lip 3-lobed, fan-shaped, and striped with purple . . . *Encyclia tampensis* p. 88

Note: For additional species often placed in *Encyclia*, see *Prosthechea*.

Encyclia rufa (Lindley) Britton & Millspaugh

rufous butterfly orchid

Florida; the Bahamas, Cuba

Florida: a single historical collection from Brevard County; proposed endangered

Plant: epiphytic or lithophytic, pseudobulb oblong-conical up to 12 cm long, inflorescence to 70 cm

Leaves: 1–3, coriaceous, to 36 × 2.5 cm

Flowers: 10–30; sepals shiny green to yellow, with a suffusion of bronze, petals similar; lip yellow with purple stripes; individual flower size 3.6–4.2 cm

Habitat: growing on low scrubby shrubs and trees or on rocky outcrops

Flowering period: May

Although not rare in the Bahamas, *Encyclia rufa* was found only once in Florida. The labels on the specimens at the New York Botanical Garden read: "*Encyclia rufa* (Lindl.) Britt. & Millsp. (annotated by Eric Hágsater in 1990). Plants of Peninsular Florida, hammock north of Eau Gallie, J. K. Small, Chas. A. Mosier & P. A. Matthaus 12938, 24 May 1926" [2 sheets]. Eau Gallie is near Melbourne in Brevard County, in a coastal area that has undergone a great deal of development in subsequent years. This is a species to be carefully searched for along the central Florida coast. *Encyclia rufa* and *Trichocentrum carthagenense,* both collected by Small, represent single collections of species never seen again in Florida. There has been, and always will be, controversy over whether they were truly native or should be treated as introductions or waifs.

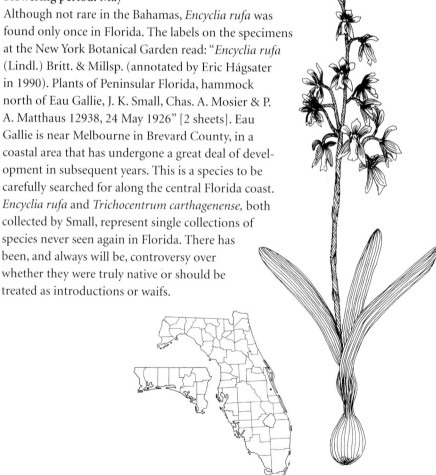

Encyclia tampensis (Lindley) Small

Florida butterfly orchid

Florida; the Bahamas, Cuba
    forma *albolabia* (A. Hawkes) E. Christensen, white-lipped form
Florida: locally abundant in the central and southern counties, especially along waterways; commercially exploitable
Plant: epiphytic, pseudobulb elliptic to ovoid up to 7 cm long, inflorescence to 80 cm
Leaves: 2, coriaceous, to 40 × 2 cm
Flowers: up to 45; sepals and petals similar, various shades of yellow, copper, green, or bronze, often suffused with purple; lip white veined with purple and with a central purple spot or striping on the midlobe; or, in the forma *albolabia,* the petals and sepals light green and the lip pure white; individual flower size 3.6–4.2 cm
Habitat: grows on a wide variety of trees, including live oak, red maple, gum, bald cypress, buttonwood, pop ash, and pond apple
Flowering period: June–July, but may flower at any other time of year
The Florida butterfly orchid is perhaps the most abundant epiphytic orchid in central and southern Florida, replaced as such in the northern part of the state by the green-fly orchis, *Epidendrum magnoliae.* The two species have a small band of overlap in central Florida from Hillsborough to Highlands Counties. Large stands of this showy and beautiful orchid can still be found along most of the major waterways from Tampa southward, and in the southern counties it is difficult to visit any good orchid habitat without encountering this species. Individual plants are highly variable in both the size of the pseudobulbs and the coloration of the flowers.

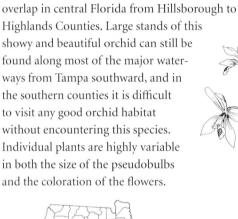

forma *albolabia*

Epidendrum

The genus *Epidendrum* contains about 2,000 neotropical species. The seven species found in Florida are all epiphytes, and with the exception of *E. magnoliae*, all are subtropical. *Epidendrum* (in Florida) is differentiated from *Encyclia* and *Prosthechea* by its elongated leafy growth and lack of pseudobulbs. Only in the Fakahatchee Swamp in Collier County can all six of the subtropical species be found. Each of the seven species found in Florida is so distinctive in its growth habit that it can usually be identified even when it is not in flower. Measurements for plants are given for a single growth, but in actuality most species produce clumps of multiple growths.

1a	inflorescence a many-flowered umbel . . . 2
1b	inflorescence otherwise . . . 4
2a	lip fringed or lacerated . . . *Epidendrum radicans,* p. 315
2b	lip entire, although often lobed . . . 3
3a	inflorescence long-stemmed; flowers bronzy green . . . *Epidendrum amphistomum,* p. 94
3b	inflorescence short-stemmed; flowers watery green . . . *Epidendrum floridense,* p. 96
4a	inflorescence a few-flowered cluster or flowers individual . . . 5
4b	inflorescence a spike . . . 7
5a	flowers large and showy with a strongly 3-lobed, white lip . . . *Epidendrum nocturnum,* p. 102
5b	flowers otherwise . . . 6
6a	flowers several in small, crowded, conelike clusters . . . *Epidendrum strobiliferum,* p. 106
6b	flowers individual at tips of long, trailing branches . . . *Epidendrum acunae,* p. 92
7a	spike a tight, zigzag arrangement . . . *Epidendrum rigidum,* p. 104
7b	spike loose and open in arrangement . . . 8
8a	flower watery green to greenish yellow, day fragrant . . . *Epidendrum magnoliae* var. *magnoliae,* p. 98
8b	flowers highly colored with bronze and pink, night fragrant . . . *Epidendrum magnoliae* var. *mexicanum,* p. 100

Note: For additional species often included in *Epidendrum,* see *Encyclia* and *Prosthechea.*

Epidendrum acunae Dressler

Acuña's star orchid

Florida; West Indies, Mexico, Central America
Florida: known from a single locality deep within the Fakahatchee Swamp in Collier County; endangered
Plant: epiphytic, to over 1 m, pendant and branching
Leaves: 2–6 on each branch, elliptic, alternating on the stem, coriaceous; 3–12 × 0.5–1.5 cm
Flowers: 1–3 at the tips of the branches; sepals and petals similar, brownish green, lip similar and suffused with purple; individual flower size 2–3 cm
Habitat: grows on pop ash and pond apple trees in deep water
Flowering period: May–June

This very distinctive and unusual species has not been seen for many years within the Fakahatchee Swamp, where it was originally found by Raleigh Burney in 1962. Several dozen plants were reported at that time. In recent years numerous—sometimes annual—searches have been made without any results. In or out of flower, the distinctive pendant, trailing stems are so diagnostic that they could not be mistaken for any other orchid within the swamp. Burney described one large plant with branches to nearly 2 meters.

Epidendrum amphistomum A. Richard

dingy-flowered star orchid

Florida; West Indies, Central America, northern South America
    forma *rubrifolium* P. M. Brown, red-leaved form

Florida: found throughout the swamps and hammocks of south Florida; endangered

Plant: epiphytic, to 110 cm tall, erect

Leaves: 5–13, green, or in the forma *rubrifolium* cranberry red, elliptic, alternating on the stem; 4–18 × 1–4 cm

Flowers: up to 25 in a compact terminal raceme; sepals and petals similar, bronzy green to brownish yellow, lip with a distinct central ridge; individual flower size 2–2.5 cm

Habitat: grows on a wide variety of trees, including live oak, bald cypress, buttonwood, pop ash, and pond apple

Flowering period: January–July, but may flower at any other time of year

This is one of the most frequently encountered species of *Epidendrum* in south Florida. The large, erect plants are very distinctive, and the long-petioled inflorescence is a sure giveaway. Plants often occur in decimated habitats that no longer support other orchids. The forma *rubrifolium,* with its cranberry-red foliage, is one of the most striking orchids that we have in the region.

forma *rubrifolium*

Epidendrum floridense Hágsater

Florida star orchid

Florida; Cuba

Florida: found primarily in the Fakahatchee Swamp and a few other scattered locales in south Florida; endangered

Plant: epiphytic, to 30 cm, pendant

Leaves: 5–10, glossy green, elliptic, alternating on the stem; 2–10 × 1–4 cm

Flowers: 3–20 in a compact, short-stemmed raceme; sepals and petals similar, watery yellow-green, lip reniform and emarginate; individual flower size 1.5–2.5 cm

Habitat: grows primarily on pop ash and pond apple along the deepwater soughs

Flowering period: August–November, but may flower at any other time of year

This beautiful and distinctive species was originally thought to be endemic to Florida. Not surprisingly, plants were subsequently found in nearby Cuba. At the time it was described (1993), no living plants could be found. It is hypothesized that the freezes of the late 1980s in Collier County destroyed most of the mature plants. But by 1997 small, immature plants were being seen regularly. Now mature, well-flowered plants can be found. The Polk County record is most curious as it is well north of the normal relatively frost-free range. The heavy, pendant umbel of watery green flowers on a short, stocky plant is very distinctive, and even the fruits, which resemble miniature pumpkins, are unique to this species in Florida.

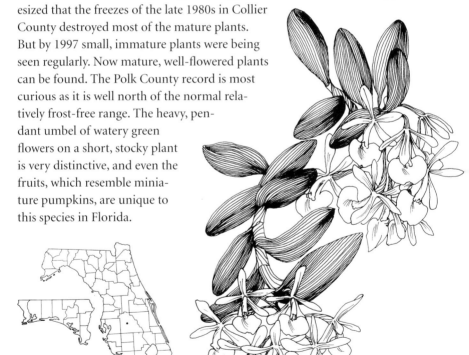

Epidendrum magnoliae Muhlenberg var. *magnoliae*

green-fly orchis

Florida west to western Louisiana and north along the coast to southeastern North Carolina
Florida; (Mexico)
Florida: very common in northern and central Florida; commercially exploitable
Plant: epiphytic, to 30 cm tall, often making enormous clumps 50–80 cm across
Leaves: 2–3, lustrous, dark green, coriaceous; 3–10 × 0.5–1.5 cm
Flowers: up to 18 in a loosely flowered terminal raceme; sepals and petals similar, yellowish green, lip distinctly 3-lobed and the column with 2 prominent pink calli; individual flower size 1.5–2.5 cm
Habitat: grows primarily on live oak, but also can be found on juniper, magnolia, sweet gum, tupelo, and red maple, often with resurrection fern
Flowering period: August–March, but can flower sporadically throughout the year
For this species, known for more than 150 years as *Epidendrum conopseum* R. Brown *ex* Aiton, Eric Hágsater recently found that the name *E. magnoliae* predates the name *E. conopseum* by a month. Both were described in 1813. Hágsater notes: "Mühlenberg's *Catalogue* was published in October, whereas Aiton was published in November of the same year. Rules of taxonomic priority require that the earlier name be used instead of the well-known name published by Robert Brown." This is not only the most frequently encountered epiphytic orchid in central and northern Florida; it is also the only epiphytic orchid in the United States that is found outside Florida. Large plants often occur and their arching flower stems of glowing green flowers are reminiscent of twinkling Christmas lights hanging from the trees.

Epidendrum magnoliae Muhlenberg var. *mexicanum* (L. O. Williams) P. M. Brown

bronze green-fly orchis

Florida; Mexico
Florida: locally common in central Florida; commercially exploitable
Plant: epiphytic, to 30 cm tall, often making enormous clumps 50–80 cm across
Leaves: 2–3, lustrous, dark green, often with a rich purple pigment, coriaceous; 3–10 × 1–2 cm
Flowers: up to 25 in a loosely flowered terminal raceme; sepals and petals similar, bronze with a pink overlay, lip distinctly scalloped; individual flower size 1.5–2.5 cm
Habitat: grows primarily on live oak, but also can be found on juniper, magnolia, sweet gum, tupelo, and red maple, often with resurrection fern
Flowering period: autumn and winter, but can flower sporadically throughout the year

This colorful variety of the green-fly orchis was only recently isolated from within the typical widespread var. *magnoliae* in Florida. It differs in several ways, including having a distinctive late night–early morning fragrance. In southern Marion County both varieties can be found in the same trees. *Epidendrum magnoliae* var. *mexicanum* does share most habit and habitat criteria with var. *magnoliae*.

Epidendrum nocturnum Jacquin

night-fragrant epidendrum

Florida; West Indies, Mexico, Central America, northern South America
Florida: found throughout the swamps and hammocks of south Florida; endangered
Plant: epiphytic, to 110 cm tall
Leaves: 4–10, dark green, elliptic, alternating on the stem; 8–15 × 0.5–2.5 cm
Flowers: up to 5, 1 or 2 produced at a time in a short-stemmed raceme; sepals yellowish, long and slender; petals similar, pale yellow; lip white, strongly 3-lobed with the middle lobe linear and extending well beyond the ovate lateral lobes; individual flower size ca. 12 cm
Habitat: grows on a wide variety of trees, including cabbage palm, pop ash, and pond apple
Flowering period: July–January, but may flower at any other time of year

This is both the largest-flowered and most distinctive species of *Epidendrum* found in Florida. The species is self-pollinating, and many of the flowers are fertilized before they fully open. Flowers in this condition look as if they were at their best the day before or will be the day after, but in reality they will never fully open. A plant with several fully open flowers is a magnificent thing to behold. The pungent fragrance is emitted at night.

Epidendrum rigidum Jacquin

rigid epidendrum

Florida; West Indies, Mexico, Central America, northern South America

Florida: found throughout the swamps and hammocks of south Florida; endangered

Plant: epiphytic, to 20 cm tall

Leaves: 2–6, green, elliptic, keeled, alternating on the stem; 3–8 × 0.8–1.5 cm

Flowers: 3–15; sessile, nonresupinate, marcescent, in a terminal spike; sepals green, ovate; petals green, linear; lip rounded, uppermost; individual flower size ca. 5 mm

Habitat: grows on a wide variety of trees, including live oak, bald cypress, buttonwood, pop ash, and pond apple

Flowering period: October–May, but may flower at any other time of year

This is perhaps the most frequently encountered of all *Epidendrum* species in Florida. Most people pass right by the plants assuming they are not in flower. It takes close examination to see if the flowers are fresh and open because they persist on the spike long after self-fertilization. The species occasionally makes large clumps but is more often seen as just a few stems. The alternating, offset flowers on the spike have given rise to a local common name of "zigzag orchid."

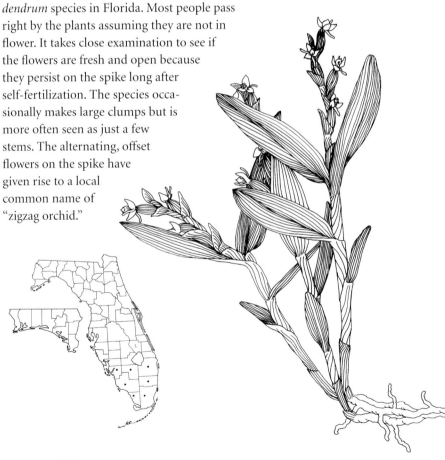

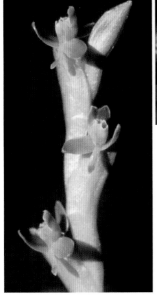

Epidendrum strobiliferum Swartz

cone-bearing epidendrum

Florida; West Indies, Mexico, Central America, northern South America
Florida: rare and local; found only in the Fakahatchee Swamp and vicinity of Collier County; endangered
Plant: epiphytic, to 18 cm long
Leaves: 2–8, reddish brown, elliptic, coriaceous, alternating on the stem; 2–5 × 0.5–1 cm
Flowers: usually 3; terminal, nonresupinate, concealed by a large floral bract; sepals pale yellow, ovate; petals white, linear; lip uppermost, concave; individual flower size 3 mm
Habitat: grows on a wide variety of trees, including red maple, bald cypress, pop ash, and pond apple
Flowering period: October and November, but may flower at any other time of year. This is the smallest and certainly the most inconspicuous of all *Epidendrum* species in Florida. The plants form dense little tangles and are often high up in the trees. The small, hard, reddish leaves and terminal inflorescence make them easier to isolate from seedlings of several other orchids. The large floral bracts that cover the flowers give the inflorescence a conelike appearance.

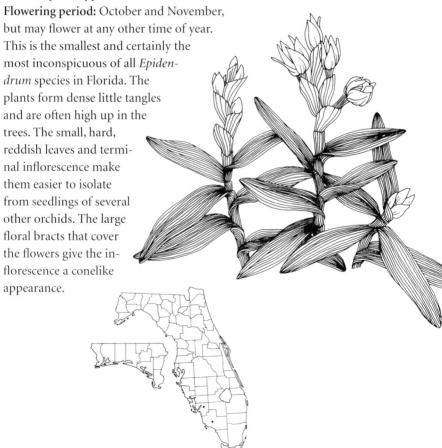

Eulophia

One of several genera in Florida having a definite African affinity, *Eulophia* is a pantropical genus of over 200 species, with only one found in Florida, the **wild coco**, *E. alta*. The flowers bear a distinctive series of keels or crests on the lip. Until recently the genus included species that are now segregated as *Pteroglossaspis*. *Eulophia alta* is widespread throughout the West Indies and Central and South America.

Eulophia alta (Linnaeus) Fawcett & Rendle

wild coco

Georgia south to Florida; Mexico, West Indies, Central America, South America, Africa
    forma *pallida* P. M. Brown, pale-colored form
    forma *pelchatii* P. M. Brown, green- and white-flowered form
Florida: widespread and often abundant from central Florida southward
Plant: terrestrial, 50–150 cm tall
Leaves: 4–6 yellow-green, plicate, lanceolate, 100 × 10 cm
Flowers: 20–50 in a tall, loose, many-flowered raceme; sepals and petals similar, lanceolate, highly variable in color from pale, in the forma *pallida*, pinks, maroons, and greens to deep rich burgundies or, in the forma *pelchatii*, light green; the lip usually richer in color, or, in the forma *pelchatii*, white, with a pair of prominent crests; individual flower size 3.5–4.5 cm
Habitat: open, lightly wooded swamps and wet woodlands, roadside ditches and riverbanks
Flowering period: (July) August–December (January)
The largest and one of the showiest of the terrestrial orchids in Florida, the wild coco is always found in damp to wet ground and flowers over a long period in the fall and early winter. It grows from a corm and would be an excellent candidate for cultivation if it could be commercially propagated. Color is quite variable; deep rich burgundies and gentle pale apple-blossom pinks can be found.

forma
pallida

forma *pelchatii*

Galeandra

A particularly beautiful genus of about six species from the neotropics, *Galeandra* contains both terrestrial and epiphytic species. The large, showy flowers have a distinctive funnel-shaped lip that forms a large thickened spur at the base of the flower. Until recently the plants in Florida were thought to be *G. beyrichii,* a wide-ranging species from Central and South America. In 2000 Romero & Brown published the **two-keeled galeandra,** *G. bicarinata,* known at present only from Florida and Cuba. It differs from *G. beyrichii* in several ways, most noticeably in having two rather than four keels on the lip.

Galeandra bicarinata G. A. Romero & P. M. Brown

two-keeled galeandra

Florida; Cuba
Florida: known only from hardwood hammocks in Miami-Dade County; endangered
Plant: terrestrial, up to 1 m tall
Leaves: 1–2, light green, plicate, lanceolate, 25 × 3 cm; not present at flowering time
Flowers: 3–17 in a terminal raceme; sepals and petals similar, lanceolate, pale green; lip white with green stripes outside and crimson stripes within, forming a prominent inflated spur; individual flower size 3.5–4.25 cm
Habitat: hardwood hammocks
Flowering period: September–November
Restricted to only a few hammocks in Miami-Dade County, this plant was previously known as *Galeandra beyrichii.* In 2000 Romero & Brown described the Florida plants as a new species restricted to Florida and Cuba. Plants do not flower every year. Leaves are present briefly from late spring to early fall and wither by the time the flowers appear. This galeandra is certainly one of the most handsome orchids we have in North America, but unfortunately few people have seen it in recent years.

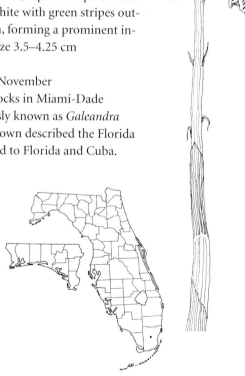

Goodyera

This is a terrestrial genus that is widespread throughout the world and known for its beautifully marked and reticulated leaves, earning the group the name of "jewel orchids." In the United States and Canada we have four species, all primarily northern or higher elevation in distribution. Only one species, the **downy rattlesnake orchis**, *G. pubescens*, is found in Florida, where it reaches the southern limit of its range in the extreme northern counties of the state.

Goodyera pubescens (Willdenow) R. Brown

downy rattlesnake orchis

Ontario east to Nova Scotia, south to Arkansas and Florida
Florida: very rare in northern Florida; endangered
Plant: terrestrial, 20–30 cm tall
Leaves: 4–6, in a basal rosette, green with white reticulations, lanceolate, 5–10 × 1–1.5 cm
Flowers: 20–50+, in a densely flowered terminal spike; white, copiously pubescent; individual flower size 3 × 4 mm
Habitat: woodlands
Flowering period: August–December (January)

Some of the rarest orchids in Florida are among the species most frequently encountered farther north. The downy rattlesnake orchis falls into this category, along with little club-spur orchis and large whorled pogonia. Like those species, it is restricted to the more northern affinity soils and woodlands of the Georgia/Alabama border with Florida. It has the most handsomely marked foliage of any of our orchids and is evergreen.

Govenia

A distinctive genus of about 18 species from the neotropics, *Govenia* historically has not been well understood. Until Ed Greenwood undertook a study of the genus, many of the species concepts were unclear and confused. He has written extensively on the genus, especially in Mexico, and has greatly aided in the understanding of the species concept within *Govenia*. Until recently the plants in Florida were poorly understood and, because of the paucity of material available, were not correctly and suitably identified. They are now known as the **Florida govenia**, *Govenia floridana,* an endemic from southern Florida.

Govenia floridana P. M. Brown

Florida govenia

Florida
Florida: known only from hardwood hammocks in Miami-Dade County; endangered
Plant: terrestrial, up to 50 cm tall
Leaves: 2, green, plicate, oblanceolate, 20–35 × 8–11 cm
Flowers: 5–15 in a terminal raceme, not fully open; sepals ovate, white; petals ovate, white with fine purple dots; lip white with 3–5 marginal purplish brown spots; individual flower size 2 cm
Habitat: hardwood hammocks
Flowering period: November–December

First discovered in 1957 by Frank Craighead, the population of this exceedingly rare orchid was a well-kept secret for many years. Unfortunately the plants nevertheless dwindled and/or were poached over the next 30 years. Destruction wrought by several hurricanes made the hammock that was home to this govenia nearly impenetrable, and then as more light came in, the vines took over. The species was originally described as *Govenia utriculata.* Greenwood (1991) and Brown (2000) have finally sorted out what the Florida plants truly are, and Brown's publication gave them a well-deserved name. Currently only a few seedlings can be found, but as more exploration is undertaken and the hammocks open up, the search for mature plants will continue.

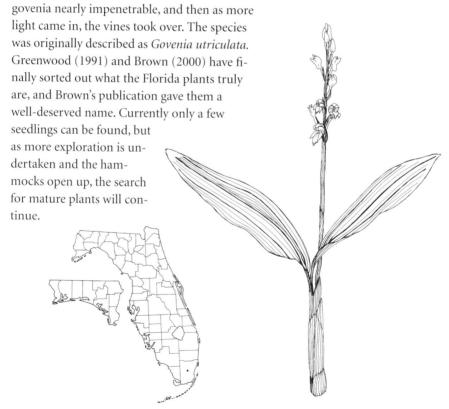

Habenaria

The genus *Habenaria* is pantropical and subtropical and consists of about 600 species. It reaches the northern limit of its range in North America in the southeastern United States. In its broadest sense, it often includes those species that are found in *Platanthera, Coeloglossum,* and *Pseudorchis.* As treated here, in the narrow sense, it contains five species, three of which are found within the United States only in Florida, the other two extending also into the southeastern and Gulf coastal plains. Four of the five species in Florida form large colonies with distinctive basal rosettes.

1a   lip and/or petals divided into linear, threadlike segments ... 2
1b   lip and/or petals merely toothed ... *Habenaria odontopetala,* p. 124
2a   leaves essentially basal or rapidly reduced upward; spur swollen
      ... *Habenaria distans,* p. 120
2b   leaves extending up the stem and gradually reduced in size,
      spur not swollen ... 3
3a   spur equal to the ovary; plants of wet habitats
      ... *Habenaria repens,* p. 128
3b   spur distinctly longer than the ovary ... 4
4a   anterior division of the lateral petal less than twice (10–18 mm) the
      length of the posterior division (6–9 mm); spur typically less than
      10 cm (in living material); plants of open pinelands, hedgerows, and
      fields ... *Habenaria quinqueseta,* p. 126
4b   anterior division of the lateral petal more than twice (20–24 mm) the
      length of the posterior division (8–11 mm); flowers, when viewed
      straight on, with a distinct rectangular aspect; spur often greater than
      10 cm (in living material); plants of rich mesic hardwood hammocks
      ... *Habenaria macroceratitis,* p. 122

Note: For other species often placed in *Habenaria,* see *Platanthera.*

Habenaria distans Grisebach

false water-spider orchis

Florida; West Indies, Central America, northern South America
Florida: very rare, known only from Collier, Lee, and Highlands Counties; endangered
Plant: terrestrial, up to 30 cm tall
Leaves: 3–6, in a basal rosette, glossy green, oblong, 3–10 × 2–3.5 cm
Flowers: 5–15, in a loosely flowered, terminal spike; sepals green, ovate to oblong, petals pale green, with 2 slender linear divisions; lip with 3 slender linear divisions; spur to 17 mm, swollen at the tip; individual flower size 3–4 × 3–4 cm
Habitat: rich, damp, hardwood hammocks
Flowering period: mid-August–October

The false water-spider orchid is currently restricted in southern Florida to Collier County. Historical specimens are known from Lee County and from Highlands Hammock State Park in Highlands County, where the habitat has been destroyed by feral hogs. There is a literature reference to Manatee County. This is one of the rarest orchids in the United States, never having been abundant. The basal leaves form a distinctive rosette and the flowering stem with slender bracts helps to distinguish it from the other species of *Habenaria*.

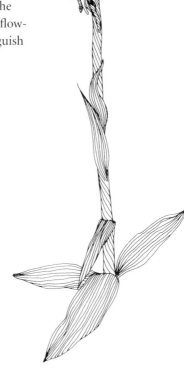

Habenaria macroceratitis Willdenow

long-horned rein orchis

Florida; Mexico, West Indies, Central America
Florida: restricted to a few of the central peninsular counties; proposed endangered
Plant: terrestrial, up to 75 cm tall
Leaves: 3–7, glossy blue-green, elliptic, to 20 × 4–6 cm; concentrated on the lower half of the stem and reduced to bracts above
Flowers: 15–25, in a loose raceme; sepals light green with dark green stripes, ovate to oblong; petals white with 2 linear divisions; lip white with 3 divisions; spur 12–25 cm long, but local clones may have shorter spurs; individual flower size ca. 6 × 8 cm, not including the spur
Habitat: rich, moist hardwood hammocks
Flowering period: August–October

The long-horned rein orchis is rare and local in rich, moist, hardwood hammocks in central Florida in Alachua, Sumter, Citrus, Hernando and (historically) Orange Counties. Although some colonies are very large and vigorous, most counties have only one or two sites. This taxon was originally described at the species level in 1805 and then over the years merged within the similar *Habenaria quinqueseta.* The most striking aspect of *H. macroceratitis* is the very long spur, but this is not the critical distinguishing aspect between the two species. The primary character, which is used in the key, is the proportional length of the segments of the lateral petals. Spur length is the most problematical of the criteria that have been traditionally used to separate this species from *H. quinqueseta,* as there can be "short-spurred" *H. macroceratitis* and "long-spurred" *H. quinqueseta.* (The epithet *macroceratitis* means long-horned rather than long-spurred.) One of the most exciting aspects of this species in Florida is the presence of a large colony in Sumter County that was first documented in 1874 and is still present today. It is vigorous and produces many spectacular flowering plants each year. In a good year, one of the three colonies in Hernando County, near Brooksville, can produce several hundred flowering stems with some up to 75 cm tall.

Habenaria odontopetala Reichenbach f.

toothed rein orchis

Florida; Mexico, West Indies, Central America
    Forma *heatonii* P. M. Brown, albino form
Florida: widespread throughout the central and southern counties; one of the most frequently seen orchids in southern Florida
Plant: terrestrial, up to 1 m tall
Leaves: 5–12, glossy green, elliptic, to 20 × 3–5 cm, or, in the forma *heatonii*, the plant entirely white
Flowers: 10–60, in an often densely flowered terminal raceme; sepals green, ovate to oblong; petals yellow-green, with 2 obscure teeth; lip with 3 divisions, the central one being noticeably longer than either the petals or sepals; spur ca. 25 mm long; individual flower size ca. 2 × 2.5 cm
Habitat: rich, damp hardwood hammocks
Flowering period: September in the north–February in southern Florida

The toothed rein orchis is common in central and southern Florida, becoming rare from Marion County northward, with single records from St. Johns and Duval Counties in northeastern Florida but no records to the northwest of Marion County. The green flowers become more pronouncedly yellow southward and the lip is more contrasting in color. The flowers have a distinctly unpleasant odor.

Habenaria quinqueseta (Michaux) Eaton

Michaux's orchis

South Carolina south to Florida and west to Texas; Mexico, West Indies, Central America

Florida: widespread throughout the entire state; less frequent in the western panhandle

Plant: terrestrial, up to 30 (50) cm tall

Leaves: 3–7, glossy bright green, elliptic, to 20 × 4–6 cm

Flowers: 15–25, in a loose raceme; sepals light green with dark green stripes, ovate to oblong; petals white with two linear divisions; lip white with three divisions; spur 5–8 cm long, but local clones may have longer spurs; individual flower size ca. 4 × 4 cm, not including the spur

Habitat: rich, moist hardwood hammocks, pine flatwoods, roadside ditches

Flowering period: August in the north–January in the south

Michaux's orchid is widespread and locally common throughout all of Florida. This is primarily a plant of damp pinelands and hedgerows. The greenish white flowers are produced on a spike to 30 cm tall and with up to 14 flowers, but more often with 6–8 flowers. The spur typically is shorter than 5 cm. Large colonies of nonflowering plants are often encountered, especially in open pine flatwoods. The flowers of *H. quinqueseta* have a "square" aspect to them whereas those of *H. macroceratitis* look more "rectangular."

Habenaria repens Nuttall

water-spider orchis

North Carolina south to Florida, west to southeastern Arkansas and Texas; Mexico, West Indies, Central America
Florida: widespread throughout the entire state
Plant: terrestrial or aquatic, up to 50 cm tall
Leaves: 3–8, yellow-green, linear-lanceolate, 3–20 × 1–2.5 cm
Flowers: 10–50 in a densely flowered terminal raceme; sepals light green, ovate to oblong; petals greenish white with two divisions; lip with three divisions, the central one being shorter than the lateral divisions; spur slender ca. 13 mm long; individual flower size ca. 2 × 2 cm, not including the spur
Habitat: open shorelines, wet ditches, stagnant pools
Flowering period: throughout the year
The water-spider orchis is one of the few truly aquatic orchids. Masses of several hundred floating plants can often be found. The plants also frequently colonize wet roadside ditches and canals. This species produces fewer sterile colonies than the other four species and is also the most wide-ranging of the five species in the United States.

Harrisella

This is a monotypic genus having as its single species the **leafless harrisella**, *Harrisella porrecta*, a diminutive little orchid that is widespread throughout its range. It occurs perhaps equally often on cultivated plants, especially old citrus trees, as on trees and shrubs in the wild. Several authors have confused the species name with *Harrisella filiformis*, which is a different species in the genus *Campylocentrum*. Recent authors have included *Harrisella* within *Campylocentrum* but retained the species epithet *porrecta*.

Harrisella porrecta (Reichenbach f.) Fawcett & Rendle

leafless harrisella

Florida; West Indies, northern South America
Florida: widespread in the central and southern counties; threatened
Plant: epiphytic, leafless, roots light gray-green, slender, less than 1 mm wide
Flowers: up to 6 very slender panicles bearing 1–6 nonresupinate flowers; sepals and petals pale yellow; lip yellow, concave with a lobulated spur; individual flower size ca. 2.5 × 3 mm
Habitat: hardwood hammocks, tramways and sloughs, cypress domes, juniper and old citrus trees
Flowering period: August–November
One of the three closely related "leafless orchids" of Florida, the diminutive *Harrisella*, once actually seen, is unmistakable. It occurs on a variety of trees and shrubs both in natural areas and especially on old citrus in cultivated areas. The fruits, which are larger (6 × 5 mm) than the flowers, hang in little clusters and have given rise to the local common name "jingle bell orchid."

Hexalectris

A genus of seven species found primarily in the southern United States and Mexico, *Hexalectris* is similar in appearance to the other mycotrophic genus, *Corallorhiza*. Although not closely related, they both have colorful flowers terminating a leafless stem that lacks all chlorophyll. The crested flowers on *Hexalectris* are much larger than those of *Corallorhiza* and more intricately beautiful. The only species to occur in Florida, the **crested coralroot**, *Hexalectris spicata*, is also the only species to occur outside the southwestern United States and adjacent Mexico.

Hexalectris spicata (Walter) Barnhardt var. *spicata*

crested coralroot

Arizona, Missouri; southern Illinois east to Maryland, south to Florida and west
to Texas; Mexico
    forma *albolabia* P. M. Brown, white-lipped form
Florida: widely scattered but primarily in the central and northern counties; endangered
Plant: terrestrial, mycotrophic, 10–80 cm tall; stems yellow-brown to deep purple
Leaves: lacking
Flowers: 5–25; sepals and petals brown–yellow with purple striations; lip pale
yellow with purple stripes (crests), 3-lobed, the lateral lobes incurved; or, in the
forma *albolabia,* the lip pure white with pale yellow stria-
tions and the petals and sepals mahogany; individual
flower size 2.5–4 cm
Habitat: dry, open hardwood forest especially under live
oak
Flowering period: April in the south–August in the
north

This being one of three species of entirely mycotrophic
orchids to be found in Florida, the plants lack all traces
of chlorophyll and therefore often blend in with their
surroundings. The crested coralroot is by far the hand-
somest of these three and is one of the most beautiful of
the summer-flowering orchids in the southern United
States. From a distance it may appear to be no more than
a dead stick, but upon close examination the striking
and colorful flowers reveal an intricate pattern of crests
upon the lip. Plants have a preference for live oak woodlands, and the number of plants, depending on the rain-
fall in a given season, may vary greatly from year to
year.

forma *albolabia*

Ionopsis

The genus *Ionopsis* has about 12 species found in the neotropics. These are primarily twig epiphytes and produce panicles of showy flowers that bloom over a long period. They all have tiny pseudobulbs that are completely hidden within the base of the leaf sheaths. Only one species, the **delicate ionopsis**, *Ionopsis utricularioides,* occurs within Florida, and it is one of the favorites of orchid hunters as well as home hobby growers, as it is readily available commercially.

Ionopsis utricularioides (Swartz) Lindley

delicate ionopsis

Florida; Mexico, West Indies, Central America, northern South America
Florida: widespread in the southern counties; endangered
Plant: epiphytic, pseudobulbs green, 2 × 0.5 cm, well concealed within the leaf bases
Leaves: 1–5, conduplicate, coriaceous, olive green, lanceolate, 2–15 × 0.5–2 cm
Flowers: 1–75; a many-branched panicle from the base of the pseudobulb; white–pink with dark pink–lilac veins; sepals and petals similar; lip very prominent, 2-lobed; individual flower size 1 × 1.7 cm
Habitat: hardwood hammocks, along tramways and sloughs, cypress domes
Flowering period: December–April

This species, along with *Harrisella porrecta* and *Lepanthopsis melanantha,* form a trio of twig epiphytes, so called because of their preference for growing on slender twigs, often on the periphery of their host. This is by far the most frequently encountered of the three and also the largest. The flowering stems can often extend to 50 cm and the branched inflorescence can flower over a two-month period. Plants almost always occur over or very near to standing water.

Isotria

The genus *Isotria* consists of only two species, both of which are found in the eastern United States and adjacent Canada. They are related to the genera *Pogonia* and, more distantly, *Triphora* and early in their history were placed in the genus *Pogonia*. We have only one species in Florida, the **large whorled pogonia**, *Isotria verticillata*. The other species, *Isotria medeoloides*, which is federally listed as threatened, occurs from Maine to Georgia and westward to Missouri. It is widely scattered, colonies often consisting of only a few plants.

Isotria verticillata (Muhlenberg *ex* Willdenow) Rafinesque

large whorled pogonia

Michigan east to Maine, south to Texas and Florida

Florida: known only from Gadsden and Washington Counties in the eastern panhandle; endangered

Plant: terrestrial, up to 30 cm tall, shorter in flower

Leaves: 5 or 6 in a whorl at the top of the stem, up to 9 × 5 cm

Flowers: 1, rarely 2; sepals purplish, wide-spreading, slender and spidery; petals pale yellow, ovate arched over the column; lip white edged in purple with a fleshy, yellow central ridge; individual flowers 10 cm across

Habitat: deciduous forest

Flowering period: April, usually before the trees leaf out

Florida is host to three northern species that are common northward but within the state are three of the rarest orchids. All occur in the central panhandle counties bordering Georgia and Alabama. *Isotria verticillata, Goodyera pubescens,* and *Platanthera clavellata* form this trio, and all have a preference for northern affinity habitats of cooler and richer woodlands. Although not sympatric here, in the north they often grow in the same community. The fanciful flowers of *Isotria* are unmistakable, and the plant has an unusual habit (as does the other species in the genus, *I. medeoloides,* which does not occur in Florida) of nearly doubling in both leaf surface and height after flowering.

Lepanthopsis

This small genus of pleurothallid orchids consists of about 30 species found mainly in the Andes of South America and the Caribbean. We have only one species, the **crimson lepanthopsis**, *L. melanantha*, in the United States. These tiny twig epiphytes with their miniscule flowers are easily overlooked.

Lepanthopsis melanantha (Reichenbach *f.*) Ames

crimson lepanthopsis

Florida; Greater Antilles
Florida: restricted to the Fakahatchee Swamp and environs in Collier County; endangered
Plant: epiphytic, 4–7 cm tall, stem with cornucopioid bracts terminating in a leaf
Leaves: 1, coriaceous, green, elliptic, 10–28 × 3–10 mm
Flowers: 5–7; on a hairlike peduncle from end of the stem; sepals ovate; petals minute, round; lip round and surrounding the column; carmine red; individual flower size 3.6 × 4 mm
Habitat: tips of cypress or pond apple branches, trunks of oak, often with bromeliads
Flowering period: primarily spring, but sporadic throughout the year

This delicate little twig epiphyte is one of the most elusive species in Florida. It has been seen only a few times over the years and is confined to the Fakahatchee Swamp–Big Cypress region. One of the last reported plants, seen in the 1980s, was collected shortly after its discovery. In addition to being a twig epiphyte it has also been found at the base of larger bromeliads. The small leaves are not unlike those of some of the smaller pepperomias (a non-orchid genus of native epiphytes), although upon close examination they are distinctive. The stem with its funnel-shaped bracts and carmine flowers is readily identified.

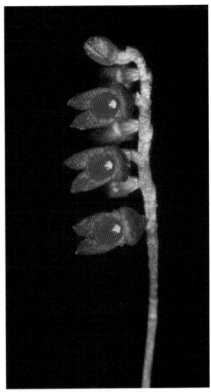

Liparis

Liparis is a cosmopolitan genus of more than 200 species occurring in a wide variety of habitats throughout the world. All members of the genus are terrestrial or semi-epiphytic and have swollen bases to the leaves that form pseudobulb-like structures. These features are not unlike those of the genus *Malaxis* and are more evident and usually above ground in the subtropical and tropical species, whereas in the temperate and more northerly species the structure is within the ground. Three species occur in the United States and Canada, but only one, the **tall tway-blade**, *Liparis elata,* in Florida.

Liparis elata Lindley

tall twayblade

Florida; Mexico, West Indies, Central America, northern South America
Florida: known from Collier, Hillsborough, and Hernando Counties; endangered
Plant: terrestrial to semi-epiphytic, up to 50 cm tall; pseudobulb conical 5–7 × 2–3 cm
Leaves: 3–7, light green, soft, and plicate, up to 25 × 13 cm
Flowers: 12–40, in a raceme terminating a winged, 5-grooved scape; sepals purple, broadly lanceolate; petals narrowly spatulate; lip deep purple to rose with recurved edges, slightly bilobed; individual flower size 1.5 cm
Habitat: rich, damp hardwood hammocks and floating logs or tree bases in open sloughs
Flowering period: July–November

This large-leaved and distinctive species is found as a terrestrial in widespread areas in the Fakahatchee Swamp, often growing upon old, rotting logs as well as in the muck of the swamp. In addition it is known from wet streamsides in the Brooksville and Tampa areas, although it has not been seen in the wide range of suitable habitat in between. The broad, plaited leaves are soft and distinctive and have earned the plant the name "elephant ear" from some local botanists in southwestern Florida. The report for Miami-Dade County is curious as neither the habitat nor flowering time given is at all typical.

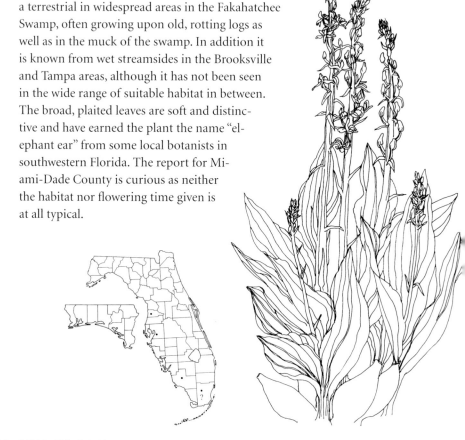

Listera

The genus *Listera* is composed of 25 species that occur in the cooler climes of both the Northern and Southern Hemispheres. Although Florida has only one species, the **southern twayblade**, *Listera australis,* eight species in the genus grow in the United States and Canada. One of these, *L. ovata,* is a common species in Europe that has become naturalized in southern Ontario.

Listera australis Lindley

southern twayblade

Quebec, Nova Scotia, New Brunswick south to Florida and west to Texas
  forma *scottii* P. M. Brown, many-leaved form
  forma *trifolia* P. M. Brown, three-leaved form
  forma *viridis* P. M. Brown, green-flowered form
Florida: widespread and somewhat scattered in the northern and central counties; threatened
Plant: terrestrial in damp soils, up to 35 cm tall
Leaves: 2, opposite midway on the stem, green, usually flushed with red, ovate 3.5 × 2 cm; or, in the forma *scottii*, leaves several scattered along the stem; or, in the forma *trifolia*, leaves 3 in a whorl
Flowers: 5–40, in a terminal raceme; sepals purple, ovate; petals purple, narrowly spatulate, recurved; lip purple, linear, split into 2 slender filaments, or, in the forma *viridis*, flowers entirely green; individual flower size 6–10 mm
Habitat: rich, damp woodlands, often in sphagnum moss
Flowering period: late December–March

A Florida spring ephemeral, the southern twayblade appears quickly in late December and throughout January and February in the north-central and northern counties, having a preference for damp, often seasonally flooded deciduous woodlands and, at many sites, for the presence of sphagnum moss. Although most populations consist of less than a dozen plants, one remarkable site in Alachua County near Paynes Prairie has over 20,000 individuals and contains an amazing degree of variation with all described forma present. The plants at this site are more robust than elsewhere, flower over a long period, and form dense, lush clumps.

The species sets seed and senesces quickly, so that a month after flowering there usually is no sign of the plants until the next season.

forma *viridis*

forma
scottii

forma
trifolia

Macradenia

A genus of 12 neotropical species that are characterized by small, slender pseudobulbs terminating in a single apical leaf. The flowers in the genus have a 3-lobed lip that in several species has the central lobe curved distinctively to the side. We have but a single species in Florida, the **Trinidad macradenia**, *Macradenia lutescens*, which has not been seen in the wild for some years.

Macradenia lutescens R. Brown

Trinidad macradenia

Florida; West Indies, northern South America
Florida: known only from Miami-Dade County and (a report from) Monroe County; endangered
Plant: epiphytic, pendant, to 30 cm long; pseudobulbs cylindrical and tapered, 3–6 cm
Leaves: 1, coriaceous, green, oblong-lanceolate, from the tip of the pseudobulb, 10–15 × 1–3 cm
Flowers: 5–22; on a pendant raceme from the base of the pseudobulb; sepals and petals similar, oblong-ovate; lip 3-lobed, the lateral lobes rounded and the center lobe a linear projection curved downward and to the side; a yellow-green base variously marked with purple, brown, and red, the lip whitish with pink stripes; individual flower size 2.5 cm
Habitat: low down on trunks and branches of a variety of trees including buttonwood and pop ash
Flowering period: October–November

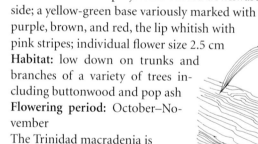

The Trinidad macradenia is among the "lost orchids" of southern Florida, its decline directly attributed to gross overcollecting. The plants have a preference for growing near ground level and are showy and easily seen, especially when in flower. A recent report for Monroe County on federal lands may represent a relic population. In the early part of the twentieth century great basketsful were collected for orchid hobbyists. Freezes in the 1980s may also have contributed to the decline of this now rare species.

Malaxis

The genus *Malaxis* is a cosmopolitan one of about 300 species. Eleven species are found in the United States and Canada, two of which occur in Florida. All species have a pseudobulbous stem, which is more evident in the subtropical and tropical species. In the temperate species it appears more cormlike. The genus possesses some of the smallest flowers in the Orchidaceae, many not more than a few millimeters in either dimension.

1a   inflorescence a slender spike . . . *Malaxis spicata,* p. 154
1b   inflorescence a flat-topped cluster . . . *Malaxis unifolia,* p. 156

Malaxis spicata Swartz

Florida adder's-mouth

Virginia south to Florida; the Bahamas, West Indies

Florida: widespread throughout the central and several of the southern counties and occasional in the northern counties

Plant: terrestrial or semi-epiphytic in damp soils and on rotted logs and old tree stumps; 8–56 cm tall

Leaves: 2, basal, ovate, keeled, 2–10 × 1–5 cm, nearly opposite, swollen at the base into a pseudobulb

Flowers: 5–115, doubly resupinate, arranged in a spike; sepals oblanceolate, brown to green; petals similar, linear and positioned behind the flower; lip orange, vermilion, brown, or green, uppermost, broadly ovate to cordate, with extended auricles at the base; individual flower size 3–5 mm

Habitat: rich, damp woodlands, riverbanks and floodplains, floating logs, tree bases and stumps

Flowering period: August–January

The Florida adder's-mouth is a widespread, if not locally common, species of peninsular Florida. It grows readily along the floodplains and in wet woods through the area. Plants in the northern part of the state tend to be small, usually under 20 cm, but southward in Collier County it is not unusual to find plants well over 30 cm in height, and the record that I have seen was 54 cm tall with over 100 minute yellow, orange, and green flowers. The leaves arise from a pea-sized pseudobulb that is nestled in the moist soil or occasionally on an old rotting stump or in a tree cavity. Plants flower successively over a very long period, often bearing flowers for more than three months.

Malaxis unifolia Michaux

green adder's-mouth

Manitoba east to Newfoundland, south to Texas and Florida; Mexico
Florida: rare and local in the northern and central counties; endangered
Plant: terrestrial in dry to damp mixed woodlands; 8–25+ cm tall
Leaves: 1, ovate, keeled, 9 × 6 cm, midway on the stem, swollen at the base into a (pseudo)bulb
Flowers: 5–80+, arranged in a compact raceme, elongating as flowering progresses; sepals oblanceolate, green; petals linear and reflexed; lip green, broadly ovate to cordate, with extended auricles at the base and bidentate at the summit; individual flower size 2–4 mm
Habitat: dry to damp woodlands, mesic pine flatwoods
Flowering period: February–April (May)

The green adder's-mouth is as rare in Florida as the Florida adder's-mouth is frequent. They have very little in common other than their morphology. Whereas the Florida adder's-mouth is a moisture lover, the green adder's-mouth prefers dry woodlands and mesic pine flatwoods. All but one of the few populations in the state are small with under 50 plants. A recently (1998) discovered population in Marion County is remarkable because it not only has in excess of 400 plants, but they occur in an area of less than two acres and with such choice companions as three birds orchis, *Triphora trianthophora;* speckled ladies'-tresses, *Cyclopogon cranichoides;* Wister's coralroot, *Corallorhiza wisteriana;* and woodland ladies'-tresses, *Spiranthes sylvatica.* The *Malaxis* plants at this site are unusually large, up to 32 cm in height, and like most members of the genus, they bear up to 100 flowers and present them over a period of up to two months.

Maxillaria

The genus *Maxillaria* is a truly subtropical and tropical genus of over 300 species. The two species found in Florida are restricted to the depths of the Fakahatchee Swamp. Occasionally rumors surface of other species of *Maxillaria* found in that same area, but none has been substantiated.

1a   leaves arranged in a loose fan, flowers individual from base of the leaves, flowers often cleistogamous . . . *Maxillaria crassifolia*, p. 160

1b   leaves arranged along a creeping stem, flowers clustered . . . *Maxillaria parviflora*, p. 162

Maxillaria crassifolia (Lindley) Reichenbach f.

false butterfly orchid

Florida; West Indies, Mexico, Central America, northern South America
Florida: known only from Collier County; endangered
Plant: epiphytic, fan-shaped and/or pendant, to 30 cm long; pseudobulbs small, to 25 mm, and completely covered by the bases of the leaves
Leaves: 6–7, coriaceous, dark green, keeled, linear, 3–30 × 1–3 cm
Flowers: 1–3; heavy textured and nestled within the base of the leaves, frequently cleistogamous; sepals and petals similar, oblong-ovate; lip elliptic; pale yellow; individual flower size ca. 2 cm
Habitat: trunks and branches of a variety of trees, including pond apple, pop ash, and live oaks, most frequently in areas of standing water
Flowering period: September–January

Rare in Florida, and known only from the region of the Fakahatchee Swamp, this species is quite widespread within that area. Although most plants are seen as individuals, there is at least one area with several hundred large, mature clumps. Unfortunately the beautiful yellow flowers do not often open wide and one usually finds a closed flower that has set seed. Plants seem to prefer trunks of larger trees in or near the various small lakes that occur throughout the swamp. Although the plant has pseudobulbs, they are always well hidden within sheathing bases of the leaves.

Maxillaria parviflora (Poeppig & Endlicher) Garay

small-flowered maxillaria

Florida; West Indies, Mexico, Central America, northern South America
Florida: known only from the Fakahatchee Swamp in Collier County; endangered
Plant: epiphytic, pendulous, to 1 m long; pseudobulbs cylindrical, 1.5–4 × 6–12 mm, distant on the rhizome
Leaves: 1, coriaceous, green, lanceolate, from the tip of the pseudobulb along a trailing stem, 6–20 × 0.6 –2 cm
Flowers: 1; densely clustered at the base of the most recent growths; sepals and petals similar, ovate; lip obscurely 3-lobed; pale orange; individual flower size 2–4 mm
Habitat: on the trunks of a pop ash in a deep slough
Flowering period: September–November?

This species has proven to be one of the most frustrating to locate within the Fakahatchee Swamp. Discovered in 1975 by Roger Hammer, it was visited a few times and then not found again. The tree that it was growing on appears to have been destroyed. Repeated searches have been unproductive. The plants were not seen in flower in the wild, but a portion of the stem was brought back to the Marie Selby Botanical Gardens, where it subsequently flowered. The *Maxillaria parviflora* complex is just that–a group of closely related species that varies from region to region. These plants have been tentatively identified as *M. parviflora* by John Atwood at Selby, but until they can be relocated we will not know more about them. The photographs shown here are of cultivated plants of the *M. parviflora* complex.

Mesadenus

Mesadenus is a small subtropical and tropical genus with about eight species. Like many others of the segregate spiranthoid genera, it is typified by having its leaves in small basal rosettes that wither at or just after flowering. The minute flowers are often presented in one–sided (secund) spikes and the petals and sepals are barely differentiated. We have but one species, the **copper ladies'-tresses**, *M. luca-yanus,* in Florida, and the best sites for it, curiously enough, are in the northern counties.

Mesadenus lucayanus (Britton) Schlechter

copper ladies'-tresses

Florida; West Indies, Mexico, Central America
Florida: known from a few widely scattered sites, with even fewer extant populations; endangered
Plant: terrestrial, spike to 40 cm tall, very slender and delicate
Leaves: 2–5 in a basal rosette, 3–6 × 1–3 cm, withering at flowering time
Flowers: 8–60; petals and sepals similar, lanceolate, coppery green; lip oblanceolate, rosy green; individual flower size 4–6 mm
Habitat: calcareous woodlands usually with live oak, juniper, and exposed limestone
Flowering period: late December–March
Of all of the *Spiranthes* segregates, this slender and delicate species is perhaps the most easily overlooked. The coppery flowers blend in with surrounding leaves on the ground, and it flowers in midwinter–early spring, when not much else is lush and green. It is definitely a "now you see it, now you don't" plant. There has been a great deal of confusion as to whether we have *Mesadenus polyanthus* or *M. lucayanus* in Florida, and recent work (Brown 2000) has solved the situation. Plants of *M. polyanthus* are from high elevations, primarily on volcanic soils in and around Mexico City, whereas *M. lucayanus* is a lowland species of scrubby oak woodlands, often calcareous, and is widespread in southern Mexico, Central America, and the West Indies as well as Florida.

Oeceoclades

This is an African genus of some 35 species, of which one, *Oeceoclades maculata,* is naturalized and widespread in Florida and the neotropics. Although perhaps becoming a nuisance in some areas of Florida, the strikingly patterned leaves with their rich, dark green base and silver mottlings rival those of the Asian tropical mottled-leaved *Paphiopedilums.* There is no evidence that *Oeceoclades* is invading and replacing our native species in the wild, and when it appears in a horticultural setting it is an added feature of the garden.

Oeceoclades maculata (Lindley) Lindley*

African spotted orchid

Florida; West Indies, Central America, Africa

Florida: rapidly spreading throughout southern Florida and moving northward into the central counties

Plant: terrestrial, pseudobulb ovoid to 4 cm tall

Leaves: 1, from apex of pseudobulb, dark green with silver mottlings, 8–25 × 1.5–5.1 cm

Flowers: 5–15; petals and sepals similar, lanceolate, lip white with purple markings; individual flower size 1–1.5 cm

Habitat: shady hammocks, cultivated gardens, especially in eucalyptus mulch

Flowering period: August–November

This is one of five non-native orchids that have become thoroughly naturalized in Florida. It first appeared in the United States via Florida in 1974 in Miami-Dade County and can now be found readily both in wild, native areas and in horticultural situations. The dark green mottled leaves are striking and the little flowers are quite attractive if and when they open fully. The species is thought to be self-fertile, as many of the flowers do not open completely and all flowers usually set seed. In Alachua County plants have naturalized from those grown within a greenhouse and set out for the summer.

Oncidium

The genus *Oncidium* is a neotropical genus of some 400 species. There are also many segregate genera that at one time were part of *Oncidium* in the larger sense. Species within this genus may be epiphytic, lithophytic, or terrestrial, and all bear pseudobulbs. The inflorescence is always lateral, coming from the base of the pseudobulb. We have only one species in Florida, the **Florida oncidium**, *Oncidium floridanum*. Three other species that were formerly in this genus are treated in *Tolumnia* and *Trichocentrum*.

Oncidium floridanum Ames

Florida oncidium

Florida; the Bahamas
Florida: very rare in Monroe and Collier Counties and widespread in southern
Miami-Dade County; endangered
Plant: terrestrial, to 1.5 m tall; pseudobulbs to 15 cm
Leaves: 3–6, linear and flexuous, green, to 1.5 m × 4 cm
Flowers: 25–80; on an arching panicle from the base of the pseudobulb; sepals
and petals similar, lanceolate; lip 3-lobed, the lateral lobes spreading, the broad
central lobe ovate with a mucronate tip; yellow irregularly marked with brown;
individual flower size 2.5 cm
Habitat: hardwood hammocks and fireroad shoulders
Flowering period: April–September

Scattered populations of this brilliant orchid can be
easily found within the many hammocks of Everglades National Park. The terrestrial habit quickly
separates it from other *Oncidium*-related species,
and the large pseudobulbs distinguish it from
other terrestrial species. The flower spike can often reach 2 meters in height and have nearly 100
flowers. Mark Chase (pers. comm., Royal Botanical
Gardens, Kew) feels strongly that *Oncidium floridanum*
should be included within *Oncidium ensatum*, but I
have maintained it as a separate species based on the lip
of *O. floridanum* having the apex apiculate and that of
O. ensatum having the apex emarginate; coloring and
markings on the flowers also differ.

Pelexia

One of the larger spiranthoid genera, *Pelexia* has about 70 species throughout the neosubtropics and neotropics. The genus bears long-petioled leaves and flowers that have the petals and sepals united to form a helmet and extending to form a distinct spur. We have only one species in Florida, the **glandular ladies'-tresses**, *P. adnata*, which has had a brief history and, if still present, has at best a tenuous hold here.

Pelexia adnata (Swartz) Sprengel

glandular ladies'-tresses

Florida; West Indies, Mexico, Central America, northern South America
Florida: known only from Miami-Dade County; endangered
Plant: terrestrial, spike to 70 cm tall, very slender and delicate
Leaves: 2–7, basal, erect, elliptic, dark green with splashes of silver, 7.5–14 × 3–5.5 cm
Flowers: 5–20; lateral sepals linear, dorsal sepal oblong, green and pubescent-glandular; petals glabrous, white enclosed within the sepals forming a hood; lip white with a yellowish throat; individual flower size 4–6 mm
Habitat: hardwood hammocks
Flowering period: June
The glandular ladies'-tresses is one of the more recent additions to the orchid flora of Florida. Thanks to the keen eyes and unflagging efforts of Roger Hammer, plants were found in 1977 in a hammock in Miami-Dade County. Thought originally to be *Eltroplectris calcarata*, the plants then flowered in June of 1978 and were subsequently identified as *Pelexia adnata*. The small colony eventually dwindled to a few plants, and by 1985 no plants could be found. A single plant was reported from Everglades National Park in 1991. To date no others have been seen.

Phaius

A showy tropical genus of about 45 species native primarily to southeastern Asia, *Phaius* has a long history of cultivation and naturalization in other parts of the world. One species, the **nun orchid**, *P. tankervilleae*, has become a permanent feature of the flora of many tropical countries and has now established itself in central Florida. Vegetatively the plants may resemble the **wild coco**, *Eulophia alta*, but florally they are distinctive, and they flower in spring rather than in autumn.

Phaius tankervilleae (Aiton) Blume*

nun orchid

northeastern Australia, southeastern Asia, Pacific Islands; naturalized in many places in the tropics, including Cuba, Jamaica, Puerto Rico, and south-central Florida

Florida: known from a single naturalized population in Hardee County
Plant: terrestrial, to 1.4 m tall, pseudobulbs green and 3–8 cm tall, the young ones concealed in the base of the sheathing leaves
Leaves: 2–8, plicate, lanceolate, 30–120 × 5–25 cm long
Flowers: 10–35; very showy; sepals and petals similar, elliptic, white on the outside with a brownish purple interior; lip trilobed, spur yellow, very short; lateral lobes of the lip suffused with maroon and incurved, forming an open tube; individual flower size ca. 4–5 cm
Habitat: dense swamps, bay heads, and hammocks
Flowering period: late March–May

This native of southeastern Asia and environs has become well naturalized in many tropical areas of the world. It is not at all surprising that this native of southeastern Asia and environs has found a suitable home in the dense wetlands of central Florida, considering how extensively it has naturalized in other tropical areas. More than 100 plants can be found in the mucky bayhead sheltered by large magnolias. It is one of the most popular orchids in cultivation and perfectly hardy in the central and southern parts of the state. The plants were first reported as palm leaves and then determined by John Tobe as *Phaius*. Plants at the original site are thriving in a private, restricted area of Hardee County. The species should be actively sought in similar adjacent areas and is unmistakable when in flower.

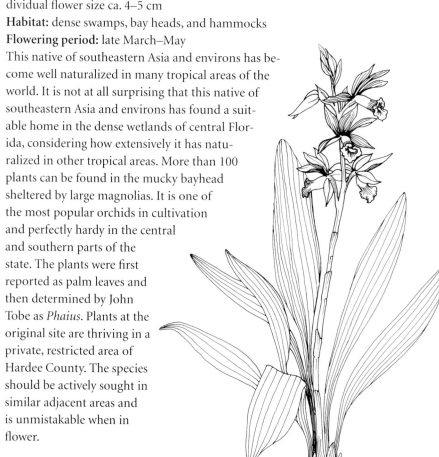

Platanthera

The genus *Platanthera* consists of about 40 North American and Eurasian species, primarily of temperate climes, and is one of the major segregates from *Habenaria*. It is the largest genus of orchids in the United States and Canada and, with eight species and several hybrids, the second largest genus in Florida. The plants are distinguished from *Habenaria* by their lack of both basal rosettes and tubers or tuberoid roots. Many of the species have large, colorful, showy flowers in tall spikes or racemes.

1a	lip margin entire . . . 2
1b	lip margin fringed or erose . . . 4
2a	lip uppermost . . . *Platanthera nivea*, p. 194
2b	lip lowermost . . . 3
3a	lip with a prominent tubercle . . . *Platanthera flava*, p. 190
3b	lip lacking a tubercle . . . *Platanthera clavellata*, p. 186
4a	lip margin merely erose . . . *Platanthera integra*, p. 192
4b	lip margin deeply fringed . . . 5
5a	flowers white . . . *Platanthera blephariglottis* var. *conspicua*, p. 180
5b	flowers yellow or orange . . . 6
6a	spur greatly exceeding the ovary . . . *Platanthera ciliaris*, p. 184
6b	spur equal to or less than the ovary . . . 7
7a	spur about equal to the ovary . . . *Platanthera chapmanii*, p. 182
7b	spur distinctly less than the ovary . . . *Platanthera cristata*, p. 188

Platanthera blephariglottis (Willdenow) Lindley var. *conspicua* (Nash) Luer

southern white fringed orchis

North Carolina south to Florida and west to Texas, primarily on the coastal plain
Florida: widespread in central and northern Florida; threatened
Plant: terrestrial, to 1 m tall
Leaves: 2–4 cauline, lanceolate, 5–35 × 1–5 cm
Flowers: 30–65; arranged in a dense terminal raceme; sepals ovate, petals linear, enclosed within the sepals forming a hood; lip ovate with a delicately fringed margin; perianth pure white; individual flower size 3 cm, not including the 3–4 cm spur
Habitat: open, wet meadows, roadside ditches and seeps, and pine flatwoods
Flowering period: August–October

The fringed orchids of eastern and central North America present some of the showiest orchids of the summer, and the stately snow white plumes of the southern white fringed orchis are no exception. Widely scattered throughout northern and central Florida, this species, like other species of fringed orchids, has fallen victim to construction. Although it prefers open damp meadows, pine flatwoods, and seeps, it now is most frequently found in narrow roadside ditches and open sphagnous areas within the woodlands. Plants flower over a long period in mid- to late summer. For those individuals that have lemon or pale coffee-colored flowers, see the hybrids following the *Platanthera* species.

Platanthera chapmanii (Small) Luer *emend.* Folsom

Chapman's fringed orchis

southern Georgia, Florida, and eastern Texas
Florida: scattered and local populations in northern Florida; proposed endangered
Plant: terrestrial, to 75 cm tall
Leaves: 2–4 cauline, lanceolate, 5–25 × 0.75–4 cm
Flowers: 30–65; arranged in a dense terminal raceme; sepals ovate, petals linear, enclosed within the sepals forming a hood; lip ovate with a delicately fringed margin; perianth brilliant orange; individual flower size 2 cm, not including the 1.75–2 cm spur
Habitat: open, wet meadows, roadside ditches and seeps, and pine flatwoods
Flowering period: late July–early September

Not always easy to identify, Chapman's fringed orchis originally arose as a hybrid between *Platanthera ciliaris,* the orange fringed orchis, and *Platanthera cristata,* the orange crested orchis. Many years of adaptation have resulted in a pollinator-specific, stable, reproducing species. Many texts still cite it as *P. ×chapmanii,* referring to its hybrid status (see Folsom 1984 for details). Because of its origins, this species falls morphologically between the two ancestors. The best character is the spur, which is equal to the lip in length. Also, unlike the contemporary hybrids of *P. ciliaris* and *P. cristata*—(*P. ×channellii;* see the hybrids following the *Platanthera* species)—*P. chapmanii* occurs in pure stands. From a global standpoint this is one of the rarest orchids we know. It is confined to one site in southern Georgia; several scattered although substantial sites in northern Florida; and a few small stands in eastern Texas. More than 90 percent of the known plants in the world are found in Florida.

Platanthera ciliaris (Linnaeus) Lindley

orange fringed orchis

southern Michigan east to Massachusetts, south to Florida and Texas
Florida: widespread in central and northern Florida; threatened
Plant: terrestrial, to 1+ m tall
Leaves: 2–5, cauline, lanceolate, 5–30 × 1–5 cm
Flowers: 30–75; arranged in a dense terminal raceme; sepals ovate, petals linear, fringed at the tip, enclosed within the sepals forming a hood; lip ovate with a delicately fringed margin; perianth yellow to orange; individual flower size 4 cm, not including the 2.5–3.5 cm spur
Habitat: open, wet meadows, roadside ditches and seeps, and pine flatwoods
Flowering period: late July–late September

The orange fringed orchis is a near mirror image of
the southern white fringed orchis, *P. blephariglottis*
var. *conspicua,* but with brilliant deep yellow to
orange plumes that can be a meter in height.
Scattered populations are well known from all
of northern Florida. With a preference for areas that stay wet to damp in the hot, dry days
of summer, populations vary from year to year
in how thrifty they are. This species often
grows with its white cousin, and their hybrid
P. ×*bicolor* often can be found too.

Platanthera clavellata (Michaux) Luer

little club-spur orchis

Ontario to Newfoundland south to Florida and Texas

Florida: exceedingly rare in northern Florida, known only from Gadsden County, with literature reports from Santa Rosa and Calhoun Counties; endangered

Plant: terrestrial, 15–35 cm tall

Leaves: 2, cauline, ovate-lanceolate, 5–15 × 1–2 cm

Flowers: 3–15; arranged in a short dense terminal raceme, flowers usually tilted to one side; sepals ovate, petals linear, enclosed within the sepals forming a hood; lip oblong, the apex obscurely 3-lobed; perianth yellow-green; individual flower size 5 mm, not including the 1 cm spur, which has a swollen tip (clavellate)

Habitat: damp woods

Flowering period: June–August

This is one of the three species of northern orchids that reach their southern limit in Florida. Again, it is one of the commonest orchids north of Florida, but here it is one of our very rarest—confined to a single location. The small, pale greenish flowers are very different from those of any other orchid we have in Florida, and they hold themselves at curious angles on the stem. The distinctive spur, with its swollen tip, is what gives this plant its common name.

Platanthera cristata (Michaux) Lindley

orange crested orchis

Massachusetts south to Florida and west to Texas, primarily on the coastal plain
  forma *straminea* P. M. Brown, pale yellow form
Florida: widespread in central and northern Florida; threatened
Plant: terrestrial, to 80 cm tall
Leaves: 2–4, cauline, lanceolate, 5–20 × 1–3 cm
Flowers: 30–80; arranged in a loose–dense terminal raceme; sepals ovate, petals spatulate with margin crested, enclosed within the sepals forming a hood; lip ovate with a delicately fringed margin; perianth deep yellow to orange; or, in the forma *straminea*, pale yellow; individual flower size 5–7 mm, not including the 7 mm spur
Habitat: open, wet meadows, roadside ditches and seeps, and pine flatwoods
Flowering period: late June–late September

The orange crested orchis is a smaller and perhaps more re-
fined version of the orange fringed orchis, *Platanthera ciliaris.*
It is more widespread in the state and often occurs without
other related species nearby. Open pine flatwoods are its
preferred habitat, although it can also be found in damp
meadows and roadside seeps, especially in the panhandle.
The raceme is usually about 2.5 cm in diameter and the
spur is always shorter than the lip, whereas in *P. ciliaris*
the spur is always much longer than the lip and the
raceme is 4.5+ cm in diameter.

forma *straminea*

Platanthera flava (Linnaeus) Lindley var. *flava*

southern tubercled orchis

southwestern Nova Scotia; Missouri east to Maryland, south to Florida and Texas
Florida: widely scattered in central and northern Florida; threatened
Plant: terrestrial, to 60 cm tall
Leaves: 2–4, cauline, lanceolate, 5–20 × 1–4 cm
Flowers: 10–40; arranged in a loose–dense terminal raceme; sepals and petals ovate, enclosed within the dorsal sepal forming a hood; lip ovate with a prominent tubercle in the center; perianth yellow-green; individual flower size 6–7 mm, not including the 8 mm spur
Habitat: open, wet meadows, roadside ditches and seeps, swamps and shaded floodplains
Flowering period: late April–July

This species is equally at home in shaded, wet woodlands, along streamsides, and on bright sunny but open and damp roadsides. Although the flowers are identical in both kinds of habitats, the habit of the plant varies greatly. Those in shaded habitats tend to be tall and slender, with flowers spaced out along the stem, whereas those in sunnier habitats have flower spikes and leaves that are very compact and crowded. The flowers in the shade tend to be greener in color and those in the sun much yellower, tending toward chartreuse. But in both instances that distinctive tubercled lip is always prominent.

Platanthera integra (Nuttall) Lindley

yellow fringeless orchis

southern New Jersey south to Florida and Texas
Florida: formerly widespread in central and northern Florida; few remaining extant sites; endangered
Plant: terrestrial, to 60 cm tall
Leaves: 1–2, cauline, lanceolate, 5–20 × 1–3 cm
Flowers: 30–65; arranged in a densely flowered terminal raceme; sepals ovate, petals oblong-ovate, enclosed within the dorsal sepal forming a hood; lip ovate, the margin erose; perianth bright yellow-orange; individual flower size 5–6 mm, not including the 6 mm spur
Habitat: open, wet meadows, seeps, damp pine flatwoods
Flowering period: late July–September

Although this species ranges from southern New Jersey to Texas, it is rapidly becoming one of the rarer orchids to be found in North America. Habitat destruction, specifically the draining of wetlands for agriculture and business, is the primary cause of decline. There are still a few scattered sites in central Florida, but the primary locales left for this species are in the Apalachicola National Forest in the central panhandle. The plants are easy to distinguish from the similarly colored fringed orchises as they are considerably smaller and more slender, with a more compact, conical raceme of flowers, and they lack the fringe on the lip.

Platanthera nivea (Nuttall) Lindley

snowy orchis

southern New Jersey south to Florida and Texas
Florida: widespread and scattered throughout Florida; threatened
Plant: terrestrial, to 60 cm tall
Leaves: 2–3, cauline, lanceolate, 5–25 × 1–3 cm
Flowers: 20–50; nonresupinate, arranged in a densely flowered terminal raceme;
sepals and petals oblong-ovate; lip uppermost, linear-elliptic and bent backward
midway; perianth stark, icy white; individual flower size 8–10 mm, not including
the 1.5 cm spur
Habitat: open, wet meadows, prairies, seeps, damp pine
flatwoods
Flowering period: late May–July

Similar in habit and habitat to the yellow fringeless orchis, *P. integra,* the snowy orchis is far more widespread
and occurs in scattered locales throughout the state.
Recently burned pine flatwoods are an excellent habitat
to search for this orchid. In addition, it has the added
feature of being deliciously fragrant. Having the uppermost lip is unique among our Florida species of
Platanthera.

Hybrids:

Platanthera ×bicolor (Rafinesque) Luer
bicolor hybrid fringed orchis

(*P. blephariglottis* var. *conspicua* × *P. ciliaris*)
Plants usually have lemon, pale coffee, or bicolored flowers and retain the overall dimensions of the parents.

Platanthera ×canbyi (Ames) Luer
Canby's hybrid fringed orchis

(*P. blephariglottis* var. *conspicua* × *P. cristata*)
Plants vary in color from nearly white to pale yellow to light orange. The spur is usually about as long as the lip.

Platanthera ×channellii Folsom

Channell's hybrid fringed orchis

(*P. ciliaris* × *P. cristata*)

This hybrid and the species *Platanthera chapmanii* can be difficult to tell apart. One of the best ways is to look about and see which other species are growing nearby. If all the plants are the same, it is most likely *P. chapmanii*, whereas if the colony shows mixed species and only a few intermediate plants are present, it is most likely *P. ×channellii*. See Folsom (1984) for more detail.

Platythelys

This neotropical genus with eight species is found primarily in damp woodlands throughout its range. To those who are familiar with the native orchids of temperate North America it appears as if intermediate between the rattlesnake orchids, *Goodyera*, and the ladies'-tresses, *Spiranthes*, to both of which it is closely related. The two species in Florida have traditionally been addressed as a single species, but careful examination easily sets them apart. Arriving at an accurate geographic distribution will require reexamination of specimens from the various counties.

1a   longest leaf proportions 4:1; central lobe of the lip cordate; capsule prominently ribbed; plants of central and northern Florida
. . . *Platythelys querceticola*, p. 200
1b   longest leaf proportions 6:1; central lobe of the lip rhomboidial, capsule indistinctly ribbed; plants of southern Florida
. . . *Platythelys sagreana*, p. 202

Platythelys querceticola (Lindley) Garay

low ground orchid

Louisiana, Florida; the Bahamas, West Indies, Mexico, Central America, northern South America
Florida: widespread in central and northern Florida; proposed endangered
Plant: terrestrial, to 5–15 cm tall
Leaves: 3–8, cauline, ovate, 5–8 × 1.5–4 cm
Flowers: 8–25; arranged in a loose–dense terminal raceme; sepals ovate; petals rhomboidial, enclosed within the dorsal sepal forming a hood; lip oblong, constricted above the tip; the apex 3-lobed with the central lobe cordate and recurved; perianth whitish green; individual flower size 3–4 mm with a saccate spur; capsule 5.5–6 mm, prominently ribbed
Habitat: swamps and shaded floodplains
Flowering period: late July–September

Although many records have been documented for this species, few extant sites appear to remain. During 1997–99, searches revealed only a few sites despite field checking of all herbarium records. Feral hogs had destroyed much of the rich wooded habitat. In August 2000 a new site was found in Goethe State Forest in Levy County with in excess of 600 flowering plants. The delicate little white spikes stand out dramatically in the dark, rich floodplain of the river bottoms. At this site the *Platythelys* are accompanied by many plants of Florida adder's-mouth, *Malaxis spicata;* fragrant ladies'-tresses, *Spiranthes odorata;* and shadow-witch, *Ponthieva racemosa*. Although *Platythelys querceticola* and the following species, *P. sagreana,* are similar, they tend to grow in different habitats and, for the most part, in different areas of Florida, flowering at different times of the year. The two species were combined for many years and only recently have they again been recognized as distinct.

Platythelys sagreana (A. Richard) Garay

Cuban ground orchid

Florida; West Indies
Florida: a few sites in southern Florida; proposed endangered
Plant: terrestrial, 10–40 cm tall
Leaves: 3–8, cauline, lanceolate, gradually reduced toward the inflorescence, 4–8 × 1 cm
Flowers: 8–25; arranged in a loose–dense terminal raceme; sepals lanceolate; petals rhomboidial, enclosed within the dorsal sepal forming a hood; lip oblong constricted above the tip, ca. 6 mm; the apex 3-lobed with the central lobe cuneate, wedge-shaped, at the base and descending; perianth creamy white; individual flower size 4–5 mm with a saccate spur; capsule 6.5–7 mm faintly ribbed
Habitat: damp to dry hardwood hammocks
Flowering period: late December–March

This, the rarer of the two ground orchids, is found primarily in south Florida. An excellent stand occurs on Long Pine Key in Everglades National Park. The plant has a preference for a much drier, more tropical habitat than that favored by *P. querceticola*. The leaves are proportionately narrower and the plants taller than in *P. querceticola*. In the park *P. sagreana* grows along with the spurred neottia, *Eltroplectris calcarata*. This combination also occurred at Highland Hammocks State Park, but that assemblage appears to have been destroyed by feral hogs.

Pleurothallis

One of the larger genera in the *Orchidaceae, Pleurothallis* has at least 1,500 species and more are described every year. It is one of the largest genera in the neotropics, but only one species, *P. gelida,* makes it as far north as Florida. Individual species in the genus vary from miniscule to massive, but all have single leaves borne by a stem, with the inflorescence arising from somewhere on the stem or at the base of the leaf, and petals—often minute—smaller than the sepals.

Pleurothallis gelida Lindley

frosted pleurothallis

Florida; West Indies, Mexico, Central America, northern South America
Florida: restricted to the Fakahatchee Swamp and environs in Collier County; endangered
Plant: epiphytic, 10–50 cm tall, stem creeping, 5–20 cm long
Leaves: 1, coriaceous, green, elliptic, to 25 × 6 cm
Flowers: 5–25; on single or multiple slender racemes 5–25 cm long; dorsal sepals ovate, lateral sepals elliptic; petals oblong, dentate; lip minute and arched; perianth frosty white; individual flower size 3 × 5 mm
Habitat: trunks of a variety of trees, including oak, pop ash, pond apple, and maple
Flowering period: December–April
This is one of our truly tropical epiphytes, found primarily in Fakahatchee Strand State Preserve. Although many large clumps occur scattered throughout the preserve, few of them flower, and many of the flowers are cleistogamous. Thus it can be a frustrating species to observe in full flower. The large, single leaves are distinctive and cannot be confused with those of any other orchids in our region.

Pogonia

This is a small genus of only three species found in Asia and North America. Formerly the genus included, among others, those species that are now treated in *Triphora, Isotria,* and *Cleistes,* although some current authors are again including *Isotria* and *Cleistes.* We have only one species in the United States and Canada, *Pogonia ophioglossoides,* which has one of the broadest ranges of any orchid in North America. In Florida its pink flowers and broad spatulate lip may remind one of roseate spoonbills. Although variable in color, form, and size, they are a true herald of a good spring of wild orchids. They are often seen in the company of grass-pinks, *Calopogon;* ladies'-tresses, *Spiranthes;* and several of the carnivores, such as pitcher-plants, sundews, and butterworts.

Pogonia ophioglossoides (Linnaeus) Ker-Gawler

rose pogonia; snake-mouth orchid

Manitoba east to Newfoundland and south to Texas and Florida
  forma *albiflora* Rand & Redfield, white-flowered form
Florida: widespread throughout most of the state; absent from the extreme southern counties; threatened
Plant: terrestrial, 8–35 cm tall
Leaves: 1, rarely 2, cauline, ovate, placed midway on the stem, 6–10 × 2 cm
Flowers: 1–3 (4); terminal; sepals and petals similar, lanceolate; the sepals wide spreading; lip spatulate with a deeply fringed margin and bright yellow beard, to 2 cm; perianth from light to dark rosy pink or lavender; or, in the forma *albiflora*, pure white; individual flower size ca. 4 cm
Habitat: moist meadows, open bogs and prairies, roadside ditches and sphagnous seeps
Flowering period: March–May

From Newfoundland to Florida and westward to the
Mississippi Valley, this little jewel adorns open bogs
and meadows, roadside ditches, borrow pits, and
sphagnous seeps. Color and form varies greatly
from colony to colony; from those with the petals
and sepals very narrow to the rare individual with
the sepals and petals broad and rounded; and
from pale lilac to intense magenta.

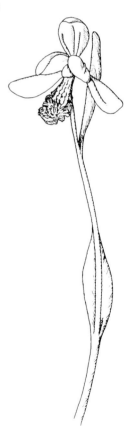

forma *albiflora*

Polystachya

This is a pantropical genus of about 150 species, most of which occur in Africa. The nonresupinate flowers, their parts joining to create a helmetlike appearance, are distinctive, as are the plants, which have a multiple-branched inflorescence. We have only one species in Florida, the **yellow helmet orchid**, *P. concreta.* This species is sometimes also known as *P. flavescens,* but if the New and Old World species are maintained as separate, then *P. flavescens* cannot be a synonym.

Polystachya concreta (Jacquin) Garay & Sweet

yellow helmet orchid

Florida; West Indies, Mexico, Central America, northern South America
Florida: uncommon; known from most of the southern counties; endangered
Plant: epiphytic, forming large masses, to 1+ m across; pseudobulbs cylindrical and tapered, 5 × 1 cm
Leaves: 2–5, thin, lanceolate-linear, from the tip of the pseudobulb, up to 30 × 4 cm
Flowers: 10–60; nonresupinate, usually on a panicle, or branched raceme, the flowers all to one side; sepals broadly ovate; petals slender and spatulate; lip 3-lobed and the floral parts arranged to form a helmet; individual flower size 5 mm
Habitat: low down on trunk and branches of a variety of trees, including buttonwood, oak, maple, and pop ash
Flowering period: September–December, but may occur at any time of year
This delightful and colorful orchid is frequently encountered. Flowering plants may vary from a single growth to massive colonies more than a meter in length and having several hundred flowers. The helmet-shaped flowers are so distinctive that there is never a question as to its identity. The species is widespread and grows farther north than do many of the tropical epiphytes.

Ponthieva

Plants in this genus of about 50 neotropical species form herbaceous basal rosettes and a pubescent to puberulent raceme of flowers, usually set at right angles
to the stem. Two species are found in Florida, one of which is exceedingly widespread while the other is restricted and rare.

1a   petal broad, prominently striped with green
       ... *Ponthieva racemosa,* p. 214
1b   petals narrow lacking the green striping
       ... *Ponthieva brittoniae,* p. 216

Ponthieva brittoniae Ames

Mrs. Britton's shadow-witch

Florida; the Bahamas, Cuba
Florida: very rare and known from only Miami-Dade County; endangered
Plant: terrestrial, 5–35 cm tall
Leaves: 4 or 5 in a basal rosette, light green, elliptic, 2–8 × 1–3 cm, often withered at flowering time
Flowers: 5–20; nonresupinate; sepals green, the dorsal hidden behind the petals; petals white, reflexed upward; lip white with 2 dark green blotches; individual flower size 5–6 mm, the flowers tipped out from the rachis at about 30° and the ovary green
Habitat: hot, dry, sunny coral-rock limestone
Flowering period: January–February

Mrs. Britton's shadow-witch was named for Elizabeth Britton, a well-recognized botanist and the wife of Nathaniel Lord Britton, then director of the New York Botanical Garden. The plant has always been very rare in the United States, and although originally named as a species by Ames in 1910, it was buried in synonymy for many years and then transferred to a variety by Luer in 1972. Reports of plants of this species from Sarasota and Collier Counties have proven all to be small-flowered *Ponthieva racemosa.* In both cases the reports were from habitats contrary to where *P. brittoniae* is found in Everglades National Park. It has been many years since live plants were last seen in the wild, despite nearly annual searches for them. The fireroad within the park where they grew was widened, and the plants were apparently destroyed.

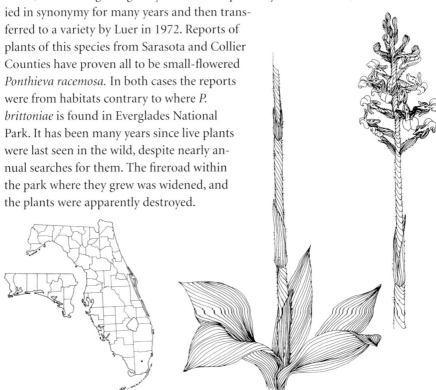

Ponthieva racemosa (Walter) Mohr

shadow-witch

southeastern Virginia south to Florida and west to eastern Texas; West Indies, Mexico, Central America, northern South America
Florida: local–frequent and widespread throughout the entire state
Plant: terrestrial, 8–60 cm tall
Leaves: 3–8 basal rosette, dark green, elliptic, 3–15 × 1–5 cm
Flowers: 8–30; nonresupinate; sepals light green, veined with darker green; petals white, veined with bright green; lip white with a green, concave center; individual flower size (6) 8–(9) 12 mm, the flowers tipped out from the rachis at about 60° and the ovary brown
Habitat: damp–wet, shaded woodlands, swamps and riverbanks
Flowering period: September–February

Ponthieva racemosa—as common as *P. brittoniae* is rare— often forms large patches in wet woods along seasonally flooded stream banks. Rarely is it found without other orchids, and most often is accompanied by the fragrant ladies'-tresses, *Spiranthes odorata;* Florida adder's-mouth, *Malaxis spicata;* and in a few areas the low ground orchid, *Platythelys querceticola* and the southern oval ladies'-tresses, *Spiranthes ovalis.*

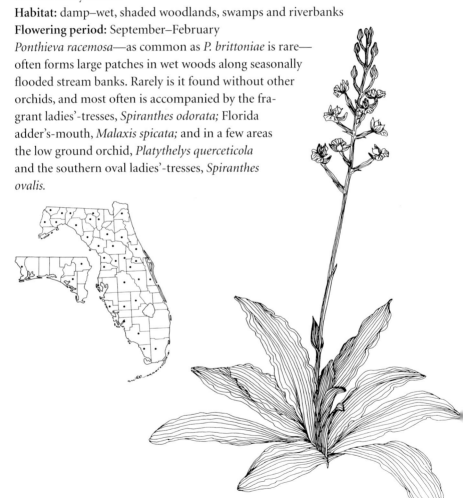

Prescottia

A small genus, this consists of about 20 neotropical species closely related to *Cranichis* and, more distantly, to *Spiranthes*. The plants all form delicate satiny rosettes and have tiny, nonresupinate flowers in slender spikes. We have but one species in Florida, the **small-flowered prescottia**, *Prescottia oligantha*, and it is restricted to the southern counties.

Prescottia oligantha (Swartz) Lindley

small-flowered prescottia

Florida; West Indies, Mexico, Central America, South America
Florida: very rare, known only from Miami-Dade County and historically from Lee (Collier) County; endangered
Plant: terrestrial, 10–30 cm tall
Leaves: 2–4 in a basal rosette, elliptic, 3–7 × 1–4 cm, often starting to wither at flowering time
Flowers: 10–50; nonresupinate; sepals ovate and recurved; petals elliptic and recurved; lip concave; individual flower size 1–2 mm, the flowers appearing green and pink, although white on the interior of the petals and lip
Habitat: dark hardwood hammocks
Flowering period: February
This slender, diminutive orchid is one of the most easily overlooked in southern Florida. It was first found in 1903 near Homestead, and although that site was destroyed for housing, it is now known from Everglades National Park. It was also found at that early time in Lee County, without a cited location other than "swamp," and may have well been in what is today the Fakahatchee Swamp in Collier County, as other collections from that date are also Fakahatchee species.

Prosthechea

The genus *Prosthechea* was revalidated in 1997 by Wesley Higgins at the University of Florida. It is among the segregate genera from the *Epidendrum* alliance and contains many of the species that were formerly in the genus *Encyclia,* itself a segregate from *Epidendrum.* The flowers are usually nonresupinate, and most are relatively showy and exhibit the "clamshell" lip.

1a   lip lowermost . . . *Prosthechea boothiana* var. *erythronioides,* p. 222
1b   lip uppermost . . . 2
2a   flowers large, to 4 or 5 cm, green and purple
     . . . *Prosthechea cochleata* var. *triandra,* p. 224
2b   flowers tiny, 2–4 mm, often cleistogamous
     . . . *Prosthechea pygmaea,* p. 226

Prosthechea boothiana (Lindley) W. E. Higgins var. *erythronioides* (Small) W. E. Higgins

Florida dollar orchid

Florida; the nominate variety throughout the West Indies, Mexico, Central America
Florida: uncommon; known from four of the southern counties; endangered
Plant: epiphytic, pseudobulbs circular and flattened; up to 3.8 × 2.8 cm
Leaves: 1–3, thin, oblanceolate, keeled, bright green, from the tip of the pseudobulb, 6–18 × 1–5 cm
Flowers: 1–10 (15); on a slender peduncle up to 30 cm long, from the apex of the pseudobulb; sepals and petals similar, oblanceolate, yellow to tan with darker brown or purplish blotches; lip white to pale yellow-green with less markings; individual flower size 2–4 cm; anthers 3 (rather than the usual 2)

Habitat: low down on trunks and branches of a variety of trees, including mangrove, buttonwood, oak, maple, and pop ash
Flowering period: August–November

The Florida dollar orchid, deriving its common name from the round, flattened pseudobulbs, is widespread within the coastal swamps of the southernmost counties and rare in freshwater habitats. It has been heavily collected over the past century, resulting in only a few thrifty sites today. The flowers are "triandrous," having three anthers instead of two anthers and a rostellum. The result is that they are self-fertilizing. This feature also occurs in other orchids in the region and is perhaps the result of an adaptation to the lack of pollinators at the periphery of the range.

Prosthechea cochleata (Linnaeus) W. E. Higgins var. *triandra* (Ames) W. E. Higgins

Florida clamshell orchid

Florida; the nominate variety throughout the West Indies, Mexico, Central America and northern South America

    forma *albidoflava* (P. M.Brown) P. M. Brown, white and yellow-flowered form

Florida: uncommon; known from most of the southern counties; endangered

Plant: epiphytic, pseudobulbs ovoid and compressed; up to 15.6 × 3.8 cm

Leaves: 1–3, thin, linear-lanceolate, keeled, from the tip of the pseudobulb, 5–30 × 1–5 cm

Flowers: 1–10 (15); nonresupinate, on a slender peduncle from the apex of the pseudobulb up to 40 cm long; sepals and petals similar, linear-lanceolate, yellow–green with a few purple spots at the base; lip uppermost, broadly cordate, concave, purple to brown with prominently colored veins radiating from the base; or, in the forma *albidoflava,* creamy white sepals and petals with a yellow lip; individual flower size 3–6 cm; anthers 3 (rather than the usual 2)

Habitat: on trunks and branches of a variety of trees, including buttonwood, oak, maple, and pop ash

Flowering period: year-round, but more heavily September–May

The Florida clamshell orchid is one of the most intriguing species to be found in the state. The fantastically arranged flowers, reminiscent of an octopus with a clamshell, never fail to delight. The three-anthered form has somewhat broader pseudobulbs than the nominate race, and different clones have flowers of varying size and color. This species is one of the most popular among hobbyist growers, for whom one of the Central American races is often the first orchid acquired. In cultivation a plant can be perpetually in flower.

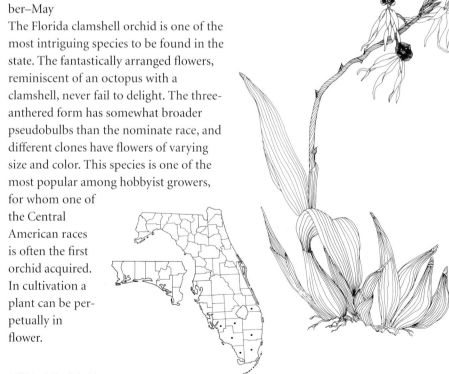

forma *albidoflava*

Prosthechea pygmaea (Hooker) W. E. Higgins

dwarf butterfly orchid

Florida; West Indies, Mexico, Central America, South America
Florida: very rare; known only from a few trees in Collier County; endangered
Plant: epiphytic, pseudobulbs slender, fusiform, up to 8 × 2 cm
Leaves: 2–3, elliptic, from the tip of the pseudobulb, 1–8 × 0.8–1.3 cm
Flowers: 1–3; sessile between the leaves at the apex of the pseudobulb; sepals, oblanceolate, light green; petals light green, linear; lip white with a bright purple tip; individual flower size 2–4 mm
Habitat: low down on trunks and branches of a variety of trees including oak, maple, pop ash, and pond apple
Flowering period: October–January
This is both the rarest and the tiniest-flowered of the epidendroid orchids in Florida. It is known not just from a single area in Collier County but from only a few individual plants on a few specific trees. The plants, surprisingly enough, can form large colonies, with the largest over a meter in length with several hundred leads. The tiny flowers often do not open fully, so that although there may be many flowers on a given plant, finding good open flowers can involve a real search.

Pteroglossaspis

A genus with strong African affinities, *Pteroglossaspis* consists of seven species, two of which occur in the New World. Only one, the **crestless plume orchid**, *P. ecristata,* is found in the southeastern United States. The tall scapes are terminated by a short spike of hooded flowers, and the leaves grow apart from the scape. The genus was formerly included within *Eulophia.*

Pteroglossaspis ecristata (Fernald) Rolfe

crestless plume orchid

North Carolina south to Florida and west to Louisiana; Cuba
    forma *flava* P. M. Brown, yellow-flowered form
Florida: becoming increasingly rare although widespread throughout most of the state; threatened, proposed endangered
Plant: terrestrial, 50–170 cm tall
Leaves: 3–4; lanceolate, yellow-green, up to 70 × 3.5 cm

Flowers: 10–30; a terminal raceme atop an elongated scape; sepals and petals similar, lanceolate, lemon yellow to grass green, forming an elaborate hood; lip 3-lobed, ovate, purple-brown to black with a green to yellow margin; or, in the forma *flava,* the perianth entirely yellow; individual flower size ca.1.5–2 cm
Habitat: old fields, orchards, pine flatwoods, prairies; usually in sandy soils
Flowering period: August–October
Perhaps one of the Florida species that looks least like an orchid, the crestless plume orchid was at one time a plant to be found fairly frequently and throughout much of the state. In recent times it has declined dramatically, and it is now difficult to find, the difficulty compounded by the fact that the plants do not appear every year. The tall scape produces a raceme of relatively few flowers, which have been described as green and black orchids on a stick. In Miami-Dade County a curious cleistogamous form occurs.

forma *flava*

Sacoila

This is the showiest and largest-flowered genus among the many *Spiranthes* segregates. Although there are only 10 species in the genus, it is exceedingly widespread throughout the New World tropics, with two of the species and one additional variety occurring in Florida. *Sacoila* can be distinguished from the closely allied *Stenorrhynchos,* which does not occur in Florida, by the presence of a mentum, or saccate spur, at the base of the flower.

1a   plants with leaves at flowering time
       ... *Sacoila lanceolata* var. *paludicola,* p. 234
1b   plants leafless at flowering ... 2
2a   mentum less than ⅓ the length of the perianth; plants puberulent
       ... *Sacoila lanceolata* var. *lanceolata,* p. 232
2b   mentum greater than ⅓, usually greater than ½ the length of
       the perianth; plants scurfy ... *Sacoila squamulosa,* p. 236

Sacoila lanceolata (Aublet) Garay var. *lanceolata*

leafless beaked orchid

Florida; West Indies, Mexico, Central America, South America
    forma *albidaviridis* Catling & Sheviak, white and green-flowered form
    forma *folsomii* P. M. Brown, golden-flowered form
Florida: throughout peninsular Florida, more frequently from Orlando southward; threatened
Plant: terrestrial, 20–60 cm tall
Leaves: 4–6; oblanceolate, 5–35 × 2–8 cm; absent at flowering time
Flowers: 10–40; in a terminal raceme atop a stout scape; sepals and petals similar, lanceolate, coral to brick red; lip lanceolate, tapered at the apex, white to pale pink; or, in the forma *albidaviridis,* the perianth white and green; or, in the forma *folsomii,* the perianth golden with a rose flush; individual flower size ca. 2 cm
Habitat: road shoulders and median strips along the highways, old fields, pine flatwoods
Flowering period: April–June

This is one of the most striking of all our Florida orchids. In early May several hundred plants can often be seen in flower along the Florida Turnpike south of Orlando and along I-75 near Port Charlotte. The two-color forms are usually mixed in with the typical red. The nomenclature of this species is perhaps the most convoluted of any orchid we have. Luer (1972) lists 34 synonyms in eight genera!

forma *folsomii*

forma *albidaviridis*

Sacoila lanceolata (Aublet) Garay var. *paludicola* (Luer) Sauleda, Wunderlin & Hansen

Fakahatchee beaked orchid

Florida; Cuba
forma *aurea* P. M. Brown, golden-yellow flowered form
Florida: known as a native only from Collier County; plants in Miami-Dade and Broward Counties may have been introduced; threatened
Plant: terrestrial, 20–50 cm tall
Leaves: 2–4; oblanceolate, 10–20 × 2–4 cm; present at flowering time
Flowers: 5–25; in a terminal raceme atop a slender scape; sepals and petals similar, lanceolate, bright red, floral bracts similar in color or, in the forma *lutea*, golden yellow; lip lanceolate, tapered at the apex, red to pale pink; individual flower size ca. 2 cm
Habitat: hammocks and tramways; old logs and stumps
Flowering period: February–March
Seen in the great swamps of Collier County, the scarlet Fakahatchee beaked orchid is striking among the verdant foliage, especially along the old tramways in the Fakahatchee Strand State Preserve. Plants at Corkscrew Swamp are primarily on old logs and stumps. Recently additional sites have been found in local county parks in Palm Beach, Broward, and Miami-Dade Counties. These may be the result of introductions. Catling (1987) discusses at length the breeding systems of this and the nominate variety.

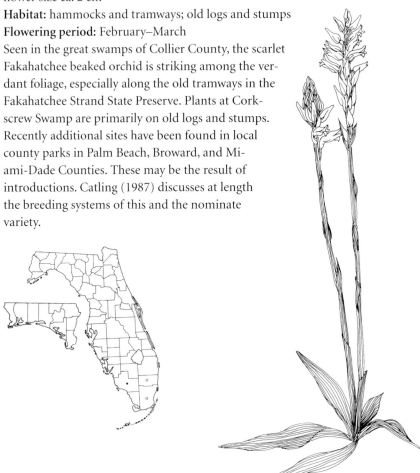

forma *aurea*

Sacoila squamulosa (Kunth) Garay

hoary beaked orchid

Florida; West Indies, Mexico, Central America
Florida: currently known from only central Florida; proposed endangered
Plant: terrestrial or lithophytic, 40–80 cm tall
Leaves: 4–6; oblanceolate, 5–35 × 3–8 cm; absent at flowering time
Flowers: 10–40; in a terminal raceme atop a stout scape; sepals and petals similar, lanceolate, brick red; lip lanceolate, tapered at the apex, pale pink; individual flower size ca. 3 cm
Habitat: (as it is currently known) damp pinelands and limestone boulders
Flowering period: April–May
This is the most recent addition to the orchid flora of Florida and the United States. Plants have been either overlooked or not well distinguished from the more common *Sacoila lanceolata* var. *lanceolata*. Nir (2000) recognized this species and listed Florida as part of the range. That resulted in determining that a large stand of nonconforming *Sacoila* in Marion County was indeed this species. It is a tall and handsome plant. Upon close examination it has the unmistakable scurfy or hoary white dots in addition to the short pubescence of *S. lanceolata*.

Spathoglottis

This is a genus of about 40 Asiatic species with large plicate leaves and showy and colorful flowers. Only one species, the **Javanese violet orchid**, *Spathoglottis plicata,* occurs in Florida, and it is also widely naturalized throughout the Caribbean. Nir (2000) reports it from 10 of the islands. This was one of the first species of plants to colonize the slopes of the mighty volcano at Krakatoa after it blew. Having been introduced for cultivation for cut flowers in Hawaii, it has been thoroughly naturalized on some of those islands.

Spathoglottis plicata Blume*

Javanese violet orchid

Florida; southeastern Asia and the Pacific islands; naturalized elsewhere
Florida: persisting and spreading in Palm Beach County
Plant: terrestrial, to 1 m tall
Leaves: 4–7; plicate, elliptic-lanceolate, 8–10 × 40–60 (100) cm; enclosing an ovoid pseudobulb to 4 cm tall and covered with the old leaf bases
Flowers: 8–27; in a terminal raceme atop a stout scape, which arises from the base of the pseudobulb; sepals and petals similar, ovate, 10–20 × 6–10 mm, rosy purple; lip strongly 3-lobed, 14–18 mm long, the lateral lobes to 18 mm across; individual flower size ca. 4 cm
Habitat: abandoned shellpits and surrounding pond shores and woodlands
Flowering period: May–July
Inclusion of this species as a naturalized orchid in Florida is no great surprise. In both of Luer's works (1972, 1975) he comments that this species occasionally survives outside local greenhouses and might someday naturalize and be more widespread. Greg Allikas (pers. comm.) of West Palm Beach reports several areas of Palm Beach County where *Spathoglottis* has naturalized in abandoned shellpits and surrounding areas. He has observed the plants since the early 1980s. They often grow with *Bletia purpurea, Eulophia alta,* and another naturalized species, *Oeceoclades maculata.*

Spiranthes

This is a cosmopolitan genus of about 50 species, treated in the strictest sense, and is one of the most easily recognized genera, although including some plants that are difficult to identify as to species. In the United States and Canada we have 25 species, of which 13 species and one variety can be found in Florida. The relatively slender, often twisted stems and spikes of small white or creamy yellow (or pink in *S. sinensis*) flowers are universally recognizable. It is possible to find a *Spiranthes* in flower somewhere in Florida every day of the year.

1a leaves present (or withering) at flowering time . . . 2
1b leaves absent at flowering time . . . 14
2a leaves linear . . . 3
2b leaves ovate to oblanceolate . . . 12
3a leaves very slender, essentially basal and withering at flowering time . . . 4
3b leaf blades broad, to 1 cm, and grasslike . . . 5
4a margin of lip crenulate . . . *Spiranthes amesiana,* p. 242
4b margin of lip ciliate-undulate . . . *Spiranthes torta,* p. 264
5a plants spring flowering . . . 6
5b plants autumn flowering . . . 9
6a sepals appressed, corolla forming a slender tube, flowers white . . . *Spiranthes praecox,* p. 260
6b sepals spreading, corolla otherwise, flowers white, cream, or green . . . 7
7a pubescence of sharp-pointed articulate hairs . . . *Spiranthes vernalis,* p. 268
7b pubescences of ball-tipped hairs . . . 8
8a flowers creamy green, lip with dark green veins . . . *Spiranthes sylvatica,* p. 262
8b flowers white, lip creamy yellow . . . *Spiranthes laciniata,* p. 250
9a flowers less than 5 mm in length . . . 10
9b flowers greater than 5 mm in length (often greater than 1 cm in length) . . . 11
10a flowers sexual, rostellum present . . . *Spiranthes ovalis* var. *ovalis,* p. 256
10b flowers asexual, rostellum absent (flowers are often cleistogamous) . . . *Spiranthes ovalis* var. *erostellata,* p. 258
11a sepals wide spreading; lip long, narrow, and descending; leaves narrow, less than 1 cm . . . *Spiranthes longilabris,* p. 252

11b sepals moderately spreading; lip broad and moderately descending; leaves often well over 1 cm wide . . . *Spiranthes odorata,* p. 254

12a plants densely pubescent . . . *Spiranthes brevilabris,* p. 244

12b plants essentially glabrous or sparingly pubescent . . . 13

13a flowers white with a green lip . . . *Spiranthes eatonii,* p. 246

13b flowers creamy yellow with a yellow lip
. . . *Spiranthes floridana,* p. 248

14a flowers pure white . . . *Spiranthes tuberosa,* p. 266

14b flowers with a green central portion on the lip . . . 15

15a margin of lip crenulate . . . *Spiranthes amesiana,* p. 242

15b margin of lip ciliate-undulate . . . *Spiranthes torta,* p. 264

Note: For other genera often treated as *Spiranthes,* see *Beloglottis, Cyclopogon, Mesadenus, Pelexia,* and *Sacoila.*

Spiranthes amesiana Schlechter *emend.* P. M. Brown

Ames' ladies'-tresses

Florida; the Bahamas, Nicaragua
Florida: known only from two collections in Miami-Dade County; proposed endangered
Plant: terrestrial, 20–50 cm tall
Leaves: 1 or 2; linear, 5–20 × 0.5 cm; absent or withering at flowering time
Flowers: 6–12; in a terminal spike; sepals and petals similar, lanceolate; lip spade-shaped, with a ciliolate margin, tapered at the apex, green with a white apron; individual flower size ca. 3–4 mm
Habitat: rocky pinelands
Flowering period: May

Schlechter's description in 1920 of *Spiranthes amesiana* was based on a herbarium sheet of specimens mixed with *S. torta*, to which it is similar. He based his segregation on the lip shape and margin and number of flowers. He also cited a specimen from the Bahamas. Until Hamer published in 1982, *S. amesiana* was placed in synonymy with *S. torta*. Hamer's discovery of plants in Central America has encouraged Florida orchidists to reexamine plants of *S. torta*. Recent reviews of *S. torta* specimens have revealed an excellent collection by George Avery in 1976 that appears to be *S. amesiana*. The distinctive smaller flowers may be a key character in finding living plants of *S. amesiana,* and the earlier flowering dates of the type may perhaps have bearing. The Avery specimen is dated June 27, and the dates on the type are nearly a month earlier, so all early-flowering *S. torta* need to be carefully examined.

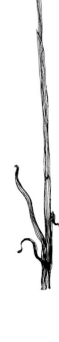

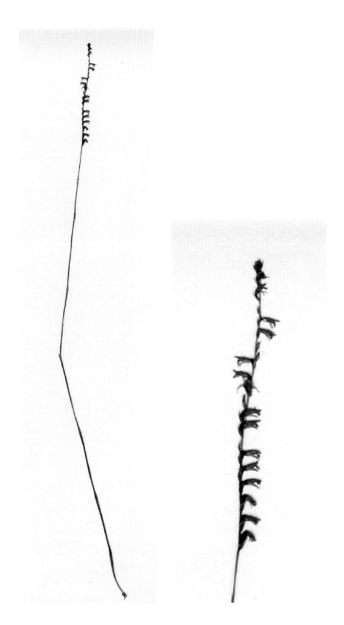

Spiranthes brevilabris Lindley

short-lipped ladies'-tresses

Alabama, Florida, Georgia, Louisiana, Mississippi, Texas
Florida: known only from a single extant site in Levy County; historically from a variety of counties scattered throughout the state; endangered
Plant: terrestrial, 20–40 cm tall, densely pubescent with capitate hairs
Leaves: 3–6; ovate, 2–6 × 1–2 cm, yellow-green; withering at flowering time
Flowers: 10–35; in a single rank, spiraled or secund; sepals and petals similar, elliptic; perianth ivory yellow with a dense pubescence; lip oblong, with the apex undulate-lacerate; individual flower size ca. 4–5 mm
Habitat: grassy roadsides, cemeteries
Flowering period: late February–April

This delicate, nearly ephemeral little ladies'-tresses is one of four species that produce winter rosettes. The leaves on *S. brevilabris* are more of a yellow-green than in the other three species. The creamy yellow, densely pubescent flowers are difficult to pick out on the roadsides when traveling, whereas the white-flowered species tend to stand out regardless of their size. After several years of intensive field work, only a single site could be found in Florida, in Levy County. Elsewhere in the southeastern United States no other extant populations could be found.

Spiranthes eatonii Ames *ex* P. M. Brown

Eaton's ladies'-tresses

eastern Texas east through all of Florida and north to southeastern Virgina, primarily on the coastal plain

Florida: specimens are known from many counties throughout the state but only a few extant populations can be found; proposed threatened

Plant: terrestrial, 20–50 cm tall

Leaves: 3–6; oblanceolate–lanceolate, 5.5 × 0.75–1 cm; withering quickly at flowering time

Flowers: 10–35; in a single rank, spiraled or secund; sepals spatulate, green at the base; petals lanceolate, green at the base; perianth white; lip oblong, centrally green with the apex undulate; individual flower size ca. 4–5 mm

Habitat: roadsides, cemeteries, drier pine flatwoods

Flowering period: late March–early May

This species has been easily confused with *Spiranthes lacera* var. *lacera* and var. *gracilis,* neither of which grows in Florida, and in herbarium specimens with *S. floridana, S. brevilabris, S. tuberosa,* and *S. torta.* However, *S. eatonii* flowers in the winter and spring. It is the only white-flowered, basal-leaved *Spiranthes* within its range to bloom at that time of year. The narrow, oblanceolate leaves are distinctive within this group. For many years plants of *S. eatonii* were identified as *S. lacera* and its southern variety *gracilis,* but neither name is a synonym.

Spiranthes floridana (Wherry) Cory *emend.* P. M. Brown

Florida ladies'-tresses

eastern Texas east through all of Florida and north to North Carolina, primarily on the coastal plain

Florida: specimens are known from many counties throughout the state but there is only one extant population; proposed endangered

Plant: terrestrial, 20–40 cm tall, glabrous to sparsely pubescent

Leaves: 3–5, ovate, 2–6 × 1–2 cm, yellow-green; withering at flowering time

Flowers: 10–35; in a single rank, spiraled or secund; sepals and petals similar; perianth creamy yellow; lip oblong, centrally yellow with the apex undulate; individual flower size ca. 4–5 mm

Habitat: roadsides, cemeteries, pine flatwoods

Flowering period: late March–early May

Spiranthes floridana and *S. brevilabris* are often and easily confused, although the degree of pubescence is an excellent diagnostic tool in the field. This species has become very rare in Florida, with only a single extant population known in 1998–2000, in Bradford County.

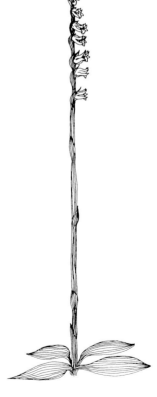

Spiranthes laciniata (Small) Ames

lace-lipped ladies'-tresses

eastern Texas east through all of Florida and north to southern New Jersey, primarily on the coastal plain; threatened

Florida: widespread and local to common throughout the state

Plant: terrestrial, 20–95 cm tall, densely pubescent with capitate hairs

Leaves: 3–5, lanceolate, 5–40 × 1–1.7 cm

Flowers: 10–50; in a single rank, spiraled or secund; sepals and petals similar, elliptic; perianth white to ivory; lip oblong, with the apex undulate-lacerate, the central portion of the lip yellow; individual flower size ca. 1 cm

Habitat: wet, grassy roadsides, ditches, swamps, and shallow open water, often in the prairies of the southern counties

Flowering period: May–July

This species is easily distinguished from *Spiranthes vernalis,* which it superficially resembles, by its ball-tipped hairs rather than the pointed articulate hairs found on *S. vernalis.* It typically flowers later than *S. vernalis* where the two are sympatric. The tall, creamy white spikes are a common sight, especially in southern Collier and Monroe Counties in the Big Cypress National Preserve, where the plant often grows with Simpson's grass-pink, *Calopogon tuberosus* var. *simpsonii.*

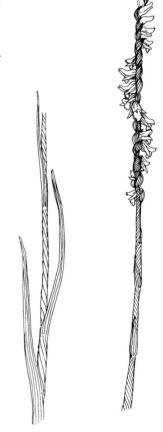

Spiranthes longilabris Lindley

long-lipped ladies'-tresses

eastern Texas east through all of Florida and north to southeastern Virginia
Florida: widespread records throughout the state but currently very rare; perhaps
known from only two sites in 1999; proposed endangered
Plant: terrestrial, 20–50 cm tall, sparsely pubescent with clubbed hairs
Leaves: 3–5, linear-lanceolate, 8–15 × 0.5 cm; often withered at flowering time
Flowers: 10–30; in a tight single rank, spiraled or secund; sepals and petals similar, lanceolate; perianth white to ivory; lip oblong, with the apex undulate-lacerate, the central portion of the lip yellow; the sepals wide spreading; individual
flower size 1–1.5 cm
Habitat: moist, grassy roadsides, pine flatwoods
Flowering period: November–December
This species is perhaps the most handsome of all the ladies'-
tresses. The close-ranked flowers spread their long sepals
like wings, and the long creamy yellow lip descends from the
front of each large flower. It is an unmistakable plant and
easily identified. Unfortunately it is becoming increasingly
difficult to locate. Several years of searching finally resulted
in finding a single locality in Levy County in 1999.

Spiranthes odorata (Nuttall) Lindley

fragrant ladies'-tresses

eastern Texas north to Oklahoma and Arkansas, east to Florida and north to Delaware

Florida: widespread throughout the state and locally abundant

Plant: terrestrial or semiaquatic, 20–110 cm tall, pubescent, stoloniferous

Leaves: 3–5, linear-oblanceolate, up to 52 × 4 cm; rigidly ascending or spreading

Flowers: 10–30; in several tight ranks; sepals and petals similar, lanceolate; perianth white to ivory; lip oblong, tapering to the apex, the central portion of lip creamy yellow or green; the sepals extending forward; individual flower size 1–1.8 cm

Habitat: moist, grassy roadsides, pine flatwoods, cypress swamps, wooded river floodplains

Flowering period: October–January

This is by far the largest of our native ladies'-tresses. Plants in wooded swamplands can reach a full meter in height. Despite the typical size of *Spiranthes odorata,* a definable ecotype that occupies mown road shoulders is often no more than 15 cm tall. This species typically occurs in seasonally inundated sites and may bloom while emerging from shallow water. Because it is at its extreme southern range limit in Florida, individual plants may bloom sporadically throughout much of the year. The rather thick, broad leaves give the plant a distinctive vegetative habit. The long, wide-spreading roots produce vegetative offshoots (stolons) often 30 cm from the parent, giving rise to extensive clonal colonies. The distinctive stoloniferous habit of this species helps set it apart from the more northerly *S. cernua,* which does not occur in Florida.

dwarf roadside habit

Spiranthes ovalis Lindley var. ovalis

southern oval ladies'-tresses

Arkansas, Texas, Louisiana, Mississippi, Florida
Florida: rare and local in north-central Florida; endangered
Plant: terrestrial, 20–40 cm tall, pubescent
Leaves: 2–4, basal and on the lower half of the stem, oblanceolate, 3–15 × 0.5–1.5 cm; present at flowering time
Flowers: 10–50; in 3 tight ranks; sepals and petals similar, lanceolate; perianth white; lip oblong, tapering to the apex with a delicate undulate margin, the sepals extending forward; individual flower size 5.5–7 mm; rostellum and viscidium, the portion of the column that permits transfer of the pollen, present, therefore the plants are sexual
Habitat: rich, damp woodlands and floodplains
Flowering period: October–December

One of the most charming of all the ladies'-tresses, *Spiranthes ovalis* is the only species exclusively of woodland habitat. The pristine small white flowers are usually carried in three distinctive, tight, vertical ranks. In variety *ovalis* the flowers are complete and therefore fertilization is effected by a pollinator. The flowers are always fully expanded. This nominate variety, var. *ovalis*, is relatively rare, found in only a few states.

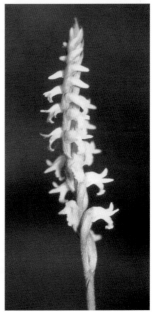

Spiranthes ovalis Lindley var. *erostellata* Catling

northern oval ladies'-tresses

Ontario south to Illinois and Arkansas, east to Ohio and western Pennsylvania, and south to northern Florida

Florida: very rare and local in three northern counties; endangered

Plant: terrestrial, 20–40 cm tall, pubescent

Leaves: 2–4, basal and on the lower half of the stem, oblanceolate, 3–15 × 0.5–1.5 cm; present at flowering time

Flowers: 10–50; in three tight ranks; sepals and petals similar, lanceolate; perianth white; lip oblong, tapering to the apex with a delicate undulate margin; the sepals extending forward; individual flower size 3.5–5 mm; rostellum lacking, therefore the plants self-pollinating; only occasionally are plants with fully open flowers seen

Habitat: rich, damp woodlands and floodplains

Flowering period: October–December

In most plants of *S. ovalis* var. *erostellata,* the flowers are never quite fully open, or in many individuals they are tiny cleistogamous flowers, and the ovaries are simultaneously swollen on each flower. Flowers of *S. ovalis* var. *ovalis* do open fully and the ovaries swell progressively. In Florida both varieties grow in the same site in Columbia and Suwannee Counties and are easy to distinguish. Also present at this site are *S. odorata* and the hybrid between it and *S. ovalis* var. *ovalis, S.* ×*itchetuckneensis.*

Spiranthes praecox (Walter) S. Watson

giant ladies'-tresses

Arkansas south to Texas, east to Florida and north to New Jersey, primarily on the coastal plain

    forma *albolabia* P. M. Brown & C. McCartney, white-lipped form

Florida: widespread and in nearly every county; one of our most common *Spiranthes*

Plant: terrestrial, 20–75 cm tall, sparsely pubescent

Leaves: 2–5; basal and on the lower third of the stem, linear-lanceolate, 8–20 × .5–1 cm; present at flowering time

Flowers: 10–40; varying from secund to a dense spiral; sepals and petals similar, lanceolate; perianth white; lip ovate-oblong, rounded to the apex with a delicate undulate margin with distinctive green veining; or, in the forma *albolabia,* the lip appearing pure white and the veins pale lemon yellow, the sepals appressed and extending forward to create a tubular flower; individual flower size 6–9 mm

Habitat: roadsides, meadows, prairies

Flowering period: February–June

This is one of the most frequently encountered orchids in Florida but like most *Spiranthes* varies from year to year. It starts flowering shortly before *Spiranthes vernalis* and continues throughout the spring. The tubular flowers are distinctive and help separate it quickly from *S. vernalis.* In rare situations the two hybridize, producing *Spiranthes* ×*meridionalis.*

forma
albolabia

forma *albolabia*

Spiranthes sylvatica P. M. Brown

woodland ladies'-tresses

East Texas to Florida, north to southeastern Virginia
Florida: local in central and northern counties
Plant: terrestrial, 25–75 cm tall, sparsely pubescent with capitate hairs
Leaves: 3–7; basal and on the lower third of the stem, linear-lanceolate, 10–35 × 0.8–1.57 cm, present at flowering time
Flowers: 10–30; in a dense spike usually appearing as multiple ranks; sepals and petals similar, lanceolate; perianth cream green; lip ovate-oblong, rounded and broadened to the apex with a delicate undulate margin with distinctive darker green veining, the sepals slightly spreading; individual flower size 1–1.7 cm
Habitat: shaded roadsides, open woodlands and live oak hammocks
Flowering period: late March–early May

This is the most recent *Spiranthes* species to be described (Brown 2001). Although the plants have been known for some time, sufficient evidence has only recently been available to satisfactorily separate this species from *Spiranthes praecox*. Although both typically have green veined lips, all similarity ceases at that point. The woodland ladies'-tresses has been passed over for many years as a disappointing example of *S. praecox*. *Spiranthes sylvatica* is usually a plant of shaded and woodland habitats and the very distinctive large, creamy green flowers are unlike any other *Spiranthes*. It is most frequently seen along roadside hedgerows bordering woodlands where the plants are tucked up into the border. Also, there are many other distinctive differences between the two species, but flower size, shape, and color are the most noticeable. At the time of this writing the full range of the species is incomplete. It will take several more seasons of searching to get a better understanding of its distribution.

Spiranthes torta (Thunberg) Garay & Sweet

southern ladies'-tresses

Florida; Bermuda, the Bahamas, West Indies, Mexico, Central America
Florida: known only from the southern counties in widely scattered populations; endangered
Plant: terrestrial, 20–50 cm tall
Leaves: 2 or 3, linear, 5–20 × 0.5 cm; absent or withering at flowering time
Flowers: 12–50; in a terminal spike, secund to loosely spiraled; nodding; sepals and petals similar, lanceolate; perianth white with green; lip ovate, with a ciliate-undulate margin, broadest at the apex, green with a white apron; individual flower size 4–5 mm
Habitat: rocky pinelands
Flowering period: late May–July

This species is restricted to the rocky pinelands in southern Florida and is easily recognized by its nodding flowers and downward-pointing lateral sepals. It could only be confused with *Spiranthes amesiana,* which needs to be reconfirmed for Florida, and with *S. tuberosa,* typically a much shorter plant with pure white flowers.

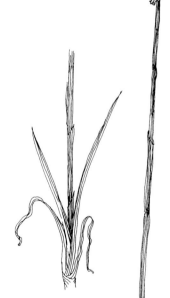

Spiranthes tuberosa Rafinesque

little ladies'-tresses

Arkansas east to southern Michigan and Massachusetts, south to Florida, and west to Texas

Florida: widespread throughout the state in dry, sandy soils; threatened
Plant: terrestrial, 10–30 cm tall, glabrous
Leaves: 2–4, ovate, dark green, 2–5 × 1–2 cm; absent at flowering time
Flowers: 10–35; in a single rank, spiraled or secund; sepals and petals similar, elliptic; perianth crystalline white; lip oblong, with the apex undulate-lacerate, exceeding the sepals; individual flower size ca. 3–4 mm
Habitat: grassy roadsides, cemeteries, open sandy areas in woodlands
Flowering period: late June–July

This is the only *Spiranthes* to flower in midsummer in Florida. One of its favorite habitats is old, dry cemeteries. The nomenclatural history of this plant is rather complex, and among the names applied to it are *Spiranthes beckii* and *S. grayi*. See Correll (1950) for a discussion. The species is easily recognized by its pure white flowers, broad crisped lip, and the absence of leaves at flowering time.

Spiranthes vernalis Engelmann & Gray

grass-leaved ladies'-tresses

Nebraska south to Texas, east to Florida, and north to New Hampshire
Florida: widespread and in nearly every county; one of our most common *Spiranthes*
Plant: terrestrial, 10–65 cm tall, pubescent with sharp-pointed hairs
Leaves: 2–7, basal and on the lower third of the stem, linear-lanceolate, 5–25 × 1–2 cm; present at flowering time
Flowers: 10–50; in a single rank or multiple ranks; sepals and petals similar, lanceolate; perianth typically creamy white; lip ovate-oblong, rounded to the apex with a delicate undulate margin, usually a deeper creamy yellow; the sepals wide spreading; individual flower size 6–9 mm
Habitat: roadsides, meadows, prairies, cultivated lawns—just about anywhere that is sunny
Flowering period: January–May

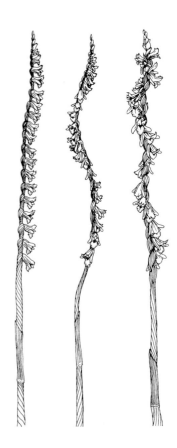

This is perhaps our most variable *Spiranthes* in habit, although the flowers remain surprisingly consistent. Plants may vary greatly in size and vigor as well as degree of spiraling, which results in a range from plants that are essentially secund to those that appear to be multiple-ranked. Plants are not consistent in habit from year to year. Color is somewhat variable from nearly pure white to cream with a contrasting, yellower lip, and some individuals have two brown or orange spots on the lip. This variation in coloring has led to a report of *S. sinensis* from Collier County, which proved to be only highly colored *S. vernalis*. The most consistent diagnostic character is the presence in the inflorescence of copious articulate, pointed hairs, which readily distinguish *S. vernalis* from other species.

Hybrids:

Spiranthes ×folsomii P. M. Brown
(*S. longilabris* × *S. odorata*)
Folsom's hybrid ladies'-tresses

Plants tend to be intermediate between the parents and have shorter leaves than *S. odorata* and more slender, wide-spreading sepals.

Spiranthes ×itchetuckneensis P. M. Brown

(*S. odorata* × *S. ovalis* var. *ovalis*)

Itchetucknee hybrid ladies'-tresses

This is a frequent hybrid where both parents are sympatric. It can be difficult to identify and looks either like a large *S. ovalis* or a small *S. odorata*.

Spiranthes ×meridionalis P. M. Brown
(*S. vernalis* × *S. praecox*)
southern hybrid ladies'-tresses

Despite the relative abundance of both parents and the fact they often occupy the same habitat, relatively few specimens have been identified as this hybrid. Look for *S. vernalis* with appressed sepals and some green in the lip or *S. praecox* with divergent sepals.

Tipularia

Tipularia is a small genus of only two species known from the Himalayas and eastern United States. The species are similar to each other, differing in the shape of the lip. The genus is characterized by having a series of tubers from which arise a single, annual winter-green leaf and then in the summer a leafless spike of flowers that has the sepals and petals all drawn to one side. The single species in Florida is the **crane-fly orchis**, *Tipularia discolor.*

Tipularia discolor (Pursh) Nuttall

crane-fly orchis

eastern Texas northeastward to southern Michigan, east to southeastern Massachusetts, and south to Florida

forma *viridifolia* P. M. Brown, green-leaved form

Florida: widespread, but local in the northern counties; threatened

Plant: terrestrial, 25–60 cm tall

Leaves: 1, basal, ovate, dark green above with raised purple spots and dark purple beneath; or, in the forma *viridifolia*, green on both sides; 8–10 × 6–7 cm, the long petiole ca. 5 cm; absent at flowering time

Flowers: 20–40; in a loose raceme; sepals and petals similar, oblanceolate; perianth greenish yellow, tinged and mottled with pale purple; lip 3-lobed, the central lobe slender, blunt, with a few shallow teeth; the sepals and petals are asymmetrical and all drawn to one side; individual flower size 2–3 × 3–3.5 cm not including spur; spur to 2.5–3 cm

Habitat: deciduous and mixed woodlands

Flowering period: late June–early August

This distinctive species is most easily found when not in flower, during the winter months and when the single leaf is most apparent. The leaf has a look of seersucker with raised purple spots on the upper surface. If one turns the leaf over, the satiny purple underside can be seen—hence the name *discolor* or "two colors." Plants with no purple present, forma *viridifolia*, have been seen in northern Marion County. The flower spike appears in midsummer, and the coloring of the stem and flowers makes it difficult to see in the woodlands, although it is not small. Spikes usually grow to 45–50+ cm tall.

Tolumnia

Tolumnia is a segregate genus from *Oncidium,* consisting of about 20 species and encompassing those plants that are in the *variegata* group, usually referred to as the dancing ladies, or "equitant oncidiums." The genus is typified by a many-flowered raceme of small, white or yellow flowers with a variety of markings in reds, purples, and browns. The leaves are all clustered at the base of the plants and are slender, conduplicate, and sharp pointed. Plants may be epiphytic or litho-phytic or, rarely, terrestrial.

Tolumnia bahamensis (Nash *ex* Britton & Millspaugh) G. J. Braem

Florida's dancing lady

Florida; the Bahamas

Florida: very local on the Palm Beach–Martin County line; endangered

Plant: terrestrial or hemi-epiphytic, scandent, 25–130 cm tall; pseudobulbs very small and hidden within the leaf bases

Leaves: 4–8, at intervals of about 5–10 cm along a scandent rhizome; to 10 × 1 cm, linear with a serrated edge, conduplicate and nearly terete

Flowers: 10–40; in a loose panicle to 50+ cm long arising from between the leaf and the pseudobulb; dorsal sepal spatulate and arching above the flower, lateral sepals linear and conjoined behind the flower, mottled with green and brown; petals spatulate, irregularly banded with yellow, brown, and green with a white tip; lip 3-lobed, the central lobe broad and spreading, white with yellow, pink, orange, and green marking at the base; individual flower size ca. 2 cm

Habitat: dry pine, palmetto, and rosemary scrub

Flowering period: late April–May

Florida's dancing lady is one of the most delightful orchids to be seen in the state. Unfortunately, only a select few have ever seen it. The plants have always been confined to a very narrow area on the Martin–Palm Beach County line. Originally described as *Oncidium bahamense,* and eventually transferred to *Tolumnia,* the Florida plants are considered distinct from other members of the *T. variegata* complex in the Bahamas and West Indies. Although the flowers are very similar to *T. variegata,* the leaf morphology of *T. bahamensis* is different. Recent unpublished reports of DNA analyses and chromosome work support this.

Trichocentrum

A segregate from the genus *Oncidium*, *Trichocentrum* contains about 54 species, widespread throughout the neosubtropics and neotropics. These species encompass the "rat-tailed" and "mule-eared" plants and quickly separate them from other *Oncidium* alliance members. Although Braem (1993) proposed segregation of the "mule-eared" species in the genus *Lophiaris* and Ackerman (2000) transferred several species, recent molecular work of Williams, Chase, and others supports the inclusion of these species in the genus *Trichocentrum*. Two species have been found in Florida, although one of them, the **spread-eagle orchid**, *T. carthagenense*, has not been seen since its original collection in 1916.

1a flowers with essentially pink markings
    . . . *Trichocentrum carthagenense* p. 282
1b flower with essentially yellow and brown markings
    . . . *Trichocentrum maculatum* p. 284

Trichocentrum carthagenense (Jacquin) M.W. Chase & N. H. Williams

spread-eagle orchid

Florida; West Indies, Mexico, Central America, northern South America

Florida: known only from a historical specimen from Monroe County; proposed endangered

Plant: epiphytic, 40 cm tall; pseudobulb hidden within the base of the leaf, ca. 1 cm long

Leaves: 1, rigid, thick and coriaceous, elliptic, green with purple flecking, to 40 × 7 cm

Flowers: 5–60; on an arching panicle from the base of the pseudobulb; sepals and petals similar, ovate; lip 3-lobed, the lateral lobes basal and central lobe reniform and undulate; a white–pale pink base variously marked with purple, brown, and red; individual flower size 2 cm

Habitat: on trunks and branches of trees, probably buttonwood and mangrove

Flowering period: April–September

This species presents a similar problem to that of *Encyclia rufa* in that it is known from a single collection by Small, housed in the herbarium of the New York Botanical Garden, with the label annotated thus: "*Oncidium carthagenense* (Jacq.) Sw. (*fide* by Donovan S. Correll in 1939 and by Richard P. Wunderlin in 1996). Hammocks, south of Coot Bay, Monroe County, J. K. Small, 1 April 1916." Also printed on the label is: "Cruise of the 'Barbee,' March–April 1916." There have been endless debates on whether to accept this as a Florida record or treat it as an introduction, escape, or waif. It is a debate that cannot be resolved unless an established colony is rediscovered. Unless in flower, the plants greatly resemble *Trichocentrum maculatum,* which grows in the same area.

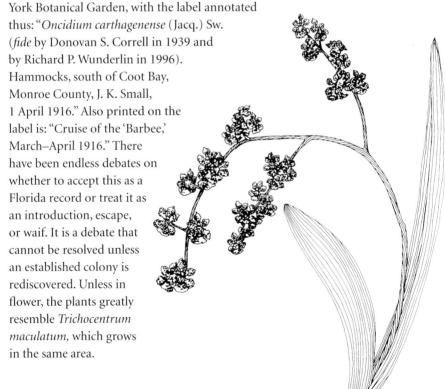

Trichocentrum maculatum (Aublet) M. W. Chase & N. H. Williams

spotted mule-eared orchid

Florida; West Indies, Mexico, Central America, northern South America
  forma *flavovirens* (P. M. Brown) P. M. Brown, unspotted, with a yellow-green
  base

Florida: rare in Collier, Monroe, and Miami-Dade Counties; endangered

Plant: epiphytic, to 1.5 m tall; pseudobulbs broad but only 1 cm long and hidden within the leaf sheaths

Leaves: 1, rigid, thick and coriaceous, elliptic, green with purple flecking, to 60 × 12 cm

Flowers: 5–60; on an arching panicle up to 2 m long from the base of the pseudobulb; sepals and petals similar, ovate; lip 3-lobed, the lateral lobes basal and very short and narrow and central lobe reniform and undulate; glossy brown to yellow-green and marked with brown; or, in the forma *flavovirens,* yellow marked with green; individual flower size 3–4 cm

Habitat: on trunks and branches of trees, usually buttonwood and mangrove in coastal forests

Flowering period: April–September

This species is one of the so-called mule-eared oncidiums that produces a tough, leathery, folded leaf and, in this case, a large, showy, many-flowered inflorescence. The only other mule-eared species we may have in Florida would be *Trichocentrum carthagenense,* and that has not been seen since its original collection. Plants of *T. maculatum* having been heavily collected for many years, there are only a few places left where this species can be seen, although much appropriate habitat still exists. It also has fallen victim to the ravages of the hurricanes that hammer southern Florida.

forma *flavovirens*

true *T. luridum* from Central America

Triphora

Consisting of about 20 species in North America, the West Indies, Mexico, and Central America, *Triphora* is a genus of small, delicate, ephemeral orchids, many of which may be largely mycotrophic. They all arise from swollen tuberoids, tuberlike roots, and some produce colorful although small flowers. Several species have flowers that do not fully open. In Florida we have five species, two of which are endemic.

1a   leaves appressed to the stem . . . *Triphora gentianoides,* p. 292
1b   leaves spreading from the stem . . . 2
2a   leaves essentially green on both surfaces (although some purple may be evident) . . . 3
2b   leaves deep purple on the reverse . . . *Triphora craigheadii,* p. 290
3a   leaves rounded to heart-shaped; flowers usually more than 1 . . . 4
3b   leaves reniform (kidney-shaped, or wider than they are long); flower always single . . . *Triphora amazonica,* p. 288
4a   flowers nodding, fully open; lip lowermost
       . . . *Triphora trianthophora* subsp. *trianthophora,* p. 296
4b   flowers upright, not fully open; lip uppermost
       . . . *Triphora rickettii,* p. 294

Triphora amazonica Schlechter

broad-leaved noddingcaps

Florida; West Indies, Central America, Brazil
Florida: restricted to two sites in central Florida; proposed endangered
Plant: terrestrial, 4–9 cm tall
Leaves: 2–4, broadly ovate to reniform, with smooth margins, green to yellow-green, 4–8 × 7–13 mm
Flowers: 1; terminal; sepals and petals similar, oblanceolate; perianth white; lip 3-lobed, the central lobe with the margin undulate and 3 parallel crests; individual flower size ca. 1 cm
Habitat: deciduous and mixed damp woodlands
Flowering period: late July–early September

This is one of the smallest of the species of *Triphora* to be found in the United States. Plants from Florida were originally named *Triphora latifolia* by George Luer in 1969. However, Jim Ackerman (2000) has recently shown they are synonymous with *T. amazonica*. Either way, this is one of the rarest and most overlooked species in our North American flora. The tiny plants prefer rich, moist soils, often with azaleas and netted chain fern. They are usually visible for only a few weeks of the year. Hence, if you are not in just the right place at just the right time, they are easily passed over.

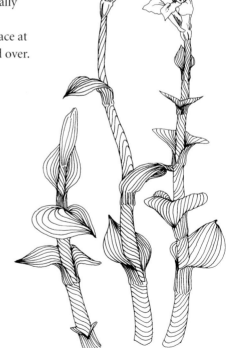

Triphora craigheadii C. A. Luer

Craighead's noddingcaps

Florida
Florida: an endemic restricted to a few sites in central Florida; endangered
Plant: terrestrial, 4–8 cm tall
Leaves: 1–4, broadly ovate to cordate, with crenulate margins, dark green with a rich purple reverse, 9–10 × 11–12 mm
Flowers: 1–3; from the axils of the upper leaves; sepals and petals similar, oblanceolate; perianth white suffused with purple and green; lip broadly triangular, 3-lobed, the central lobe with the margin erose and with 3 parallel crests, spotted with purple; individual flower size 6–8 mm
Habitat: rich, deciduous and mixed damp woodlands
Flowering period: late June–early July

This miniscule little gem is the crowning jewel of the tiny-flowered triphoras. The richly colored flowers and dramatically colored leaves set it apart from any other *Triphora*. It is difficult to conceive of the size of the plants of this, *T. amazonica*, and *T. rickettii*, until one actually sees them in the wild. The specimens from Highlands and Collier Counties are but leaves that are similar to leaves of this species, but flowering plants have never been seen.

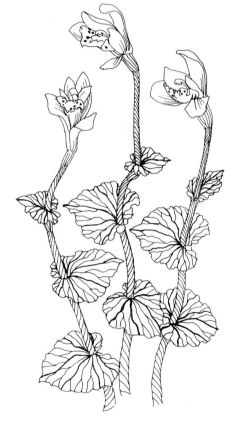

Triphora gentianoides (Swartz) Ames & Schlechter

least-flowered triphora; gentian noddingcaps

Florida; West Indies, Central America, northern South America
Florida: found primarily in the southern counties
Plant: terrestrial, 8–20 cm tall
Leaves: 3–10, ovate, green tinged with brown; clasping the stem, 10–18 × 5–10 mm
Flowers: 3–10; in a raceme; sepals and petals similar, lanceolate; perianth whitish yellow to pale green; lip 3-lobed, the central lobe ovate and tapered with the margin cleft and with 3 parallel green crests; individual flower size ca. 8 mm
Habitat: primarily as a weed in cultivated gardens and bark mulch; occasionally in natural areas
Flowering period: late June–early August
This curious little *Triphora* may or may not be native. It was first reported in 1919, and although it may be abundant where it is found, it has been seen in only a few areas. Planter boxes and mulched beds seem to be its preferred habitat.

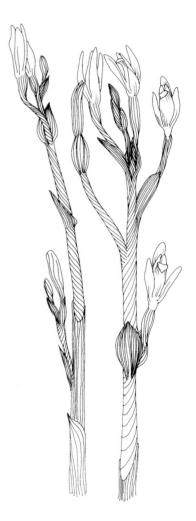

Triphora rickettii C. A. Luer

Rickett's noddingcaps

Florida
Florida: restricted to a few sites in central Florida; proposed endangered
Plant: terrestrial, 8–20 cm tall
Leaves: 5–10, broadly ovate to cordate, with undulate margins, dark green, 1–2 × 1–2 cm
Flowers: 1–8, erect, from the axils of the leaves; sepals and petals similar, oblanceolate; perianth yellow, flowers not opening fully; lip 3-lobed, uppermost, the central lobe with the margin undulate and 3 parallel crests; individual flower size ca. 1 cm
Habitat: deciduous and mixed damp woodlands
Flowering period: late July–early October

This species was known for many years from central Florida before it was described by Luer in 1966. The tiny yellow flowers, which never fully open, are similar in appearance to those of *T. gentianoides,* but the leaves are totally different. They resemble the leaves of *T. craigheadii* in shape but are green on both sides. Some authors have reduced *T. rickettii* to synonymy with *T. yucatenensis,* but there are too many differences, including color and position of the flowers, to accept that opinion. This is one of the three endemic orchids of Florida.

Triphora trianthophora (Swartz) Rydberg subsp. *trianthophora*

three birds orchis; nodding pogonia

Texas north to Minnesota, east to Maine, south to Florida
>forma *albidoflava* Keenan, white-flowered form
>forma *caerulea* P. M. Brown, blue-flowered form
>forma *rossii* P. M. Brown, pink and white form

Florida: primarily in north-central Florida, where it is locally abundant; threatened

Plant: terrestrial, 8–25 cm tall

Leaves: 2–8, broadly ovate to cordate, with smooth margins, dark green often with a purple cast; or, in the forma *rossii,* the stem and leaves white, pink, and yellow; 10–15 × 2–15 mm

Flowers: 1–25, nodding, from the axils of the upper leaves; sepals and petals similar, oblanceolate; perianth white to pink; lip 3-lobed, the central lobe with the margin sinuate and with 3 parallel green crests; or, in the forma *albidoflava,* the perianth pure white and the crests yellow; or, in the forma *caerulea,* lilac-blue; individual flower size ca. 1–2 cm

Habitat: deciduous and mixed woodlands, often with partridge-berry

Flowering period: late July–mid December

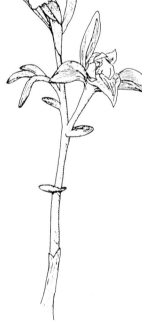

This is the largest-flowered and showiest of our native triphoras. Elsewhere in its range plants usually flower for only a few days each year, but in Florida they can be found in flower for several months. Also, the number of flowers here is much greater than elsewhere. One colony in Marion County has about 500,000 plants and many individuals have more than 12 flowers per plant. This colony also supports both the forma *rossi* and the forma *albidoflava* as well as several other interesting variations.

    Triphora trianthophora subsp. *mexicana* has recently been mentioned by several workers in Florida, but after considerable comparison with both herbarium specimens and living material in the field, no plants of the subspecies could be found.

forma *rossii*

forma *caerulea*

forma *albidoflava*

Tropidia

A genus of tall, terrestrial, branched herbs with a curious distribution. There are about 35 species in *Tropidia,* and all but one are in Asia and Oceania. The plants carry a heavily branched floral panicle that has many flowers. The flowers themselves are relatively small and do not always open fully during the day. The single species in the Americas, the **many-branched tropidia,** *Tropidia polystachya,* is widespread throughout the West Indies and Central America as well as eastern Mexico and northern South America.

Tropidia polystachya (Swartz) Ames

many-branched tropidia

Florida; West Indies, Mexico, Central America, and northern South America
Florida: known only from a single location in Miami-Dade County; endangered
Plant: terrestrial, 10–35 cm tall
Leaves: 1–5, elliptic-lanceolate, plicate, and strongly veined; 5–15 × 2–5 cm
Flowers: 10–60; a terminal panicle, or branched raceme; sepals and petals similar, oblanceolate; perianth greenish white; lip oblong, the central portion with a bright yellow disc; individual flower size ca. 1.5–2 cm
Habitat: hardwood limestone hammocks
Flowering period: late September–October

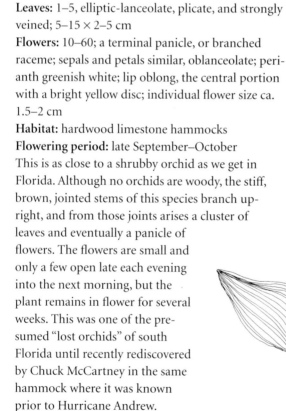

This is as close to a shrubby orchid as we get in Florida. Although no orchids are woody, the stiff, brown, jointed stems of this species branch upright, and from those joints arises a cluster of leaves and eventually a panicle of flowers. The flowers are small and only a few open late each evening into the next morning, but the plant remains in flower for several weeks. This was one of the presumed "lost orchids" of south Florida until recently rediscovered by Chuck McCartney in the same hammock where it was known prior to Hurricane Andrew.

Vanilla

Vanilla is a pantropical genus of about 100 species and contains the only orchid that is important commercially, other than those in the cut-flower trade. As a food flavoring and fragrance, vanilla is one of the most important of spices. It is derived from the fruit or "bean" of *Vanilla planifolia*, which is grown on large-scale plantations in Mexico and Madagascar as well as on a lesser scale in a few other countries. All members of the genus are climbing vines with alternate fleshy or rudimentary leaves. The flowers are large and showy, and several species have limited geographic distributions. Four species are native to Florida and two additional species are escapes from cultivation.

1a	mature vines leafless . . . 2
1b	mature vines leafy . . . 3
2a	sepals and petals slender, ca. 1 cm wide, 5+ cm long . . . *Vanilla dilloniana*, p. 304
2b	sepals and petals broad, ca. 1.5 cm wide, less than 5 cm long . . . *Vanilla barbellata*, p. 302
3a	leaves longer than the internodes . . . 4
3b	leaves shorter than the internodes . . . *Vanilla phaeantha*, p. 308
4a	sepals and petal margins undulate and tips reflexed . . . *Vanilla mexicana*, p. 306
4b	sepal and petal margins not undulate . . . 5
5a	lip entire . . . *Vanilla pompona*, p. 318
5b	lip 3-lobed . . . *Vanilla planifolia*, p. 317

Vanilla barbellata Reichenbach *f.*

worm-vine; leafless vanilla

Florida; West Indies
Florida: known from Miami-Dade and Monroe Counties; endangered
Plant: epiphytic vine, to 20 m long
Leaves: 1 per node, bractlike, up to 4 × 1.5 cm on the newest growth only, soon withering; the nodes spaced every 8–12 cm
Flowers: 1–12; a raceme at a lateral node; sepals and petals similar, oblanceolate; perianth buff to greenish-yellow; lip broadly triangular, 3-lobed, the central portion pink and yellow with a white margin, the side lobes upcurved to form a tubular lip; individual flower size 5–7 cm across
Habitat: coastal mangrove thickets from Florida City to Cape Sable and inland along the brackish marshes, especially at Hell's Bay and Nine Mile Bend
Flowering period: June–July

The worm-vine is a frequently encountered leafless vanilla of the coastal waterways. On a good day a plant may have several dozen flowers open simultaneously. In the full sunlight the green stems become bright orange. The best sites for this orchid are to be seen by canoe in the Hell's Bay area of Everglades National Park.

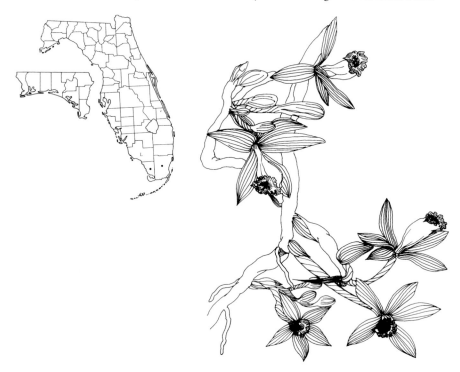

Vanilla dilloniana Correll

Dillon's vanilla

Florida; West Indies
Florida: known only from Miami-Dade County; endangered
Plant: epiphytic vine, much branched, to 5 m long
Leaves: 1 per node, 10 × 1.5 cm on the newest growth only, soon withering; the nodes spaced every 8–12 cm
Flowers: 1–8; a raceme at a lateral node; sepals and petals similar, oblanceolate ca. 1 cm wide; perianth light green; lip broadly triangular, 3-lobed, the central portion deep reddish purple without a white margin, the side lobes upcurved to form a tubular lip; individual flower size 6–9 cm across
Habitat: tropical hardwood limestone hammocks
Flowering period: June–July

Vanilla dilloniana is known only from a few collections from Brickell and Madiera Hammocks south of Miami, although Humes collected a specimen in 1944 labeled "from the Cape Sable region," which may be from Monroe County. A plant was then grown at the Lott home in South Miami and eventually developed into a large plant. The type specimen and drawing were made from this plant. Vegetatively it is almost identical to *Vanilla barbellata,* but florally, although similar, it differs in several aspects. The petals and sepals are longer, more slender, and green, and the fluted lip is colored all the way to the apex.

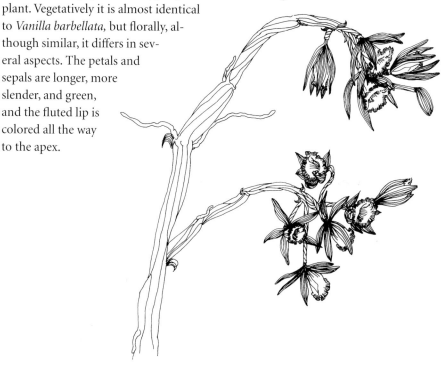

Vanilla mexicana Miller

scentless vanilla

Florida; West Indies, Mexico, Central America, and northern South America
Florida: known only from Miami-Dade and Martin Counties; endangered
Plant: epiphytic vine, much branched, 5–15 m long
Leaves: 1 per node, broadly ovate, thin, 25 × 12 cm; the nodes spaced every 5–8 cm
Flowers: 1–5; a raceme at a lateral node; sepals and petals similar, oblanceolate, undulate, recurved; chartreuse; lip 3-lobed, the central portion ovate tapering to a point, white, the side lobes upcurved to form a tubular lip; individual flower size 1.5–3 cm across
Habitat: clearings in coastal marshes
Flowering period: April–September; very sporadic

This is the most recent *Vanilla* to be discovered in Florida. The white and green undulate flowers are totally different from those of any other vanillas. The short internodes with leaves longer than the nodes are helpful in identifying this species when it is not in flower. Plants have not been seen in south Florida for many years, but the Martin County site is thriving on protected land.

Vanilla phaeantha Reichenbach f.

oblong-leaved vanilla

Florida; West Indies
Florida: known only from Collier County; endangered
Plant: epiphytic vine, much branched, to 25 m or more long
Leaves: 1 per node, oblong, 11–15 × 3.5–5 cm; the nodes spaced every 10–15 cm; the leaves usually equaling or shorter than the internodes
Flowers: 1–12; a raceme at a lateral node; sepals and petals similar, oblanceolate; perianth pale green; lip narrowly triangular, tubular, and appearing unlobed, white with fine yellow stripes; individual flower size 8–14 cm across
Habitat: swamps, climbing on a variety of trees
Flowering period: June–July

This is the most common *Vanilla* to be seen in Florida, although it is confined to Collier County. Reports for other counties need veri-
fication. The plants are high climbing and have a
distinctive zigzag growth habit. They flower
only on the highest growths reaching for
light. The flowers open early in the
morning and sometimes close
as early as 10:00 A.M.

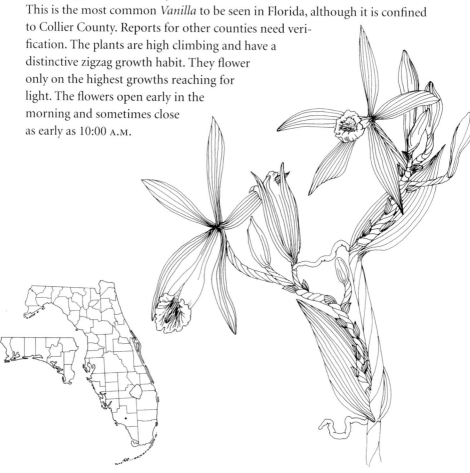

Zeuxine

An African and Asiatic genus of about 30 species, *Zeuxine* is allied to *Spiranthes*, *Platythelys*, and *Goodyera*. One species, the **lawn orchid**, *Zeuxine strateumatica*, is naturalized in the New World. Plants appear to be both apomictic and annual. They often appear in greenhouses as well as throughout the landscape.

Zeuxine strateumatica (Linnaeus) Schlechter*

lawn orchid

Texas, Louisiana, Georgia, Florida; West Indies
Florida: widespread throughout the state in nearly every county
Plant: terrestrial, 4–25 cm tall
Leaves: 5–12, lanceolate, green with purple or tan pigmentation (also seen on the stem), 1–8 × 0.3–1 cm
Flowers: 5–50+; in a densely flowered terminal spike, the flowers twisted to an angle; sepals and petals similar, oblanceolate; perianth white; lip narrowed at the base and broadly spreading at the apex, bright yellow; individual flower size 6–8 mm
Habitat: lawns, shrub borders, roadsides, and now in out of the way natural areas
Flowering period: (late October) December–April

This interesting introduction from Asia or Africa is an abundant and attractive orchid throughout the state. It often appears in unlikely spots around homes or even in nursery pots. The plants vary greatly in size and vigor, but at the time of year that they bloom, no other species can be confused with their distinctive white and yellow flowers. To some the lawn orchid may look like a *Spiranthes*, but close examination reveals a very different lip. The plants are annuals that move around as the seed blows. Capsules mature in a matter of one to two weeks after flowering. Despite its widespread habits, it is in no danger of being a threat to our native orchid populations.

Introduced, Escaped, and Waifs

Seven additional species may be considered as aliens in the Florida orchid flora.

Bletia florida (Salisbury) R. Brown

slender pine-pink

Native to Cuba and Jamaica: escaped in gardens near Homestead, Miami-Dade County. The escapes have been persistent for many years but are not spreading to the surrounding countryside.

Bletia patula Graham

broad-lipped pine-pink

Native to a few islands in the West Indies: a single record from Miami-Dade County. In 1947 a plant was discovered by Roy Woodbury, not in flower, and it subsequently flowered in a greenhouse and was identified as this species. No other plants have been collected or seen that are referable to *B. patula*.

Bletilla striata (Thunberg) Reichenbach *f.*

Chinese orchid

Native to China: a single record from Escambia County. A popular garden plant, this appears to have persisted, although not spreading. It may have been established through discarded garden waste.

Epidendrum radicans Pavón *ex* Lindley

flame star-orchid

Native to Mexico, Central America, and northern South America: Lee County, persistent on Captiva Island; apparently a garden escape in southern Miami-Dade County. This very showy, brilliant orange-flowered species is a common orchid for home growers and readily available at garden centers. It has many adventitious roots along the aerial stems and easily propagates. A broken stem piece roots easily and then perpetuates itself. It is possible that the plants in both counties are actually hybrids that closely resemble the species.

Laelia rubescens Lindley

pink laelia

Native to Mexico and Central America: naturalized in a single site in Miami-Dade County. Plants were found by Blanca Alvarez and Russ Clusman in a hammock south of Miami in 1999. The plants show evidence of having originated from seed rather than having been planted out.

Vanilla planifolia Jackson *ex* Andrews

commercial vanilla

Native to the West Indies, Mexico, Central America, and South America: a single 1976 collection of an escaped or naturalized plant from Miami-Dade County. There have also been numerous reports over the years, including one from Collier County by Roger Hammer. Although represented by only a single herbarium specimen, this species is a popular horticultural subject. As the plant grows readily from stem cuttings, it is not at all surprising to find an occasional plant that has escaped.

Vanilla pompona Schiede

showy vanilla

Native to the West Indies, Mexico, Central America, and South America: a single 1946 collection of an escaped or naturalized plant in Miami-Dade County. Less common than *Vanilla planifolia*, this is nonetheless an attractive species for the home garden or nursery. It is not known if the escaped plant persisted.

Note: *Cymbidium aloifolium* (Linnaeus) Swartz, a native to southeastern Asia, is reported to have escaped and self-seeded within a grower's yard in Homestead, Miami-Dade County, in the 1970s; no specimen exists, nor has it spread other than at the base of a pygmy date palm.

3 ❧

Resources and References

Determining what is native and what is an alien can sometimes be more difficult than one might think. Given both the climate and the many orchid growers throughout Florida, it sometimes is difficult to determine if a record for a one-time collection is a truly native species. Some such examples might be Small's collections of the **spread-eagle orchid**, *Trichocentrum carthagenense,* and the **rufous butterfly orchid**, *Encyclia rufa*—neither having been seen before or after—and there is no satisfactory answer to the debate. They are both treated as natives herein.

Conversely, some species are well documented as non-natives that have naturalized within the state, such as the **lawn orchid**, *Zeuxine strateumatica;* the **yellow cowhorn orchid**, *Cyrtopodium polyphyllum;* and the **African spotted orchid,** *Oeceoclades maculata.* Other natives, such as some of the many **ladies'-tresses**, *Spiranthes* spp., are definitely opportunistic and will seed in wherever the habitat presents itself. These are species that like disturbed areas and frequent mowing to keep the competition down. Even species like the lawn orchid and African spotted orchid are now showing up in what otherwise appears to be a remote, thoroughly native habitat. Given the great number of people who grow orchids in Florida, both as a hobby and professionally, it is amazing that more non-natives have not found their way into our natural habitats.

Checklist of Native and Naturalized Orchids of Florida

(* = naturalized species)

Basiphyllaea corallicola (Small) Ames
Carter's orchid

Beloglottis costaricensis (Reichenbach *f.*) Schlechter
Costa Rican ladies'-tresses

Bletia purpurea (Lamark) de Candolle
pine-pink
    forma *alba* (Ariza-Julia & J. Jiménez Alm.) P. M. Brown, white-flowered form

Brassia caudata (Linnaeus) Lindley
spider orchid

Bulbophyllum pachyrachis (A. Richard) Grisebach
rat-tail orchid

Calopogon barbatus (Walter) Ames
bearded grass-pink
Calopogon multiflorus Lindley
many-flowered grass-pink
Calopogon pallidus Chapman
pale grass-pink
    forma *albiflorus* P. M. Brown, white-flowered form
Calopogon tuberosus (Linnaeus) Britton, Sterns & Poggenberg var. *tuberosus*
common grass-pink
    forma *albiflorus* Britton, white-flowered form
Calopogon tuberosus (Linnaeus) Britton, Sterns & Poggenberg var. *simpsonii* (Small) Magrath

Simpson's grass-pink
    forma *niveus* P. M. Brown, white-flowered form

Campylocentrum pachyrrhizum (Reichenbach *f.*) Rolfe
crooked-spur orchid; ribbon orchid

Cleistes bifaria (Fernald) Catling & Gregg
upland spreading pogonia
Cleistes divaricata (Linnaeus) Ames
large spreading pogonia
    forma *leucantha* P. M. Brown, white-flowered form

Corallorhiza odontorhiza (Willdenow) Poiret var. *odontorhiza*
autumn coralroot
Corallorhiza wisteriana Conrad
Wister's coralroot
    forma *albolabia* P. M. Brown, white-lipped, yellow-stemmed form
    forma *rubra* P. M. Brown, red-stemmed form

Cranichis muscosa Swartz
moss-loving cranichis

Cyclopogon cranichoides (Grisebach) Schlechter
speckled ladies'-tresses
    forma *albolabium* (Brown & McCartney) P. M. Brown, white-lipped form
Cyclopogon elatus (Swartz) Schlechter
tall neottia

Cyrtopodium polyphyllum (Vell) Pabst *ex* F. Barrios*
yellow cowhorn orchid
Cyrtopodium punctatum (Linnaeus) Lindley
cowhorn orchid; cigar orchid

Dendrophylax lindenii (Lindley) Bentham *ex* Rolfe
ghost orchid; frog orchid

Eltroplectris calcarata (Swartz) Garay & Sweet
spurred neottia

Encyclia rufa (Lindley) Britton & Millspaugh
rufous butterfly orchid
Encyclia tampensis (Lindley) Small
Florida butterfly orchid
    forma *albolabia* (A. Hawkes) E. Christensen, white-lipped form

Epidendrum acunae Dressler
Acuña's star orchid
Epidendrum amphistomum A. Richard
dingy-flowered star orchid
    forma *rubrifolium* P. M. Brown, red-leaved form
Epidendrum floridense Hágsater
Florida star orchid
Epidendrum magnoliae Muhlenberg var. *magnoliae*
green-fly orchis
Epidendrum magnoliae Muhlenberg var. *mexicanum* (L. O. Williams) P. M. Brown
bronze green-fly orchis
Epidendrum nocturnum Jacquin
night-fragrant epidendrum
Epidendrum rigidum Jacquin
rigid epidendrum
Epidendrum strobiliferum Swartz
cone-bearing epidendrum

Eulophia alta (Linnaeus) Fawcett & Rendle
wild coco
    forma *pallida* P. M. Brown, pale-colored form
    forma *pelchatii* P. M. Brown, green- and white-flowered form

Galeandra bicarinata G. A. Romero & P. M. Brown
two-keeled galeandra

Goodyera pubescens (Willdenow) R. Brown
downy rattlesnake orchis

Govenia floridana P. M. Brown
Florida govenia

Habenaria distans Grisebach
false water-spider orchis
Habenaria macroceratitis Willdenow
long-horned rein orchis
Habenaria odontopetala Reichenbach f.
toothed rein orchis
    forma *heatonii* P. M. Brown, albino form
Habenaria quinqueseta (Michaux) Eaton
Michaux's orchis
Habenaria repens Nuttall
water-spider orchis

Harrisella porrecta (Reichenbach *f.*) Fawcett & Rendle
leafless harrisella

Hexalectris spicata (Walter) Barnhardt var. *spicata*
crested coralroot
    forma *albolabia* P. M. Brown, white-lipped form

Ionopsis utricularioides (Swartz) Lindley
delicate ionopsis

Isotria verticillata (Muhlenberg *ex* Willdenow) Rafinesque
large whorled pogonia

Lepanthopsis melanantha (Reichenbach *f.*) Ames
crimson lepanthopsis

Liparis elata Lindley
tall twayblade

Listera australis Lindley
southern twayblade
    forma *scottii* P. M. Brown, many-leaved form
    forma *trifolia* P. M. Brown, three-leaved form
    forma *viridis* P. M. Brown, green-flowered form

Macradenia lutescens R. Brown
Trinidad macradenia

Malaxis spicata Swartz
Florida adder's-mouth
Malaxis unifolia Michaux
green adder's-mouth

Maxillaria crassifolia (Lindley) Reichenbach *f.*
false butterfly orchid
Maxillaria parviflora (Poeppig & Endlicher) Garay
small-flowered maxillaria

Mesadenus lucayanus (Britton) Schlechter
copper ladies'-tresses

Oeceoclades maculata (Lindley) Lindley*
African spotted orchid

Oncidium floridanum Ames
Florida oncidium

Pelexia adnata (Swartz) Sprengel
glandular ladies'-tresses

Phaius tankervilleae (Aiton) Blume*
nun orchid

Platanthera blephariglottis (Willdenow) Lindley var. *conspicua* (Nash) Luer
southern white fringed orchis
Platanthera chapmanii (Small) Luer *emend.* Folsom
Chapman's fringed orchis
Platanthera ciliaris (Linnaeus) Lindley
orange fringed orchis
Platanthera clavellata (Michaux) Luer
little club-spur orchis
Platanthera cristata (Michaux) Lindley
orange crested orchis
    forma *straminea* P. M. Brown, pale yellow form
Platanthera flava (Linnaeus) Lindley var. *flava*
southern tubercled orchis
Platanthera integra (Nuttall) Lindley
yellow fringeless orchis
Platanthera nivea (Nuttall) Luer
snowy orchis

PLATANTHERA HYBRIDS
Platanthera ×bicolor (Rafinesque) Luer
bicolor hybrid fringed orchis
(*P. blephariglottis* var. *conspicua* × *P. ciliaris*)
Platanthera ×canbyi (Ames) Luer
Canby's hybrid fringed orchis
(*P. blephariglottis* var. *conspicua* × *P. cristata*)
Platanthera ×channellii Folsom
Channell's hybrid fringed orchis
(*P. ciliaris* × *P. cristata*)

Platythelys querceticola (Lindley) Garay
low ground orchid
Platythelys sagreana (A. Richard) Garay
Cuban ground orchid

Pleurothallis gelida Lindley
frosted pleurothallis

Pogonia ophioglossoides (Linnaeus) Ker-Gawler
rose pogonia; snake-mouth orchid
    forma *albiflora* Rand & Redfield, white-flowered form

Polystachya concreta (Jacquin) Garay & Sweet
yellow helmet orchid

Ponthieva brittoniae Ames
Mrs. Britton's shadow-witch
Ponthieva racemosa (Walter) Mohr
shadow-witch

Prescottia oligantha (Swartz) Lindley
small-flowered prescottia

Prosthechea boothiana (Lindley) W. E. Higgins var. *erythronioides* (Small) W. E.
Higgins
Florida dollar orchid
Prosthechea cochleata (Linnaeus) W. E. Higgins var. *triandra* (Ames) W. E.
Higgins
Florida clamshell orchid
    forma *albidoflava* (P. M. Brown) P. M. Brown, white- and yellow-flowered form
Prosthechea pygmaea (Hooker) W. E. Higgins
dwarf butterfly orchid

Pteroglossaspis ecristata (Fernald) Rolfe
crestless plume orchid
    forma *flava* P. M. Brown, yellow-flowered form

Sacoila lanceolata (Aublet) Garay var. *lanceolata*
leafless beaked orchid
    forma *albidaviridis* Catling & Sheviak, white and green-flowered form
    forma *folsomii* P. M. Brown, golden-flowered form
Sacoila lanceolata (Aublet) Garay var. *paludicola* (Luer) Sauleda, Wunderlin &
Hansen
Fakahatchee beaked orchid
    forma *aurea* P. M. Brown, golden-yellow flowered form
Sacoila squamulosa (Kunth) Garay
hoary beaked orchid

Spathoglottis plicata Blume*
Javanese violet orchid

Spiranthes amesiana Schlechter *emend.* P. M. Brown
Ames' ladies'-tresses
Spiranthes brevilabris Lindley
short-lipped ladies'-tresses
Spiranthes eatonii Ames *ex* P. M. Brown
Eaton's ladies'-tresses
Spiranthes floridana (Wherry) Cory *emend.* P. M. Brown
Florida ladies'-tresses
Spiranthes laciniata (Small) Ames
lace-lipped ladies'-tresses
Spiranthes longilabris Lindley
long-lipped ladies'-tresses
Spiranthes odorata (Nuttall) Lindley
fragrant ladies'-tresses
Spiranthes ovalis Lindley var. *ovalis*
southern oval ladies'-tresses
Spiranthes ovalis Lindley var. *erostellata* Catling
northern oval ladies'-tresses
Spiranthes praecox (Walter) S. Watson
giant ladies'-tresses
    forma *albolabia* Brown & McCartney, white-lipped form
Spiranthes sylvatica P. M. Brown
woodland ladies'-tresses
Spiranthes torta (Thunberg) Garay & Sweet
southern ladies'-tresses
Spiranthes tuberosa Rafinesque
little ladies'-tresses
Spiranthes vernalis Engelmann & Gray
grass-leaved ladies'-tresses

SPIRANTHES HYBRIDS
Spiranthes ×folsomii P. M. Brown
(*S. longilabris* × *S. odorata*)
Folsom's hybrid ladies'-tresses
Spiranthes ×itchetuckneensis P. M. Brown
(*S. odorata* × *S. ovalis* var. *ovalis*)
Itchetucknee hybrid ladies'-tresses

Spiranthes ×*meridionalis* P. M. Brown
(*S. praecox* × *S. vernalis*)
southern hybrid ladies'-tresses

Tipularia discolor (Pursh) Nuttall
crane-fly orchis
    forma *viridifolia* P. M. Brown, green-leaved form

Tolumnia bahamensis (Nash *ex* Britton & Millspaugh) G. J. Braem
Florida's dancing lady

Trichocentrum carthagenense (Jacquin) M. W. Chase & N. H. Williams
spread-eagle orchid
Trichocentrum maculatum (Aublet) M. W. Chase & N. H. Williams
spotted mule-eared orchid
    forma *flavovirens* (P. M. Brown) P. M. Brown, unspotted with a
    yellow-green base

Triphora amazonica Schlechter
broad-leaved noddingcaps
Triphora craigheadii C. A. Luer
Craighead's noddingcaps
Triphora gentianoides (Swartz) Ames & Schlechter
least-flowered triphora; gentian noddingcaps
Triphora rickettii C. A. Luer
Rickett's noddingcaps
Triphora trianthophora (Swartz) Rydberg subsp. *trianthophora*
three birds orchis; nodding pogonia
    forma *albidoflava* Keenan, white-flowered form
    forma *caerulea* P. M. Brown, blue-flowered form
    forma *rossii* P. M. Brown, pink and white form

Tropidia polystachya (Swartz) Ames
many-flowered tropidia

Vanilla barbellata Reichenbach f.
worm-vine; leafless vanilla
Vanilla dilloniana Correll
Dillon's vanilla
Vanilla mexicana Miller
scentless vanilla

Vanilla phaeantha Reichenbach f.
oblong-leaved vanilla

Zeuxine strateumatica (Linnaeus) Schlechter*
lawn orchid

Introduced, Escaped, and Waifs

Bletia florida (Salisbury) R. Brown
slender pine-pink
Bletia patula Graham
broad-lipped pine-pink

Bletilla striata (Thunberg) Reichenbach f.
Chinese orchid

Epidendrum ef. radicans Pavón *ex* Lindley
flame star-orchid

Laelia rubescens Lindley
pink laelia

Vanilla planifolia Jackson *ex* Andrews
commercial vanilla
Vanilla pompona Scheide
showy vanilla

Recent Literature References for New Taxa, Combinations, and Additions to the Orchid Flora of Florida

In the thirty years since Luer's monumental work on the native orchids of Florida was published, no single reference addressing all of the changes (new taxa, combinations, and additions) has followed. Various journal articles and occasional references in other books have dealt with the Florida orchids. The references that follow should enable the reader to find information concerning all these changes more easily.

Note: *NANOJ = North American Native Orchid Journal*

Bletia purpurea (Lamark) de Candolle
forma *alba* (Ariza-Julia & J. Jiménez Alm.) P. M. Brown
Brown, P. M. 2000. *NANOJ* 6(4):335.

Calopogon tuberosus (Linnaeus) Britton, Sterns & Poggenberg var. *simpsonii* (Small) Magrath
forma *niveus* P. M. Brown
Brown, P. M. 1995. *NANOJ* 1(2):130.
Magrath, L. K., and J. L. Norman. 1989. *Sida* 13(3):371–72.

Cleistes bifaria (Fernald) Catling & Gregg
Catling, P. M., and K. B. Gregg. 1992. *Lindleyana* 7(2):57–73.

Cleistes divaricata (Linnaeus) Ames
forma *leucantha* P. M. Brown
Brown, P. M. 1995. *NANOJ* 1(1):7.

Corallorhiza wisteriana Conrad
forma *albolabia* P. M. Brown
Brown, P. M. 1995. *NANOJ* 1(1):9–10.

Corallorhiza wisteriana Conrad
forma *rubra* P. M. Brown
Brown, P. M. 2000. *NANOJ* 6(1):62.

Cyclopogon cranichoides (Grisebach) Schlechter
forma *albolabium* (Brown & McCartney) P. M. Brown
Brown, P. M. 1995. *NANOJ* 1(1):8.

Encyclia rufa (Lindley) Britton & Millspaugh
Sauleda, R. P., and R. M. Adams. 1983. *Rhodora* 85 (842):127–74.
Wunderlin, R. A. 1998. *Guide to the Vascular Plants of Central Florida.*

Epidendrum amphistomum A. Richard
Hágsater, E. 2000. *NANOJ* 6(4):299–309.
forma *rubrifolium* P. M. Brown
Brown, P. M. 2000. *NANOJ* 6(1):63.

Epidendrum floridense Hágsater
Hágsater, E. 2000. *NANOJ* 6(4):299–309.
Hágsater, E., and G. Salazar. 1993. *Icones Orchidacearum* pl. 133.
Romero, G. A. 1994. *American Orchid Society Bulletin* 63(10):1168–70.

Epidendrum magnoliae Muhlenberg
Hágsater, E. 2000. *NANOJ* 6(4):299–309.

Epidendrum magnoliae Muhlenberg var. *mexicanum* (L. O. Williams) P. M. Brown
Brown, P. M. 1999. *NANOJ* 5(1):3.
———. 2000. *NANOJ* 6(4):335–36.

Eulophia alta (Linnaeus) Fawcett & Rendle
forma *pallida* P. M. Brown
Brown, P. M. 1995. *NANOJ* 1(2):131.
forma *pelchatii* P. M. Brown
P. M. Brown. 1998. *NANOJ* 4(1):46.

Galeandra bicarinata G. A. Romero & P. M. Brown
Romero, G. A., and P. M. Brown. 2000. *NANOJ* 6(2):77–87.

Govenia floridana P. M. Brown
Brown, P. M. 2000. *NANOJ* 6(3):230–40.
Greenwood, E. W. 1991. *American Orchid Society Bulletin* 60(9):867–69.

Habenaria macroceratitis Willdenow
Brown, P. M. 2000. *NANOJ* 6(2):142–53.

Harrisella porrecta (Reichenbach *f.*) Fawcett & Rendle
Ackerman, J. D. 1995. *Orchids of Puerto Rico and the Virgin Islands.* P. 87.

Maxillaria parviflora (Poeppig & Endlicher) Garay
Atwood, J. T. 1993. *Lindleyana* 8(1):25–31.
Hammer, R. L. 1981. *Fairchild Tropical Garden Bulletin* 36(3):16–18.
McCartney, C. L., Jr. 1993. *Florida Orchidist* 36(3):25–29.

Mesadenus lucayanus (Britton) Schlechter
Brown, P. M. 2000. *NANOJ* 6(4):333–34.

Pelexia adnata (Swartz) Sprengel
Hammer, R. L. 1981. *Fairchild Tropical Garden Bulletin* 36(3):16–18.
McCartney, C. L., Jr. 1983. *Florida Orchidist* 26(3):124–29.

Platanthera chapmanii (Small) Luer *emend.* Folsom
Platanthera ×*channellii* Folsom
Folsom, J. P. 1984. *Orquidea* (Mex) 9(2):344.

Platythelys querceticola (Lindley) Garay
Platythelys sagreana (A. Richard) Garay
Brown, P. M. 1999 *NANOJ* 5(1):4.

Ponthieva brittoniae Ames
McCartney, C. L., Jr. 1995. *NANOJ* 1(2):106–16.

Prosthechea boothiana (Lindley) W. E. Higgins var. *erythronioides* (Small) W. E. Higgins
Brown, P. M. 1998. *NANOJ* 4(1):52.
———. 1999. *NANOJ* 5(1):15.
Higgins, W. E. 1997(1998). *Phytologia* 82(5):370–83.

Prosthechea cochleata (Linnaeus) W. E. Higgins var. *triandra* (Ames) W. E. Higgins
Brown, P. M. 1998. *NANOJ* 4(1):53.
———. 1999. *NANOJ* 5(1):16.
Higgins, W. E. 1997 (1998). *Phytologia* 82(5):370–83.
    forma *albidoflava* (P. M. Brown) P. M. Brown
Brown, P. M. 1995. *NANOJ* 1(2):131.
———. 1998. *NANOJ* 4(1):53.
———. 1999 *NANOJ* 5(1):16.

Prosthechea pygmaea (Hooker) W. E. Higgins
Brown, P. M. 1998. *NANOJ* 4(1):52.
Higgins, W. E. 1997 (1998). *Phytologia* 82(5):370–83.

Pteroglossaspis ecristata (Fernald) Rolfe
forma *flava* P. M. Brown
Brown, P. M. 2000. *NANOJ* 6(1):64.

Sacoila lanceolata (Aublet) Garay var. *lanceolata*
forma *albidaviridis* Catling & Sheviak
Catling, P. M., and C. J. Sheviak. 1993. *Lindleyana.* 8(2):77–81.
forma *folsomii* P. M. Brown
Brown, P. M. 1999. *NANOJ* 5(2):198.

Sacoila lanceolata (Aublet) Garay var. *paludicola* (Luer) Sauleda, Wunderlin & Hansen
Catling, P. M. 1987. *Annals of the Missouri Botanical Garden.* 74:58–68.
Catling, P. M., and C. J. Sheviak. 1993. *Lindleyana* 8(2):77–81.
forma *aurea* P. M. Brown
Brown, P. M. 2001. *NANOJ* 7(1):95–96.

Sacoila squamulosa (Kunth) Garay
Brown, P. M. 2000. *NANOJ* 6(4):332–33.
Nir, M. 2000. *Orchidaceae Antillanae.* P. 362.

Spiranthes amesiana Schlechter *emend.* P. M. Brown
Brown, P. M. 2001. *NANOJ* 7(1):91–93.

Spiranthes eatonii Ames *ex* P. M. Brown
Brown, P. M. 1999. *NANOJ* 5(1):5.

Spiranthes floridana (Wherry) Cory *emend.* P. M. Brown
Brown, P. M. 2001. *NANOJ* 7(1):91–93.

Spiranthes ovalis Lindley var. *ovalis*
Spiranthes ovalis Lindley var. *erostellata* Catling
Catling, P. M. 1983. *Brittonia* 35:120–25.

Spiranthes praecox (Walter) S. Watson
forma *albolabia* Brown & McCartney
Brown, P. M. 1995. *NANOJ* 1(1):13.

Spiranthes sylvatica P. M. Brown
Brown, P. M. 2001. *NANOJ* 7(3):193–205.

Spiranthes ×*folsomii* P. M. Brown
Brown, P. M. 2000. *NANOJ* 6(1):16.

Spiranthes ×*itchetuckneensis* P. M. Brown
Brown, P. M. 1999. *NANOJ* 5(4):358–67.

Spiranthes ×*meridionalis* P. M. Brown
Brown, P. M. 1999. *NANOJ* 5(4):358–67.
———. 2000. *NANOJ* 6(2):139.

Tipularia discolor (Pursh) Nuttall
   forma *viridifolia* P. M. Brown
Brown, P. M. 2000. *NANOJ* 6(4):334–35.

Tolumnia bahamensis (Nash *ex* Britton & Millspaugh) G. J. Braem
Sauleda, R. P., and R. M. Adams. 1989. *Rhodora* 91(866):188–200.

Trichocentrum carthagenense (Jacquin) M. W. Chase & N. H. Williams
Braem, G. J. 1993. *Schlechteriana* 4(1–2):17.
Williams, N. H., and M. W. Chase, T. Fulcher, W. M. Whitten. 2001. *Lindleyana* 16(2):137.

Trichocentrum maculatum (Aublet) M. W. Chase & N. H. Williams
Ackerman, J. D. 2000. *Lindleyana* 15(2):92–93.
Williams, N. H., and M. W. Chase. 2001. *Lindleyana* 16(3):218–19.
   forma *flavovirens* (P. M. Brown) P. M. Brown
Brown, P. M. 2000. *NANOJ* 6(4):335.
———. 2001. *NANOJ* 7(3):249.

Triphora amazonica Schlechter
Ackerman, J. D. 2000. *Lindleyana* 15(2):92–93.

Triphora trianthophora (Swartz) Rydberg subsp. *trianthophora*
   forma *albidoflava* Keenan
Keenan, P. 1992. *Rhodora* 94(877):38–39.
   forma *caerulea* P. M. Brown
Brown, P. M. 1999. *NANOJ* 7(1):3.
   forma *rossii* P. M. Brown
Brown, P. M. 1999. *NANOJ* 5(1):5.
Medley, M. E. 1991. *Selbyana* 12:102–3.

Synonyms and Misapplied Names

Synonyms and misapplied names are often confused in the literature and in the understanding of orchid enthusiasts. A synonym is simply another name previously published for a given plant. From among the synonyms, authors must select a name that they feel best suits the currently accepted genus and species for the plant. Although the genus names may vary, the species epithet often may be the same. In such large groups as the spiranthoid orchids (*Spiranthes* and its allied genera), many synonyms may exist for the same species—all within different genera.

The rules of priority, as set forth in the *International Code of Botanical Nomenclature*, dictate that the earliest validly published name must be used. A good example involves *Epidendrum magnoliae* Muhlenberg, which was published in October 1813, and *Epidendrum conopseum* R. Brown, published in November 1813. Although the latter name is in widespread usage, priority indicates that the former is the valid name. It rarely comes down to months, as in this example, and usually the year of publication is sufficient for determining the valid name.

Spiranthes adnata would be a synonym for *Pelexia adnata*, *Pelexia* being the currently accepted genus. *Habenaria* is another group that has undergone a great deal of scrutiny in the past 25 years. Several groups of species formerly included within *Habenaria* are now treated as distinct genera. This is not always a case of correct or incorrect names but often a matter of the author's preference for one genus over another. A synonym may also be a validly published name that duplicates a previously published taxon and therefore is rendered a synonym.

A misapplied name is an incorrect name for a given plant that may have resulted from reassessment of the genus or species, such that two or more species have been described from within the original species, or it may simply be a wrong name assigned to the plant. This is especially common in geographic areas at the edge of a group's range. *Epidendrum anceps* would be a misapplied name for *E. amphistomum*, *E. anceps* not occurring in Florida, or it could be an error in the original identification. A more frequently encountered example would be *Govenia floridana,* which is a recently described species in Florida. The Florida plants that were formerly identified as *G. utriculata* are now known to be *G. floridana,* with *G. utriculata* not known from Florida. The term *auct.* (*auctorum,* meaning "of authors") is used to indicate a misapplied name, and occasionally an author incorrectly appends the phrase "in part" after a name listed under synonymy. Misapplied names are not synonyms and refer only to the specific geographic area being treated—in this case Florida.

An issue can arise as to whether a name is a synonym or misapplied, and answers depend on whether one takes a broad or narrow view of the taxonomy—the lumpers vs. the splitters. Such a situation would best be described thus: if *Liparis elata* is considered to be synonymous with *L. nervosa, L. elata* becomes a synonym of *L. nervosa;* but if *L. elata* is considered a good species on its own, *L. nervosa* becomes a misapplied name for *L. elata* (in Florida). At times this appears to be an endless argument, and authors must make their own decisions regarding synonymy and misapplied names.

Cross references to all taxa with synonyms and misapplied names are presented later in part 3. Synonyms and misapplied names are given for the Florida taxa found in the following publications and for occasional references to specific journal articles:

Small, J. K. 1933. *Manual of the Southeastern Flora.*
Correll, D. S. 1950. *Native Orchids of North America.*
Luer, C. A. 1972. *Native Orchids of Florida.*
Ackerman, J. D. 1995. *An Orchid Flora of Puerto Rico and the Virgin Islands.*
Wunderlin, R. P. 1998. *Guide to the Vascular Plants of Florida.*
Nir, M. 2000. *Orchidaceae Antillanae.*

Segregate Genera

Five genera within Florida have several segregate genera that have been variously treated by different authors. Those are:

> *Epidendrum*
> > *Encyclia*
> > *Prosthechea*
> *Habenaria*
> > *Platanthera*
> *Oncidium*
> > *Tolumnia*
> > *Trichocentrum*

Pogonia
   Cleistes
   Isotria
Spiranthes
   Beloglottis
   Cyclopogon
   Pelexia
   Sacoila

Synonyms

Most current taxonomic treatments recognize the numerous segregate genera of the spiranthoid orchids (Garay 1980) as well as of *Encyclia* and *Prosthechea* from within the *Epidendrum* alliance. References given are not necessarily the taxonomic work that first designated the new combination but often to the work that best shows the example. *The Flora of North America* (*FNA*), volume 26 (2001), treats many of the following taxa as well.

Beloglottis costaricensis (Reichenbach *f.*) Schlechter
SYNONYM
Spiranthes costaricensis Reichenbach *f.*
Garay 1980; Ackerman 1995; Nir 2000.

Cleistes bifaria (Fernald) Catling & Gregg
SYNONYMS
Cleistes divaricata var. *bifaria* Fernald
Catling, P. M., and K. B. Gregg. 1992. *Lindleyana* 7(2):57–73.
Pogonia bifaria P. M. Brown & R. P. Wunderlin
Brown, P. M., and R. P. Wunderlin. 1997. *NANOJ* 3(4):450–51.

Cyclopogon cranichoides (Grisebach) Schlechter
SYNONYMS
Beadlea cranichoides (Grisebach) Small
Spiranthes cranichoides (Grisebach) Cogniaux
Ackerman 1995; Nir 2000.

Cyclopogon elatus (Swartz) Schlechter
SYNONYMS
Beadlea elata (Swartz) Small
Spiranthes elata (Swartz) L. C. Richard
Ackerman 1995; Nir 2000.

Dendrophylax lindenii (Lindley) Bentham *ex* Rolfe
SYNONYMS
Polyradicion lindenii (Lindley) Garay
Polyrrhiza lindenii (Lindley) Cogniaux
Nir 2000.

The most recent work on this group indicates that both *Polyrrhiza* and *Polyradicion* belong within *Dendrophylax* (Nir 2000).

Eltroplectris calcarata (Swartz) Garay & Sweet
SYNONYM
Centrogenium setaceum (Lindley) Schlechter
Ackerman 1995; Nir 2000.

Encyclia rufa (Lindley) Britton & Millspaugh
SYNONYMS
Encyclia bahamensis (Grisebach) Britton & Millspaugh
Epidendrum bahamense Grisebach
Epidendrum rufum Lindley
Nir 2000.

Encyclia tampensis (Lindley) Small
SYNONYM
Epidendrum tampense Lindley
Luer 1972; Ackerman 1995; Wunderlin 1998; Nir 2000.

Epidendrum acunae Dressler
MISAPPLIED
Epidendrum blancheanum Urban

Although Luer uses *E. acunae*, recent Florida workers have used *E. blancheanum* (Wunderlin 1998). Nir (2000) clearly describes the differences between the two species and demonstrates that the difference in the lip shape is conclusive—*E. blancheanum* having a lip that is as wide as it is long and *E. acunae* having a lip that is narrower than it is long. Luer's photographs and drawings clearly show a lip that is narrow and long.

Epidendrum amphistomum A. Richard
MISAPPLIED
Epidendrum anceps Jacquin
Hágsater, E. 2000. *NANOJ* 6(4):299–309.

Epidendrum floridense Hágsater

MISAPPLIED

Epidendrum difforme Jacquin
Neolehmannia difformis (Jacquin) Pabst
Epidendrum umbellatum Swartz

In 1993 Hágsater and Salazar (*Icones Orchidacearum*) published numerous new species segregated from *E. difforme* based both on plant morphology and geographic range. Nir (2000) combines this and two other species under *E. umbellatum.*

Hágsater, E. 2000. *NANOJ* 6(4):299–309.

Epidendrum magnoliae Muhlenberg

SYNONYM

Epidendrum conopseum R. Brown
Hágsater, E. 2000. *NANOJ* 6(4):299–309.

Galeandra bicarinata G. A. Romero & P. M. Brown

MISAPPLIED

Galeandra beyrichii Reichenbach *f.*
Romero, G. A., and P. M. Brown. 2000. *NANOJ* 6(2):77–87.

Govenia floridana P. M. Brown

MISAPPLIED

Govenia utriculata (Swartz) Lindley
Brown, P. M. 2000. *NANOJ* 6(3):230–40.

Habenaria macroceratitis Willdenow

SYNONYM

Habenaria quinqueseta var. *macroceratitis* (Willdenow) Luer
Nir 2000.

Habenaria odontopetala Reichenbach *f.*

SYNONYM

Habenaria strictissima Reichenbach *f.* var. *odontopetala* (Reichenbach *f.*) L. O. Williams
Habenaria garberi Porter
Luer, Ackerman, Nir.

MISAPPLIED

Habenaria floribunda Lindley

Wunderlin (1998) used *H. floribunda,* considering it a polymorphic umbrella species for several other taxa. Sheviak (pers. comm.; *FNA* 2001) could find no evidence for including *H. odontopetala* within *H. floribunda.*

Harrisella porrecta (Reichenbach *f.*) Fawcett & Rendle
SYNONYM
Campylocentrum porrectum Reichenbach *f.*
Luer 1972; Ackerman 1995.
MISAPPLIED
Harrisella filiformis (Swartz) Cogniaux
   Ackerman has clearly discussed the synonyms and misapplied names for this often confusing taxon. He shows that *H. filiformis* is a synonym for *Campylocentrum filiforme* (Swartz) Cogniaux *ex* Kuntze.

Isotria verticillata (Muhlenberg *ex* Willdenow) Rafinesque
SYNONYM
Pogonia verticillata Nuttall
Wunderlin 1998.

Liparis elata Lindley
MISAPPLIED
Liparis nervosa (Thunberg) Lindley
   If *L. nervosa* is viewed as a pantropical species (in both the Eastern and Western Hemispheres), then *L. elata* is a synonym; otherwise it is misapplied. Garay (1971, Orchidaceae, in Wiggins and Porter *Flora of the Galapagos Islands*. Stanford, Calif.: Stanford University Press) indicated that *L. nervosa* is pantropical, but recent work in Florida indicates to the contrary.

Malaxis spicata Swartz
SYNONYM
Malaxis floridana (Chapman) O. Kuntze
Luer 1972; Wunderlin 2000.

Maxillaria parviflora (Poeppig & Endlicher) Garay
SYNONYM
Maxillaria conferta (Grisebach) Schweinfurth *ex* Leon
Ackerman 1995; Wunderlin 1998; Nir 2000.

Mesadenus lucayanus (Britton) Schlechter
SYNONYMS
Ibidium lucayanum Britton
Spiranthes lucayana (Britton) Cogniaux
MISAPPLIED
Mesadenus polyanthus (Reichenbach *f.*) Schlechter
   Recent examination of numerous specimens of *M. polyanthus* from Mexico

compared to the material from the West Indies and Florida clearly indicates that two species are present. *M. polyanthus* is confined to higher elevations in central Mexico and *M. lucayanus* to lower elevations in Florida, the West Indies, southern Mexico, and Guatemala.

Brown, P. M. 2000. *NANOJ* 6(4):333–34.

Oncidium floridanum Ames
MISAPPLIED
Oncidium ensatum Lindley

Mark Chase (pers. comm.) feels strongly that *O. floridanum* should be included with *O. ensatum*, although my examination of the Florida material compared with *O. ensatum* has not proven conclusive.

Nir 2000.

Pelexia adnata (Swartz) Sprengel
SYNONYM
Spiranthes adnata (Swartz) Bentham *ex* Fawcett
Ackerman 1995; Wunderlin 1998; Nir 2000.

Platanthera blephariglottis (Willdenow) Lindley var. *conspicua* (Nash) Luer
SYNONYMS
Blephariglottis conspicua (Nash) Small
Habenaria blephariglottis (Willdenow) Hooker var. *conspicua* (Nash) Ames
Luer 1972; Wunderlin 1998.

Platanthera chapmanii (Small) Luer *emend.* Folsom
SYNONYMS
Blephariglottis chapmanii Small
Habenaria ×chapmanii (Small) Ames
Luer 1972; Wunderlin 1998.

Platanthera ciliaris (Linnaeus) Lindley
SYNONYMS
Blephariglottis ciliaris (Linnaeus) Rydberg
Habenaria ciliaris (Linnaeus) R. Brown
Luer 1972; Wunderlin 1998.

Platanthera clavellata (Michaux) Luer
SYNONYMS
Gymnadenopsis clavellata (Michaux) Rydberg *ex* Britton

Habenaria clavellata (Michaux) Sprengel
Luer 1972; Wunderlin 1998.

Platanthera cristata (Michaux) Lindley
SYNONYMS
Blephariglottis cristata (Michaux) Rafinesque
Habenaria cristata (Michaux) R. Brown
Luer 1972; Wunderlin 1998.

Platanthera flava (Linnaeus) Lindley var. *flava*
SYNONYM
Habenaria flava (Linnaeus) R. Brown
Luer 1972; Wunderlin 1998.

Platanthera integra (Nuttall) Lindley
SYNONYM
Habenaria integra (Nuttall) Sprengel
Luer 1972; Wunderlin 1998.

Platanthera nivea (Nuttall) Lindley
SYNONYM
Habenaria nivea (Nuttall) Sprengel
Luer 1972.

Platanthera ×*bicolor* (Rafinesque) Luer
SYNONYM
Habenaria ×*bicolor* (Rafinesque) Beckner
Luer 1972; Wunderlin 1998.

Platanthera ×*canbyi* (Ames) Luer
SYNONYMS
Blephariglottis canbyi (Ames) W. Stone
Habenaria canbyi Ames
Luer 1972; Wunderlin 1998.

Platythelys querceticola (Lindley) Garay
SYNONYMS
Erythrodes querceticola (Lindley) Ames
Physurus querceticola Lindley
Ackerman 1995; Nir 2000.

Platythelys sagreana (A. Richard) Garay

Erythrodes sagreana (A. Richard) Leon
Physurus sagreanus A. Richard
Nir 2000.

Polystachya concreta (Jacquin) Garay & Sweet
SYNONYM OR MISAPPLIED
Polystachya flavescens (Lindley) J. K. Small
Ackerman 1995; Wunderlin 1998; Nir 2000.

    If *P. flavescens* is viewed as a pantropical species (in both the Eastern and Western Hemispheres), then *P. flavescens* is a synonym; otherwise it is misapplied.

Ponthieva brittoniae Ames
SYNONYM
Ponthieva racemosa (Walter) C. Mohr var. *brittonae* (Ames) Luer
Wunderlin 1995; Nir 2000.

Prosthechea boothiana (Lindley) W. E. Higgins var. *erythronioides* (Small) W. E. Higgins
SYNONYMS
Encyclia boothiana (Lindley) Dressler var. *erythronioides* (Small) Luer
Epicladum boothianum (Lindley) Small
Epidendrum boothianum Lindley
Epidendrum erythronioides Small
Nir 2000.

    Higgins's reinstatement of the genus *Prosthechea* (*Phytologia* 82[5]):370–383, 1997 [1998]) follows upon the earlier work of Small and more recent work of Dressler to segregate species from within the greater *Epidendrum* alliance.

Prosthechea cochleata (Linnaeus) W. E. Higgins var. *triandra* (Ames) W. E. Higgins
SYNONYMS
Anacheilum cochleatum (Linnaeus) Hoffmansegg var. *triandrum* (Ames) Sauleda et al.
Encyclia cochleata (Linnaeus) Dressler var. *triandra* (Ames) Dressler
Encyclia cochleata (Linnaeus) Dressler subsp. *triandra* (Ames) Hágsater
Epidendrum cochleatum Linnaeus
Prosthechea cochleata (Linnaeus) W. E. Higgins subsp. *triandra* (Ames) Nir
Nir 2000.

Prosthechea pygmaea (Hooker) Higgins
SYNONYMS
Encyclia pygmaea (Hooker) Dressler
Epidendrum pygmaceum Hooker
Hormidium pygmaeum (Hooker) Bentham & Hooker *f.*
Nir 2000.

Pteroglossaspis ecristata (Fernald) Rolfe
SYNONYM
Eulophia ecristata (Fernald) Ames
Ackerman 1995; Wunderlin 1998; Nir 2000.

Sacoila lanceolata (Aublet) Garay var. *lanceolata*
SYNONYMS
Spiranthes lanceolata (Aublet) Leon
Spiranthes orchioides (Swartz) A. Richard
Stenorrhynchos lanceolatum (Aublet) Richard *ex* Sprengel
Wunderlin 1998.

Sacoila lanceolata (Aublet) Garay var. *paludicola* (Luer) Sauleda, Wunderlin & Hansen
SYNONYM
Spiranthes lanceolata (Aublet) Leon var. *paludicola* Luer
Wunderlin 1998.

Sacoila squamulosa (Kunth) Garay
SYNONYMS
Sacoila lanceolata (Aublet) Garay var. *squamulosa* (Kunth) Szlachetko
Spiranthes squamulosa (H.B.K.) Leon
Stenorrhynchos squamulosum (H.B.K.) Sprengel
Nir 2000.

All of the *Spiranthes* synonyms have had a long and somewhat checkered history. Small used the genus *Ibidium* for virtually all of the *Spiranthes* he treated, and Correll tended to merge many of the segregate genera as well as several species in his 1950 publication. Reevaluation to address this situation has been a long and slow process. Although Garay (1980) restored some genera and designated new genera, many of the following have not appeared in current literature, other than in a few journal articles, until the publication of *Flora of North America* (2001).

Spiranthes brevilabris Lindley
SYNONYM
Spiranthes gracilis (Bigelow) L. C. Beck var. *brevilabris* (Lindley) Correll
Wunderlin 1998.

Spiranthes cernua (Linnaeus) Richard
SYNONYM
Ibidium cernuum (Linnaeus) House
Luer 1972; Wunderlin 1998.

Spiranthes floridana (Wherry) Cory *emend.* P. M. Brown
SYNONYMS
Ibidium floridanum Wherry
Spiranthes brevilabris Lindley var. *floridana* (Wherry) Luer
Spiranthes gracilis (Bigelow) L. C. Beck var. *floridana* (Wherry) Correll
Wunderlin 1998.

Spiranthes laciniata (Small) Ames
SYNONYM
Ibidium laciniatum (Small) House
Luer 1972; Wunderlin 1998.

Spiranthes longilabris Lindley
SYNONYM
Ibidium longilabre (Lindley) House
Luer 1972; Wunderlin 1998.

Spiranthes odorata (Nuttall) Lindley
SYNONYMS
Spiranthes cernua (Linnaeus) Richard var. *odorata* (Nuttall) Correll
Ibidium odoratum (Nuttall) House
Wunderlin 1998.

Spiranthes praecox (Walter) S. Watson
SYNONYM
Ibidium praecox (Walter) House
Luer 1972; Wunderlin 1998.

Spiranthes torta (Thunberg) Garay & Sweet
SYNONYMS
Spiranthes tortilis (Swartz) Richard
Ibidium tortile (Swartz) House
Wunderlin 1998.

Spiranthes tuberosa Rafinesque
SYNONYMS
Spiranthes grayi Ames
Spiranthes tuberosa var. *grayi* (Ames) Fernald
Spiranthes beckii Lindley
Ibidium beckii House, misapplied
Wunderlin 1992.

Spiranthes vernalis Engelmann & A. Gray
SYNONYM
Ibidium vernale (Engelmann & A. Gray) House
Luer 1972; Wunderlin 1998.

Tolumnia bahamensis (Nash *ex* Britton & Millspaugh) G. J. Braem
SYNONYMS
Oncidium bahamense Nash *ex* Britton & Millspaugh
MISAPPLIED
Tolumnia variegata (Swartz) G. J. Braem
Wunderlin 1998; Nir 2000; Ackerman 1995.

Trichocentrum carthagenense (Jacquin) M. W. Chase & N. H. Williams
SYNONYMS
Lophiaris carthagenensis (Jacquin) G. J. Braem
Oncidium carthagenense (Jacquin) Swartz

Trichocentrum maculatum (Aublet) M. W. Chase & N. H. Williams
SYNONYMS
Lophiaris maculata (Aublet) Ackerman
Oncidium undulatum (Swartz) Salisbury
MISAPPLIED
Lophiaris lurida (Lindley) G. J. Braem
Oncidium luridum Lindley
Trichocentrum luridum (Lindley) M. W. Chase & N. H. Williams
   Luer's photos clearly compare the Florida material (*Trichocentrum undulatum*) with the Central American material (*T. luridum*), although at that time he addressed all as *O. luridum*. This is a case of simple misidentification. See also R. P. Sauleda and R. M. Adams, 1989, *Rhodora* 91(866):188–200.

Triphora amazonica Schlechter
SYNONYM
Triphora latifolia G. Luer

Ackerman, J. D. 2000. *Lindleyana* 15(2):92–93.

Triphora rickettii Luer
MISAPPLIED
Triphora yucatanensis Ames
    Although Medley (*Selbyana* 12:102–3, 1991) considered these two species the same, detailed examination of *T. rickettii* in the field has shown several differences, and I feel that it should be maintained as a good species.

Vanilla mexicana Miller
SYNONYM
Vanilla inodora Schiede
Ackerman 1995.

Cross References for Synonyms and Misapplied Names

= synonym for
≠ misapplied name for
Anacheilum cochleatum (Linnaeus) Small var. *triandrum* (Ames) Sauleda et al.
    = *Prosthechea cochleata* (Linnaeus) W. E. Higgins var. *triandra* (Ames) W. E.
    Higgins
Beadlea cranichoides (Grisebach) Small = *Cyclopogon cranichoides* (Grisebach)
    Schlechter
Beadlea elata (Swartz) Small = *Cyclopogon elatus* (Swartz) Schlechter
Blephariglottis canbyi (Ames) W. Stone = *Platanthera* ×*canbyi* (Ames) Luer
Blephariglottis chapmanii Small = *Platanthera chapmanii* (Small) Luer *emend.*
    Folsom
Blephariglottis ciliaris (Linnaeus) Rydberg = *Platanthera ciliaris* (Linnaeus)
    Lindley
Blephariglottis conspicua (Nash) Small = *Platanthera blephariglottis*
    (Willdenow) Lindley var. *conspicua* (Nash) Luer
Blephariglottis cristata (Michaux) Rafinesque = *Platanthera cristata* (Michaux)
    Lindley
Campylocentrum porrectum Reichenbach f. = *Harrisella porrecta* (Reichenbach
    f.) Fawcett & Rendle
Centrogenium setaceum (Lindley) Schlechter = *Eltroplectris calcarata* (Swartz)
    Garay & Sweet
Cleistes divaricata var. *bifaria* Fernald = *Cleistes bifaria* (Fernald) Catling &
    Gregg

Encyclia bahamensis (Grisebach) Britton & Millspaugh = *Encyclia rufa* (Lindley) Britton & Millspaugh

Encyclia boothiana (Lindley) Dressler var. *erythronioides* (Small) Luer = *Prosthechea boothiana* (Lindley) W. E. Higgins var. *erythronioides* (Small) W. E. Higgins

Encyclia cochleata (Linnaeus) Dressler subsp. *triandra* (Ames) Hágsater = *Prosthechea cochleata* (Linnaeus) W. E. Higgins var. *triandra* (Ames) W. E. Higgins

Encyclia cochleata (Linnaeus) Dressler var. *triandra* (Ames) Dressler = *Prosthechea cochleata* (Linnaeus) W. E. Higgins var. *triandra* (Ames) W. E. Higgins

Encyclia pygmaea (Hooker) Dressler = *Prosthechea pygmaea* (Hooker) W. E. Higgins

Epicladum boothianum (Lindley) Small = *Prosthechea boothiana* (Lindley) W. E. Higgins var. *erythronioides* (Small) W. E. Higgins

Epidendrum anceps Jacquin ≠ *Epidendrum amphistomum* A. Richard

Epidendrum bahamense Grisebach ≠ *Encyclia rufa* (Lindley) Britton & Millspaugh

Epidendrum blancheanum Urban ≠ *Epidendrum acunae* Dressler

Epidendrum boothianum Lindley = *Prosthechea boothiana* (Lindley) W. E. Higgins var. *erythronioides* (Small) W. E. Higgins

Epidendrum cochleatum Linnaeus = *Prosthechea cochleata* (Linnaeus) W. E. Higgins var. *triandra* (Ames) W. E. Higgins

Epidendrum conopseum R. Brown = *Epidendrum magnoliae* Muhlenberg

Epidendrum conopseum R. Brown var. *mexicanum* L. O. Williams = *Epidendrum magnoliae* Muhlenberg var. *mexicanum* (L. O. Williams) P. M. Brown

Epidendrum difforme Jacquin ≠ *Epidendrum floridense* Hágsater

Epidendrum erythronioides Small = *Prosthechea boothiana* (Lindley) W. E. Higgins var. *erythronioides* (Small) W. E. Higgins

Epidendrum pygmaceum Hooker = *Prosthechea pygmaea* (Hooker) W. E. Higgins

Epidendrum rufum Lindley = *Encyclia rufa* (Lindley) Britton & Millspaugh

Epidendrum tampense Lindley = *Encyclia tampensis* (Lindley) Small

Epidendrum umbellatum Swartz ≠ *Epidendrum floridense* Hágsater

Erythrodes querceticola (Lindley) Ames = *Platythelys querceticola* (Lindley) Garay

Erythrodes sagreana (A. Richard) Leon = *Platythelys sagreana* (A. Richard) Garay

Eulophia ecristata (Fernald) Ames = *Pteroglossaspis ecristata* (Fernald) Rolfe

Galeandra beyrichii Reichenbach *f.* ≠ *Galeandra bicarinata* G. A. Romero & P. M. Brown

Govenia utriculata (Swartz) Lindley ≠ *Govenia floridana* P. M. Brown

Gymnadenopsis clavellata (Michaux) Rydberg *ex* Britton = *Platanthera clavellata* (Michaux) Luer

Habenaria blephariglottis (Willdenow) Hooker var. *conspicua* (Nash) Ames = *Platanthera blephariglottis* (Willdenow) Lindley var. *conspicua* (Nash) Luer

Habenaria canbyi Ames = *Platanthera ×canbyi* (Ames) Luer

Habenaria ciliaris (Linnaeus) R. Brown = *Platanthera ciliaris* (Linnaeus) Lindley

Habenaria clavellata (Michaux) Sprengel = *Platanthera clavellata* (Michaux) Luer var. *clavellata*

Habenaria cristata (Michaux) R. Brown = *Platanthera cristata* (Michaux) Lindley

Habenaria flava (Linnaeus) R. Brown = *Platanthera flava* (Linnaeus) Lindley var. *flava*

Habenaria floribunda Lindley ≠ *Habenaria odontopetala* Reichenbach *f.*

Habenaria garberi Porter = *Habenaria odontopetala* Reichenbach *f.*

Habenaria integra (Nuttall) Sprengel = *Platanthera integra* (Nuttall) Lindley

Habenaria nivea (Nuttall) Sprengel = *Platanthera nivea* (Nuttall) Lindley

Habenaria quinqueseta var. *macroceratitis* (Willdenow) Luer = *Habenaria macroceratitis* Willdenow

Habenaria strictissima Reichenbach *f.* var. *odontopetala* (Reichenbach *f.*) L. O. Williams = *Habenaria odontopetala* Reichenbach *f.*

Habenaria ×bicolor (Rafinesque) Beckner = *Platanthera ×bicolor* (Rafinesque) Luer

Habenaria ×chapmanii (Small) Ames = *Platanthera chapmanii* (Small) Luer *emend.* Folsom

Harrisella filiformis (Swartz) Cogniaux ≠ *Harrisella porrecta* (Reichenbach *f.*) Fawcett & Rendle

Hormidium pygmaeum (Hooker) Bentham & Hooker *f.* = *Prosthechea pygmaea* (Hooker) W. E. Higgins

Ibidium beckii House = *Spiranthes tuberosa* Rafinesque

Ibidium floridanum Wherry = *Spiranthes floridana* (Wherry) Cory *emend.* P. M. Brown

Ibidium laciniatum (Small) House = *Spiranthes laciniata* (Small) Ames

Ibidium longilabre (Lindley) House = *Spiranthes longilabris* Lindley

Ibidium lucayanum Britton = *Mesadenus lucayanus* (Britton) Schlechter

Ibidium odoratum (Nuttall) House = *Spiranthes odorata* (Nuttall) Lindley

Ibidium praecox (Walter) House = *Spiranthes praecox* (Walter) S. Watson

Ibidium tortile (Swartz) House = *Spiranthes torta* (Thunberg) Garay & Sweet

Ibidium vernale (Engelmann & A. Gray) House = *Spiranthes vernalis* Englemann & A. Gray

Liparis nervosa (Thunberg) Lindley ≠ *Liparis elata* Lindley

Malaxis floridana (Chapman) O. Kuntze = *Malaxis spicata* Swartz

Maxillaria conferta (Grisebach) Schweinfurth *ex* Leon = *Maxillaria parviflora* (Poeppig & Endlicher) Garay

Mesadenus polyanthus (Reichenbach f.) Schlechter ≠ *Mesadenus lucayanus* (Britton) Schlechter

Neolehmannia difformis (Jacquin) Pabst ≠ *Epidendrum floridense* Hágsater

Oncidium bahamense Nash *ex* Britton & Millspaugh = *Tolumnia variegata* (Swartz) G. J. Braem

Oncidium carthagenense (Jacquin) Swartz = *Trichocentrum carthagenense* (Jacquin) M. W. Chase & N. H. Williams

Oncidium ensatum Lindley ≠ *Oncidium floridanum* Ames

Oncidium luridum Lindley = *Trichocentrum luridum* (Lindley) M. W. Chase & N. H. Williams

Oncidium undulatum (Swartz) Salisbury = *Trichocentrum maculatum* (Aublet) M. W. Chase & N. H. Williams

Oncidium variegatum (Swartz) ≠ *Tolumnia bahamensis* (Nash *ex* Britton & Millspaugh) G. J. Braem

Physurus querceticola Lindley = *Platythelys querceticola* (Lindley) Garay

Physurus sagreanus A. Richard = *Platythelys sagreana* (A. Richard) Garay

Pogonia bifaria P. M. Brown & R. P. Wunderlin = *Cleistes bifaria* (Fernald) Catling & Gregg

Pogonia divaricata (Linnaeus) R. Brown = *Cleistes divaricata* (Linnaeus) Ames

Pogonia verticillata (Muhlenberg *ex* Willdenow) Nuttall = *Isotria verticillata* (Muhlenberg *ex* Willdenow) Rafinesque

Polyradicion lindenii (Lindley) Garay = *Dendrophylax lindenii* (Lindley) Bentham *ex* Rolfe

Polyrrhiza lindenii (Lindley) Cogniaux = *Dendrophylax lindenii* (Lindley) Bentham *ex* Rolfe

Polystachya flavescens (Lindley) J. K. Small ≠ *Polystachya concreta* (Jacquin) Garay & Sweet

Ponthieva racemosa (Walter) C. Mohr var. *brittonae* (Ames) Luer = *Ponthieva brittoniae* Ames

Sacoila lanceolata (Aublet) Garay var. *squamulosa* (Kunth) Szlachetko = *Sacoila squamulosa* (Kunth) Garay

Spiranthes adnata (Swartz) Bentham *ex* Fawcett = *Pelexia adnata* (Swartz) Sprengel

Spiranthes beckii Lindley = *Spiranthes tuberosa* Rafinesque

Spiranthes brevilabris Lindley var. *floridana* (Wherry) Luer = *Spiranthes floridana* (Wherry) Cory

Spiranthes cernua (Linnaeus) Richard var. *odorata* (Nuttall) Correll = *Spiranthes odorata* (Nuttall) Lindley

Spiranthes costaricensis Reichenbach *f.* = *Beloglottis costaricensis* (Reichenbach *f.*) Schlechter

Spiranthes cranichoides (Grisebach) Cogniaux = *Cyclopogon cranichoides* (Grisebach) Schlechter

Spiranthes elata (Swartz) L. C. Richard = *Cyclopogon elatus* (Swartz) Schlechter

Spiranthes gracilis (Bigelow) L. C. Beck var. *brevilabris* (Lindley) Correll = *Spiranthes brevilabris* Lindley

Spiranthes gracilis (Bigelow) L. C. Beck var. *floridana* (Wherry) Correll = *Spiranthes floridana* (Wherry) Cory *emend.* P. M. Brown

Spiranthes grayi Ames = *Spiranthes tuberosa* Rafinesque

Spiranthes lanceolata (Aublet) Leon = *Sacoila lanceolata* (Aublet) Garay var. *lanceolata*

Spiranthes lanceolata (Aublet) Leon var. *paludicola* Luer = *Sacoila lanceolata* (Aublet) Garay var. *paludicola* (Luer) Sauleda, Wunderlin & Hansen

Spiranthes lucayana (Britton) Cogniaux = *Mesadenus lucayanus* (Britton) Schlechter

Spiranthes orchioides (Swartz) A. Richard = *Sacoila lanceolata* (Aublet) Garay

Spiranthes squamulosa (H.B.K.) Leon = *Sacoila squamulosa* (Kunth) Garay

Spiranthes tortilis (Swartz) Richard = *Spiranthes torta* (Thunberg) Garay & Sweet

Spiranthes tuberosa var. *grayi* (Ames) Fernald = *Spiranthes tuberosa* Rafinesque

Stenorrhynchos lanceolatum (Aublet) Richard *ex* Sprengel = *Sacoila lanceolata* (Aublet) Garay var. *lanceolata*

Stenorrhynchos squamulosum (H.B.K.) Sprengel = *Sacoila squamulosa* (Kunth) Garay

Tolumnia variegata (Swartz) G. J. Braem ≠ *Tolumnia bahamensis* (Nash *ex* Britton & Millspaugh) G. J. Braem

Triphora latifolia G. Luer = *Triphora amazonica* Schlechter

Triphora yucatanensis Ames ≠ *Triphora rickettii* Luer

Vanilla mexicana Miller = *Vanilla inodora* Schiede

Species Pairs

When two species appear to be very closely related and have similar morphology, they are often referred to as species pairs. Although not necessarily a scientific or taxonomic term, the designation is often helpful in recognizing two species that may be difficult to distinguish both in the field and in herbaria. Their taxonomic history usually involves synonyms and/or recognition at different taxonomic levels—subspecies, varieties, or, rarely, forma. Validation of the two taxa at species level usually involves studies of pollinators, habit, habitat, range, morphology, and in recent years DNA analyses. Eight such species pairs are to be found in Florida. Fortunately a few simple morphological characters easily separate the taxa. In each case these are characters that are to be found within the key to the species. Also, range and habitat are often well separated.

Calopogon barbatus (Walter) Ames
bearded grass-pink
common and widespread throughout most of the state; petals widest below the middle

Calopogon multiflorus Lindley
SYNONYM *Calopogon barbatus* var. *multiflorus* (Lindley) Correll
many-flowered grass-pink
rare and local throughout the state; petals widest above the middle; see descriptions on pages 40 and 42 for details

Cleistes bifaria (Fernald) Catling & Gregg
SYNONYM *Cleistes divaricata* var. *bifaria* Fernald
upland spreading pogonia
widespread throughout the northern peninsula and the panhandle; lip about 27 mm long, broadly pointed at the apex

Cleistes divaricata (Linnaeus) Ames
large spreading pogonia
very rare and local in northeastern Florida; lip 34–56 mm long, narrowly pointed
at the apex; see descriptions on pages 54 and 56 for details

Habenaria macroceratitis Willdenow
SYNONYM *Habenaria quinqueseta* var. *macroceratitis* (Willdenow) Luer
long-horned rein orchis
rare and local in central Florida; plants of rich mesic hardwood hammocks; anterior division of the lateral petal more than twice (20–24 mm) the length of the
posterior division (8–11 mm); flowers, when viewed straight on, with a distinct
rectangular aspect; spur often greater than 10 cm (in living material)

Habenaria quinqueseta (Michaux) Eaton
Michaux's orchis
widespread throughout most of the state; plants of open pinelands, hedgerows
and fields; anterior division of the lateral petal less than twice (10–18 mm) the
length of the posterior division (6–9 mm); spur typically less than 10 cm (in living material); see descriptions on pages 122 and 126 for details

Platythelys querceticola (Lindley) Garay
low ground orchid
rare and local in central and northern Florida; longest leaf proportions 4:1; central lobe of the lip cordate; capsule prominently ribbed

Platythelys sagreana (A. Richard) Garay
SYNONYM *Erythrodes querceticola* var. *sagreana* (A. Richard) Leon
Cuban ground orchid
rare and local in the southernmost counties; longest leaf proportions 6:1; central
lobe of the lip rhomboidal, capsule indistinctly ribbed; see descriptions on pages
200 and 202 for details

Ponthieva brittoniae Ames
SYNONYM *Ponthieva racemosa* var. *brittonae* (Ames) Luer
Mrs. Britton's shadow-witch
very rare in Miami–Dade County; plants of rocky dry pinelands; may be extirpated; flowers nonresupinate, ovaries green, petals white

Ponthieva racemosa (Walter) Mohr
shadow-witch
widespread and locally common throughout most of Florida; plants of wet woodlands; flowers resupinate; ovaries brown, petals white with green striping; see descriptions on pages 214 and 216 for details

Spiranthes amesiana Schlechter *emend.* P. M. Brown
Ames' ladies'-tresses
very rare (2 collections) in Miami-Dade County; may be overlooked or extirpated; lip spade shaped, margin ciliolate, flowers 3–4 mm long

Spiranthes torta (Thunberg) Garay & Sweet
southern ladies'-tresses
widespread and local in southern Florida; lip ovate, margin lacerate-undulate; flowers 5–6 mm long; see descriptions on pages 242 and 264 for details

Spiranthes brevilabris Lindley
short-lipped ladies'-tresses
plants densely pubescent

Spiranthes floridana (Wherry) Cory *emend.* P. M. Brown
SYNONYM *Spiranthes brevilabris* var. *floridana* (Wherry) Luer
Florida ladies'-tresses
plants essentially glabrous; ranges and habitats overlap throughout Florida; see descriptions on pages 244 and 248 for details

Vanilla barbellata Reichenbach *f.*
worm-vine; leafless vanilla
lip with a distinct white margin

Vanilla dilloniana Correll
Dillon's vanilla
lip colored (purple) to the margin; very rare and perhaps extirpated in Florida, but ranges overlap; never reduced to synonymy; see descriptions on pages 302 and 304 for details

Some Florida Orchid Statistics

About half of the orchid species in Florida are listed as endangered or threatened, and more are proposed for addition to these listings. The state has several species that exist nowhere else and many for which Florida is the only habitat in the United States.

Endangered and Threatened Species

The following listings of threatened and endangered orchid species are taken from the latest *Regulated Plant Index* published by the Division of Plant Industry (DPI) in Gainesville in December 2000. Fifty-six species are listed as endangered, 17 are listed threatened, and 2 as commercially exploitable. Those species that have been proposed for listing either as endangered (14) or as threatened (2) are also noted. The listing process is exceedingly cumbersome and highly political, hence changes to the official list of protected plants are slow to come. Changes to current nomenclature, revisions of species not present in the state, and replacement with the correct plant names are even more arduous. Although the nomenclature in the DPI index is open to challenge, the intent to protect the species is there. Cross references are given for the nomenclature used in this book and for species that listings are intended to protect, even though those species are not listed. Subspecific taxa are not recognized. Common names and spellings are as used by DPI. More information may be found at *http://doacs.state.fl.us/~pi/5B-40.htm*.

Listed as Endangered

Basiphyllaea corallicola, Carter's orchid
Brassia caudata, spider orchid
Bulbophyllum pachyrrachis, rat-tail orchid

Calopogon multiflorus, many-flowered grass-pink

Campylocentrum pachyrrhizum, leafless orchid

Corallorhiza odontorhiza, autumn coralroot

Cranichis muscosa, moss orchid

Cyrtopodium punctatum, cowhorn orchid; cigar orchid

Eltroplectris calcarata, spurred neottia

Encyclia boothiana, dollar orchid = *Prosthechea boothiana* var. *erythronioides;* nominate variety does not grow in Florida

Encyclia cochleata, Florida clamshell orchid = *Prosthechea cochleata* var. *triandra;* nominate variety does not grow in Florida

Encyclia pygmaea, dwarf epidendrum = *Prosthechea pygmaea*

Epidendrum acunae, Acuña's epidendrum

Epidendrum anceps, dingy-flowered epidendrum; does not grow in Florida; intent is to protect *Epidendrum amphistomum*

Epidendrum difforme, umbelled epidendrum; does not grow in Florida; intent is to protect *Epidendrum floridense*

Epidendrum nocturnum, night-scented epidendrum

Epidendrum rigidum, rigid epidendrum

Epidendrum strobiliferum, matted epidendrum

Galeandra beyrichii, helmet orchid; does not grow in Florida; intent is to protect *Galeandra bicarinata*

Goodyera pubescens, downy rattlesnake orchid

Govenia utriculata, Gowen's orchid; does not grow in Florida; intent is to protect *Govenia floridana*

Habenaria distans, distans habenaria

Hexalectris spicata, crested coral-root

Ionopsis utricularioides, delicate ionopsis orchid

Isotria verticillata, whorled pogonia

Leochilus labiatus, lipped orchid; does not grow in Florida

Lepanthopsis melanantha, tiny orchid

Liparis nervosa, tall twayblade = *Liparis elata*

Macradenia lutescens, Trinidad macradenia

Malaxis unifolia, green adder's-mouth orchid

Maxillaria crassifolia, hidden orchid

Maxillaria parviflora, minnie-max

Oncidium bahamense, dancing-lady orchid = *Tolumnia bahamensis*

Oncidium floridanum, Florida oncidium

Oncidium luridum, mule-ear orchid; does not grow in Florida; intent is to
   protect *Trichocentrum maculatum*, spotted mule-eared orchid
Platanthera clavellata, green rein orchid
Platanthera integra, orange rein orchid
Pleurothallis gelida, frosted orchid
Polyradicion lindenii, ghost orchid = *Dendrophylax lindenii*
Polystachya concreta, pale-flowered polystachya
Ponthieva brittoniae, Mrs. Britton's shadow witch
Prescottia oligantha, small-flowered orchid
Spiranthes adnata, pelexia = *Pelexia adnata*, glandular ladies'-tresses
Spiranthes brevilabris, small ladies'-tresses
Spiranthes costaricensis, Costa Rican ladies'-tresses = *Beloglottis costari-*
   censis
Spiranthes elata, tall neottia = *Cyclopogon elatus*
Spiranthes ovalis, lesser ladies'-tresses
Spiranthes polyantha, Ft. George ladies'-tresses; does not grow in Florida;
   intent is to protect *Mesadenus lucayanus*
Spiranthes torta, southern ladies' tresses
Triphora craigheadii, Craighead's orchid
Triphora latifolia, wide-leaved triphora = *Triphora amazonica*
Tropidia polystachya, young-palm orchid
Vanilla barbellata, worm-vine orchid
Vanilla dilloniana, Dillon's vanilla
Vanilla mexicana, unscented vanilla
Vanilla phaeantha, leafy vanilla

Listed as Threatened

Bletia purpurea, pine-pink orchid
Cleistes divaricata, spreading pogonia: proposed endangered
Harrisella filiformis, threadroot orchid; does not grow in Florida; intent is
   to protect *Harrisella porrecta*, leafless harrisella
Listera australis, southern twayblade
Platanthera blephariglottis, white-fringed orchid; only var. *conspicua*
   grows in Florida
Platanthera ciliaris, yellow-fringed orchid
Platanthera cristata, crested fringed orchid
Platanthera flava, gypsy-spikes

Platanthera nivea, snowy orchid
Pogonia ophioglossoides, rose pogonia
Pteroglossaspis ecristata, non-crested Eulophia: proposed endangered
Spiranthes laciniata, lace-lipped ladies'-tresses
Spiranthes longilabris, long-lipped ladies'-tresses: proposed endangered
Spiranthes tuberosa, little pearl-twist
Stenorrhynchos lanceolatum, leafless beaked orchid = *Sacoila lanceolata*
Tipularia discolor, crane-fly orchid
Triphora trianthophora, three-birds orchid

Commercially Exploited

Encyclia tampensis, butterfly orchid
Epidendrum conopseum, green-fly orchid = *Epidendrum magnoliae*

Proposed for Listing as Endangered

Cleistes divaricata, large spreading pogonia
Cyclopogon cranichoides, speckled ladies'-tresses
Encyclia rufa, rufous butterfly orchid
Habenaria macroceratitis, long-horned rein orchis
Platythelys querceticola, low ground orchid
Platythelys sagreana, Cuban ground orchid
Pteroglossaspis ecristata, crestless plume orchid
Sacoila squamulosa, hoary beaked orchid
Spiranthes amesiana, Ames' ladies'-tresses
Spiranthes floridana, Florida ladies'-tresses
Spiranthes longilabris, long-lipped ladies tresses
Spiranthes sylvatica, woodland ladies'-tresses
Trichocentrum carthagenense, spread-eagle orchid
Triphora rickettii, Rickett's noddingcaps

Proposed for Listing as Threatened

Cleistes bifaria, upland spreading pogonia
Spiranthes eatonii, Eaton's ladies'-tresses

Species of Regional Interest

Endemics

Three species are endemic to Florida.

Govenia floridana
Triphora craigheadii
Triphora rickettii

Species with Limited Distribution outside Florida

Six species and two varieties are found only in Florida and one or two other countries.

Dendrophylax lindenii Cuba
Encyclia rufa the Bahamas
Epidendrum floridense Cuba
Epidendrum magnoliae var. *mexicanum* Mexico
Galeandra bicarinata Cuba
Oncidium floridanum the Bahamas, Cuba
Ponthieva brittoniae the Bahamas, Cuba
Sacoila lanceolata var. *paludicola* Cuba

Species with U.S. Occurrence Limited to Florida

Within the United States and Canada there are 56 species and five varieties that are found only in Florida.

Basiphyllaea corallicola
Beloglottis costaricensis
Bletia purpurea
Brassia caudata
Bulbophyllum pachyrachis
Calopogon tuberosus var. *simpsonii*
Campylocentrum pachyrrhizum
Cranichis muscosa
Cyclopogon cranichoides
Cyclopogon elatus
Cyrtopodium punctatum
Dendrophylax lindenii
Eltroplectris calcarata

Encyclia rufa
Encyclia tampensis
Epidendrum acunae
Epidendrum amphistomum
Epidendrum floridense
Epidendrum magnoliae var. *mexicanum*
Epidendrum nocturnum
Epidendrum rigidum
Epidendrum strobiliferum
Galeandra bicarinata
Govenia floridana
Habenaria distans
Habenaria macroceratitis
Habenaria odontopetala
Harrisella porrecta
Ionopsis utricularioides
Lepanthopsis melanantha
Liparis elata
Macradenia lutescens
Maxillaria crassifolia
Maxillaria parviflora
Mesadenus lucayanus
Oncidium floridanum
Pelexia adnata
Platythelys sagreana
Pleurothallis gelida
Polystachya concreta
Ponthieva brittoniae
Prescottia oligantha
Prosthechea boothiana var. *erythronioides*
Prosthechea cochleata var. *triandra*
Prosthechea pygmaea
Sacoila lanceolata var. *lanceolata*
Sacoila lanceolata var. *paludicola*
Sacoila squamulosa
Spiranthes amesiana
Spiranthes torta

Tolumnia bahamensis
Trichocentrum carthagenense
Trichocentrum maculatum
Triphora amazonica
Triphora craigheadii
Triphora gentianoides
Triphora rickettii
Tropidia polystachya
Vanilla barbellata
Vanilla dilloniana
Vanilla mexicana
Vanilla phaeantha

Species Limited to One County

Within Florida, 25 species and one variety are found only in one county (although reports may exist for additional counties).

Beloglottis costaricensis
Brassia caudata
Bulbophyllum pachyrachis
Campylocentrum pachyrrhizum
Corallorhiza odontorhiza
Encyclia rufa
Epidendrum acunae
Epidendrum strobiliferum
Galeandra bicarinata
Goodyera pubescens
Govenia floridana
Lepanthopsis melanantha
Macradenia lutescens
Maxillaria crassifolia
Maxillaria parviflora
Pelexia adnata
Platanthera clavellata
Pleurothallis gelida
Ponthieva brittoniae
Prosthechea pygmaea

Sacoila lanceolata var. *paludicola*
Sacoila squamulosa
Spiranthes amesiana
Trichocentrum carthagenense
Vanilla dilloniana
Vanilla phaeantha

Occurrence Uncertain

There are 13 species that have not been verified in the wild since 1990, some for much longer than that.

Brassia caudata, 1977
Bulbophyllum pachyrachis, 1968? (1978 report)
Cranichis muscosa, 1903 (1991 report)
Cyclopogon elatus, 1980
Encyclia rufa, single collection 1926
Epidendrum acunae, 1978
Macradenia lutescens, 1966 (1994 report)
Maxillaria parviflora, 1990
Pelexia adnata, prior to 1985 (1991 report)
Ponthieva brittoniae, 1987
Spiranthes amesiana, 1976
Trichocentrum carthagenense, single collection 1916
Vanilla dilloniana, 1928; type from cultivated plant 1946

Naturalized or Escaped Species

Five species are truly naturalized, with reproducing populations that are, to some extent, spreading.

Cyrtopodium polyphyllum: Miami-Dade and Highlands Counties
Oeceoclades maculata: Alachua, Broward, Collier, Hendry, Martin, Miami-Dade, Palm Beach, Pinellas, St. Lucie, and Sarasota Counties
Phaius tankervilleae: Hardee County
Spathoglottis plicata: Palm Beach County
Zeuxine strateumatica: abundantly naturalized throughout the state

Seven species are known in Florida from one-time collections or are represented by a few established plants.

Bletia florida: escaped in gardens near Homestead, Miami-Dade County

Bletia patula: single record from Miami-Dade County, 1947

Bletilla striata: Escambia County, garden escape

Epidendrum radicans: Lee County, persistent on Captiva Island; an apparent garden escape in southern Miami-Dade County

Laelia rubescens: Miami-Dade County, naturalized in a single site, 1999

Vanilla planifolia: Miami-Dade County single collection of an escaped or naturalized plant, 1976; numerous reports over the years

Vanilla pompona: Miami-Dade County single collection of an escaped or naturalized plant, 1946

Excluded Species

Some species periodically attributed to Florida have never been documented or the documentation presented has proven to be erroneous. The following are some of those species most frequently reported.

Brassavola caudata Lindley

Cattleya spp.

Cypripedium parviflorum Salisbury

Encyclia hodgeana (A. D. Hawkes) Beckner

Leochilus labiatus Cogniaux *ex* Urban

Maxillaria coccinea (Jacquin) L. O. Williams *ex* Hodge

Restrepiella ophiocephala (Lindley) Garay & Dunsterville

Spiranthes cernua (Linnaeus) L. C. Richard

Spiranthes lacera var. *gracilis* (Bigelow) Luer

Spiranthes sinensis (Persoon) Ames

Tetramicra cf. *caniculata* Urban

Triphora trianthophora subsp. *mexicana* (S. Watson) M. E. Medley

Chuck McCartney (1997) discusses several of these records more fully. Strictly speaking, all the plants given in the present work as having misapplied names could also be included here.

Orchid Hunting in Florida

Many people have the misconception that the state of Florida consists of nothing but sand. Although sand certainly prevails, there is much more to Florida, and it therefore offers many superb habitats for orchids. From the rough coral-rock pinelands of the Everglades to the rich hammocks of the central counties and the sand and seeps of the panhandle, Florida offers several geographic and geologic habitats. Limestone underlies all of the state, and when it is encountered as an outcrop or eroded area, it can greatly alter the pH of the soils. Acidic soils found in the pinelands can quickly change to alkaline soils in the exposed limestone areas—often side by side. The counties listed for each area lie either wholly or in part within the geographic area and habitat being discussed. The orchid species listed are selections of those species that have been found in these counties.

Northern Florida: Panhandle and Greater Jacksonville

Panhandle counties presented here are Bay, Calhoun, Escambia, Franklin, Gadsden, Gulf, Hamilton, Holmes, Jackson, Jefferson, Leon, Liberty, Madison, Okaloosa, Santa Rosa, Taylor, Wakulla, Walton, and Washington Counties. Although primarily a sandy Gulf coastal plain region, the panhandle has several major rivers that bisect it, and these present rich, shaded floodplains. The pine flatwoods that comprise so much of the panhandle are widespread and often managed with both controlled burns and logging. The Apalachicola National Forest occupies much of the central portion of the panhandle, and because of the extensive river systems, many seeps and shallow valleys exist. All of the state parks and the national forest are excellent places to search for orchids, with Ocklockonee River State Park, Mariana Caverns State Park, and Three Rivers State Park being especially good. Some species found throughout the panhandle include:

Calopogon barbatus, bearded grass-pink
Calopogon multiflorus, many-flowered grass-pink
Calopogon pallidus, pale grass-pink
Calopogon tuberosus var. *tuberosus,* common grass-pink
Cleistes bifaria, upland spreading pogonia
Corallorhiza wisteriana, Wister's coralroot
Epidendrum magnoliae var. *magnoliae,* green-fly orchis
Hexalectris spicata, crested coralroot
Listera australis, southern twayblade
Malaxis spicata, Florida adder's-mouth
Malaxis unifolia, green adder's-mouth
Platanthera blephariglottis var. *conspicua,* southern white fringed orchis
Platanthera chapmanii, Chapman's fringed orchis
Platanthera integra, yellow fringeless orchis
Platanthera nivea, snowy orchis
Platanthera ×canbyi, Canby's hybrid fringed orchis
Platanthera ×channellii, Channell's hybrid fringed orchis
Tipularia discolor, crane-fly orchid

In addition, the following three are also found in the panhandle but are known from few sites and represent the southern limits for species more common northward:

Goodyera pubescens, downy rattlesnake orchis
Isotria verticillata, large whorled pogonia
Platanthera clavellata, little club-spur orchis

The greater Jacksonville area—Baker, Duval, Nassau, and Union Counties—is essentially a southern extension of the central Atlantic coastal plain. In addition to many of the species found along the Gulf Coast of the panhandle, this area has several specialties. Found only in the greater Jacksonville area is the large spreading pogonia, *Cleistes divaricata,* and this area represents the northern limit for the southern Florida species for *Habenaria odontopetala,* the toothed rein orchis, and for *Mesadenus lucayanus,* copper ladies'-tresses. Fort George State Park and Cary State Forest are two exceptional areas in the Jacksonville vicinity.

North-Central Florida: The Great Temperate Hammocks

North-central Florida presents more temperate live oak hammocks and open wet prairies in Alachua, Bradford, Citrus, Clay, Columbia, Dixie, Gilchrist, Hernando,

Hillsborough, Levy, Marion, Orange, Osceola, Pasco, Polk, Seminole, Sumter, Suwannee, and Taylor Counties. The oak island hammocks, often surrounded by either sandhills and pinelands or wet prairie, are the choicest of habitats and never fail to present a variety of orchids. The intermediate zones from the prairie edge to the hammock uplands—although involving only a few feet of difference in elevation—often harbor species not seen in either the open wet areas or the drier hammocks. The deeply shaded and rich mucky river bottoms and their floodplains, usually with extensive colonies of red maples and a variety of other hardwoods, are the very thriftiest in orchids.

The list of good orchid-hunting areas in north-central Florida is lengthy, but some highlights would include many portions of the Marjorie Harris Carr Cross Florida Greenway, particularly the Ross Prairie section; Ocala National Forest, especially Alexander Springs Recreation Area; Jennings State Forest; San Felasco State Preserve; Devil's Millhopper State Geologic Site; Goethe State Forest; Ichetucknee Springs, Weikiva Springs, and Hillsborough state parks; and almost any woodland in and around Brooksville.

Some of the species found in the rich wooded hammocks of north-central Florida include:

Corallorhiza odontorhiza, autumn coralroot
Corallorhiza wisteriana, Wister's coralroot
Cyclopogon cranichoides, speckled ladies'-tresses
Epidendrum magnoliae var. *magnoliae,* green-fly orchis
Epidendrum magnoliae var. *mexicanum,* bronze green-fly orchis
Habenaria macroceratitis, long-horned rein orchis
Habenaria odontopetala, toothed rein orchis
Habenaria quinqueseta, Michaux's orchis
Listera australis, southern twayblade
Malaxis spicata, Florida adder's-mouth
Malaxis unifolia, green adder's-mouth
Mesadenus lucayanus, copper ladies'-tresses
Platythelys querceticola, low ground orchid
Ponthieva racemosa, shadow-witch
Sacoila squamulosa, hoary beaked orchid
Spiranthes sylvatica, woodland ladies'-tresses
Triphora amazonica, broad-leaved noddingcaps
Triphora craigheadii, Craighead's noddingcaps
Triphora rickettii, Rickett's noddingcaps
Triphora trianthophora, three birds orchis

Species to be found along the roadsides and in meadows, grasslands, and open pine flatwoods of north-central Florida are:

Calopogon barbatus, bearded grass-pink
Calopogon multiflorus, many-flowered grass-pink
Calopogon pallidus, pale grass-pink
Calopogon tuberosus var. *tuberosus,* common grass-pink
Eulophia alta, wild coco
Platanthera blephariglottis var. *conspicua,* southern white fringed orchis
Platanthera ciliaris, orange fringed orchis
Platanthera cristata, orange crested orchis
Platanthera flava, southern tubercled orchis
Platanthera integra, yellow fringeless orchis
Platanthera nivea, snowy orchis
Platanthera ×bicolor, bicolor hybrid fringed orchis
Platanthera ×canbyi, Canby's hybrid fringed orchis
Pogonia ophioglossoides, rose pogonia
Pteroglossaspis ecristata, crestless plume orchid
Sacoila lanceolata var. *lanceolata,* leafless beaked orchid
Spiranthes brevilabris, short-lipped ladies'-tresses
Spiranthes eatonii, Eaton's ladies'-tresses
Spiranthes floridana, Florida ladies'-tresses
Spiranthes laciniata, lace-lipped ladies'-tresses
Spiranthes longilabris, long-lipped ladies'-tresses
Spiranthes odorata, fragrant ladies'-tresses
Spiranthes praecox, giant ladies'-tresses
Spiranthes sylvatica, woodland ladies'-tresses (shaded areas)
Spiranthes vernalis, grass-leaved ladies'-tresses
Spiranthes ×folsomii, Folsom's hybrid ladies'-tresses
Spiranthes ×meridionalis, southern hybrid ladies'-tresses

In addition, the northernmost records for two epiphytes are in this area: in Lake County for *Harrisella porrecta,* leafless harrisella, and in Levy and Volusia Counties for *Encyclia tampensis,* Florida butterfly orchid.

Coastal Plain and Pine Scrublands

The coastal plain sandlands on the east and west sides of the peninsula lie in Brevard, Charlotte, DeSoto, Flagler, Glades, Hardee, Indian River, Manatee, Martin, Pinellas, Sarasota, St. Johns, St. Lucie, and Volusia Counties. The coastal plain has its share of orchid habitat, and the highway system in these coastal areas often offers the best habitats for the open grassland species. The grasslands of the road shoulders and center strips are periodically mown, which keeps down the competition so that many species of ladies'-tresses, *Spiranthes* and *Sacoila*, abound.

One of the choicest of all of Florida's state parks is Jonathan Dickinson State Park just north of West Palm Beach. The coastal pine and palmetto scrublands and open shallow pools host many species. Some of the orchids that can be expected would include:

Calopogon barbatus, bearded grass-pink
Calopogon pallidus, pale grass-pink
Calopogon tuberosus var. *tuberosus,* common grass-pink
Spiranthes laciniata, lace-lipped ladies'-tresses
Spiranthes odorata, fragrant ladies'-tresses
Spiranthes vernalis, grass-leaved ladies'-tresses
Tolumnia bahamensis, Florida's dancing lady

South-Central Florida: Lake and Ridge Country

In Highlands, Lake, Okeechobee, Osceola, Orange, Polk, and Seminole Counties, the lake country and Lake Wales Ridge (extending south from Haines City) from Wildwood to Sebring are dotted with bordering wetlands and higher rocky sandhills. Although few species grow within these areas because of extensive citrus cultivation and urban sprawl, there are still orchid-rich habitats, often in sight of major development. Three species often associated with these sandhill roadsides are:

Pteroglossaspis ecristata, crestless plume orchid
Sacoila lanceolata var. *lanceolata,* leafless beaked orchid
Spiranthes vernalis, grass-leaved ladies'-tresses

Many of Florida's theme parks fall within this province. Although these parks have destroyed much choice habitat, one large area that was set aside in mitigation is the Disney Wilderness Preserve of The Nature Conservancy. Located south of Kissimmee, the preserve covers many acres of expansive wet prairies and pine flatwoods. After a prescribed burn in late winter several areas abound with the many-flowered grass-pink, *Calopogon multiflorus,* in what is likely the largest remaining colony known.

Perhaps the premier gem of the state park system lies in this general area. It is

Highlands Hammock State Park in Sebring. This is the southern terminus of the Lake Wales Ridge and also the southernmost of the central Florida live oak hammocks. In addition to the hammocks there are extensive damp pine flatwoods and great roadsides. The oldest of the state parks, Highlands Hammock is one of the most beautiful places in North America. The orchid list is long and impressive. Unfortunately, feral hogs have wrought destruction throughout the park, but as they are brought under control, more areas are returning to their former glory. Every visit to this park yields more orchids. Species that have been observed in Highlands Hammock State Park are:

Corallorhiza wisteriana, Wister's coralroot
Cyclopogon cranichoides, speckled ladies'-tresses
Eltroplectris calcarata, spurred neottia
Encyclia tampensis, Florida butterfly orchid
Epidendrum magnoliae var. *mexicanum*, bronze green-fly orchis
Habenaria distans, false water-spider orchis
Habenaria odontopetala, toothed rein orchis
Habenaria quinqueseta, Michaux's orchis
Harrisella porrecta, leafless harrisella
Habenaria repens, water-spider orchis
Malaxis spicata, Florida adder's-mouth
Platythelys querceticola, low ground orchid
Ponthieva racemosa, shadow-witch
Triphora trianthophora, three birds orchis

Species of the flatwoods and roadsides include:
Calopogon barbatus, bearded grass-pink
Calopogon multiflorus, many-flowered grass-pink
Calopogon pallidus, pale grass-pink
Calopogon tuberosus var. *tuberosus*, common grass-pink
Eulophia alta, wild coco
Platanthera blephariglottis var. *conspicua*, southern white-fringed orchis
Platanthera ciliaris, orange fringed orchis
Platanthera cristata, orange crested orchis
Platanthera flava, southern tubercled orchis
Platanthera integra, yellow fringeless orchis
Platanthera nivea, snowy orchis
Platanthera ×bicolor, bicolor hybrid fringed orchis

Platanthera ×canbyi, Canby's hybrid fringed orchis
Pogonia ophioglossoides, rose pogonia
Pteroglossaspis ecristata, crestless plume orchid
Sacoila lanceolata var. *lanceolata,* leafless beaked orchid
Spiranthes eatonii, Eaton's ladies'-tresses
Spiranthes floridana, Florida ladies'-tresses
Spiranthes laciniata, lace-lipped ladies'-tresses
Spiranthes longilabris, long-lipped ladies'-tresses
Spiranthes odorata, fragrant ladies'-tresses
Spiranthes praecox, giant ladies'-tresses
Spiranthes tuberosa, little ladies'-tresses
Spiranthes vernalis, grass-leaved ladies'-tresses
Spiranthes ×meridionalis, southern hybrid ladies'-tresses

South Florida: Parks, Preserves, and Pinelands

South Florida—taking in Broward, Collier, Hendry, Lee, Maimi-Dade, Monroe, and Palm Beach Counties—offers a dramatic and distinctive change in climate and habitats relative to the rest of the state. The remaining rocky pinelands of Everglades National Park and the dense swamps of Collier County are home to most of the truly tropical species to be found in Florida. The many local, county, state, and federal conservation areas and parklands all abound in native orchids. The choicest of areas to search for the native orchids would include Corkscrew Swamp Sanctuary, Fakahatchee Strand State Preserve, Big Cypress National Preserve, Collier-Seminole State Park, Everglades National Park, Big Pine Key, and virtually any of the multitude of smaller local parks and preserves.

The list of species found within these southern counties comprises half of the orchids known from Florida. These are some of the highlights that can be expected:

Bletia purpurea, pine-pink
Calopogon tuberosus var. *simpsonii,* Simpson's grass-pink
Campylocentrum pachyrrhizum, crooked-spur orchid
Cyclopogon cranichoides, speckled ladies'-tresses
Cyrtopodium punctatum, cowhorn orchid; cigar orchid
Dendrophylax lindenii, ghost orchid; frog orchid
Eltroplectris calcarata, spurred neottia
Encyclia tampensis, Florida butterfly orchid
Epidendrum amphistomum, dingy star orchid

Epidendrum floridense, Florida star orchid
Epidendrum nocturnum, night-fragrant epidendrum
Epidendrum rigidum, rigid epidendrum
Eulophia alta, wild coco
Galeandra bicarinata, two-keeled galeandra
Habenaria distans, false water-spider orchis
Habenaria odontopetala, toothed rein orchis
Habenaria quinqueseta, Michaux's orchis
Habenaria repens, water-spider orchis
Harrisella porrecta, leafless harrisella
Ionopsis utricularioides, delicate ionopsis
Liparis elata, tall twayblade
Malaxis spicata, Florida adder's-mouth
Maxillaria crassifolia, false butterfly orchid
Oncidium floridanum, Florida oncidium
Platanthera nivea, snowy orchis
Platythelys sagreana, Cuban ground orchid
Polystachya concreta, yellow helmet orchid
Ponthieva racemosa, shadow-witch
Prosthechea boothiana var. *erythronioides,* Florida dollar orchid
Prosthechea cochleata var. *triandra,* Florida clamshell orchid
Sacoila lanceolata var. *lanceolata,* leafless beaked orchid
Sacoila lanceolata var. *paludicola,* Fakahatchee beaked orchid
Spiranthes torta, southern ladies'-tresses
Trichocentrum maculatum, spotted mule-eared orchid
Vanilla barbellata, worm-vine
Vanilla phaeantha, oblong-leaved vanilla

Tips and Trips

Because the flowering season is so drawn out in Florida, it can be difficult to see several species in flower at a single site in one visit. For those who would like to make extended trips, the seasonal suggestions that follow offer some excellent orchid hunting.

Spring in North-Central Florida

On a visit in mid- to late April, starting in Baker and Union counties in north

Florida and proceeding southward through Clay, Bradford, and Marion Counties to end in Levy County, many orchids can be seen, in appropriate habitat, along the roadsides. Some of the species are fairly common while a few are known from single sites. This trip can be a real test of your observational skills and ability to back up and turn around frequently. Be sure to stop at cemeteries along the way as they often have excellent orchids growing in the infrequently mown areas. Our primary route is SR 23 south through Union and Baker counties, connecting with SR 121 in MacClenny and then down US 301, with a side trip to Jennings State Forest in Clay County near Middleburg.

Return to US 301 in Starke and continue down to Ocala. From Ocala, go southwest on SR 200 to CR 484, through Dunnellon onto SR 40, and right on CR 336, passing through Goethe State Forest on one of the best orchid roads in Florida. Species that can be seen from late April to early May along this route include:

> *Calopogon barbatus,* bearded grass-pink
> *Calopogon multiflorus,* many-flowered grass-pink
> *Calopogon pallidus,* pale grass-pink
> *Calopogon tuberosus,* common grass-pink
> *Cleistes bifaria,* upland spreading pogonia
> *Cyclopogon cranichoides,* speckled ladies'-tresses
> *Epidendrum magnoliae* var. *magnoliae,* green-fly orchis
> *Epidendrum magnoliae* var. *mexicanum,* bronze green-fly orchis
> *Malaxis unifolia,* green adder's-mouth
> *Platanthera flava,* southern tubercled orchis
> *Pogonia ophioglossoides,* rose pogonia
> *Sacoila lanceolata* var. *lanceolata,* leafless beaked orchid
> *Sacoila squamulosa,* hoary beaked orchid
> *Spiranthes brevilabris,* short-lipped ladies'-tresses
> *Spiranthes eatonii,* Eaton's ladies'-tresses
> *Spiranthes floridana,* Florida ladies'-tresses
> *Spiranthes praecox,* giant ladies'-tresses
> *Spiranthes sylvatica,* woodland ladies'-tresses
> *Spiranthes vernalis,* grass-leaved ladies'-tresses

Summer in the Panhandle

Early August in the Apalachicola National Forest presents a suite of spectacular fringed orchids and their cousins and hybrids. Watch carefully along CR 65 and CR 379 for seep areas, damp pine flatwoods, and recently burned areas for all of the following:

Platanthera blephariglottis var. *conspicua,* southern white fringed orchis
Platanthera chapmanii, Chapman's fringed orchis
Platanthera ciliaris, orange fringed orchis
Platanthera cristata, orange crested orchis
Platanthera integra, yellow fringeless orchis
Platanthera nivea, snowy orchis
Platanthera ×*bicolor,* bicolor hybrid fringed orchis
Platanthera ×*canbyi,* Canby's hybrid fringed orchis
Platanthera ×*channellii,* Channell's hybrid fringed orchis

Autumn in Levy County

Goethe State Forest in Levy County is one of the most productive orchid habitats in the state. Driving the many paved and woodland roads always produces a variety of flowering species. Although spring is good, early November presents several of the ladies'-tresses, *Spiranthes,* in full flower. If you are adventuresome, step off the roadways into some of the small wooded swamps and hammocks that border the roads. The following species are regularly to be found, especially along the forest roads:

Epidendrum magnoliae var. *magnoliae,* green-fly orchis
Malaxis spicata, Florida adder's-mouth
Ponthieva racemosa, shadow-witch
Spiranthes longilabris, long-lipped ladies'-tresses
Spiranthes odorata, fragrant ladies'-tresses
Spiranthes ovalis var. *ovalis,* southern oval ladies'-tresses
Spiranthes ×*folsomii,* Folsom's hybrid ladies'-tresses
Spiranthes ×*itchetuckneensis,* Itchetucknee hybrid ladies'-tresses

Everglades National Park

A trip to Everglades National Park can be both exceedingly productive and frustrating. Because of gross overcollecting throughout the years, many of the orchids of the park are no longer found along the roadsides. The good news is that most species can easily be seen within only a few hundred feet of many designated parking areas. Long Pine Key offers several hiking trails through the various hammocks, and the fire roads offer a good, safe hiking environment. A word of warning: be especially careful if you venture into the pinnacle rock hammocks. They look harmless, but the sharp limestone coupled with small (or large) sinkholes can be accidents waiting to happen. Always carry a walking stick for support and watch every step. October is prime flowering time for several species that are specialties of the Everglades. Bring your insect repellent, be prepared for wet feet in places, and enjoy! A single day in October can easily yield the following:

Encyclia tampensis, Florida butterfly orchid
Epidendrum nocturnum, night-fragrant epidendrum
Epidendrum rigidum, rigid epidendrum
Eulophia alta, wild coco
Galeandra bicarinata, two-keeled galeandra
Habenaria odontopetala, toothed rein orchis
Habenaria quinqueseta, Michaux's orchis
Polystachya concreta, yellow helmet orchid
Prosthechea boothiana var. *erythronioides,* Florida dollar orchid
Prosthechea cochleata var. *triandra,* Florida clamshell orchid

If you are both exceedingly watchful and fortunate, perhaps you will find the elusive Carter's orchid, *Basiphyllaea corallicola.*

Fakahatchee Strand State Preserve

Almost everyone who has an interest in the native orchids of Florida at some point wants to visit the Fakahatchee Swamp within the Fakahatchee Strand State Preserve east of Naples. This is not roadside viewing, but there are a few trails that do pass by some of the orchids. The best way to see these hidden gems is to make arrangements to join one of the swamp walks held by the preserve naturalist. Call the office of the preserve for details, as these walks are held periodically throughout the season. November is perhaps the best month for seeing the greatest number of orchids in flower in a single day. A clear, crisp November day can produce many of the following:

Campylocentrum pachyrrhizum, crooked-spur orchid
Encyclia tampensis, Florida butterfly orchid
Epidendrum amphistomum, dingy-flowered star orchid
Epidendrum floridense, Florida star orchid
Epidendrum nocturnum, night-fragrant epidendrum
Epidendrum rigidum, rigid epidendrum
Epidendrum strobiliferum, cone-bearing epidendrum
Eulophia alta, wild coco
Habenaria odontopetala, toothed rein orchis
Habenaria repens, water-spider orchis
Harrisella porrecta, leafless harrisella
Liparis elata, tall twayblade

Malaxis spicata, Florida adder's-mouth
Polystachya concreta, yellow helmet orchid
Ponthieva racemosa, shadow-witch
Prosthechea cochleata var. *triandra,* Florida clamshell orchid
Prosthechea pygmaea, dwarf butterfly orchid
Spiranthes odorata, fragrant ladies'-tresses

Plant Records and County Lines

Plant records are usually maintained by county. In most states this makes for clear delimitation, but in Florida the counties have undergone many changes over the past 200 years. For this reason it is important to understand how the counties evolved and that the present county lines are not necessarily those of the early or mid-twentieth century. One example would be that plants collected in the early 1900s and labeled from Lee County could actually be from what is today Collier County. If the specimen is labeled Fakahatchee Swamp, that is decisive, but if it merely says "swamp," it is difficult to be sure where the plants were found. Likewise, Dade County (renamed Miami-Dade County in 1998) included all of what is now Broward County until 1915. There are numerous records with the location given as "Ft. Lauderdale, Dade Co." Granted, this affects only a small portion of the orchid flora of Florida, but it can nonetheless raise fascinating conundrums.

The following listing provides a better understanding of the evolution of Florida's counties; their locations are given on the map on page 21. Plant collection records to double-check for the correct county:

Prior to 1925

St. Lucie included Indian River
Palm Beach included Martin
Alachua included Gilchrist
Calhoun included Gulf

Prior to 1923

Lee included Hendry and Collier

Prior to 1921

DeSoto included Charlotte, Glades, Highlands, and Hardee

Manatee included Sarasota and Manatee
Lafayette included Dixie and Lafayette

Prior to 1910

Miami-Dade included Palm Beach
Hillsborough included Pinellas
Washington included Bay
Orange included Seminole
Dade and Palm Beach included Broward
Santa Rosa and Walton included Okaloosa
St. Johns and Volusia included Flagler
Osceola and St. Lucie included Okeechobee

Prior to 1887

Hernando included Citrus
Manatee included DeSoto
Orange, Sumter, and Volusia included Lake
Monroe included Lee
Brevard and Orange included Osceola
Hernando included Pasco
Sumter was redrawn with creation of Lake

Chronological List of Florida Counties with Date of Creation

Escambia	1821	Franklin	1832
St. Johns	1821	Hillsborough	1834
Duval	1822	Dade	1836, renamed
Jackson	1822		Miami-Dade in 1998
Gadsden	1823	Calhoun	1838
Monroe	1823	Santa Rosa	1842
Alachua	1824	Hernando	1843
Leon	1824	Wakulla	1843
Nassau	1824	Marion	1844
Walton	1824	St. Lucie	1844
Washington	1825	Levy	1845
Hamilton	1827	Orange	1845
Jefferson	1827	Holmes	1848
Madison	1827	Putnam	1849
Columbia	1832	Volusia	1854

Brevard	1855		Bay	1913
Liberty	1855		Seminole	1913
Manatee	1855		Broward	1915
Lafayette	1856		Okaloosa	1915
Taylor	1856		Flagler	1917
Clay	1858		Okeechobee	1917
Suwannee	1858		Charlotte	1921
Baker	1861		Dixie	1921
Bradford	1861		Glades	1921
Polk	1861		Hardee	1921
Citrus	1887		Highlands	1921
DeSoto	1887		Sarasota	1921
Lake	1887		Union	1921
Lee	1887		Collier	1923
Osceola	1887		Hendry	1923
Pasco	1887		Gilchrist	1925
Sumter	1887		Gulf	1925
Palm Beach	1909		Indian River	1925
Pinellas	1911		Martin	1925

Florida Counties with Date of Creation

Alachua	1824		Flagler	1917
Baker	1861		Franklin	1832
Bay	1913		Gadsden	1823
Bradford	1861		Gilchrist	1925
Brevard	1855		Glades	1921
Broward	1915		Gulf	1925
Calhoun	1838		Hamilton	1827
Charlotte	1921		Hardee	1921
Citrus	1887		Hendry	1923
Clay	1858		Hernando	1843
Collier	1923		Highlands	1921
Columbia	1832		Hillsborough	1834
Dade	1836, renamed		Holmes	1848
	Miami-Dade in 1998		Indian River	1925
DeSoto	1887		Jackson	1822
Dixie	1921		Jefferson	1827
Duval	1822		Lafayette	1856
Escambia	1821		Lake	1887

Lee	1887	Pinellas	1911
Leon	1824	Polk	1861
Levy	1845	Putnam	1849
Liberty	1855	Santa Rosa	1842
Madison	1827	Sarasota	1921
Manatee	1855	Seminole	1913
Marion	1844	St. Johns	1821
Martin	1925	St. Lucie	1844
Monroe	1823	Sumter	1887
Nassau	1824	Suwannee	1858
Okaloosa	1915	Taylor	1856
Okeechobee	1917	Union	1921
Orange	1845	Volusia	1854
Osceola	1887	Wakulla	1843
Palm Beach	1909	Walton	1824
Pasco	1887	Washington	1825

The Southeastern Atlantic
and Gulf Coastal Plains

Many of the orchids in this field guide also grow in the nearby
Atlantic and Gulf coastal plain states—Virginia, North and
South Carolina, Georgia, Alabama, Mississippi, Louisiana, and
Texas. The distribution information that follows is presented
to encourage use of this book in those areas as well. Only two
additional species are normally found in this wider zone:
(a) the **nodding ladies'-tresses**, *Spiranthes cernua*, and
(b) the **southern slender ladies'-tresses**, *Spiranthes lacera* var.
gracilis, both of which occur in all eight states. The species
listed may also occur well away from the coastal plain; parentheses indicate presence in the state but not necessarily
on the coastal plain. Many of those species with southern
affinities are relatively rare and have few occurrences,
whereas those that are more northerly in their centers of
distribution occur with greater frequency.

   The status given for each state is based on a combination
of official and unofficial state lists from the Natural Heritage

b

Program of The Nature Conservancy, natural resource agencies, and personal communications. These indications of status are thus by no means definitive but are included to offer some feel for frequency. Meanings of the symbols used are E = endangered, T = threatened, R = rare, H = historical, and U = undetermined. Absence of any symbol for status indicates that the species is widespread throughout appropriate habitat. No attempt has been made to differentiate between extant sites and historical records except in well-documented cases.

Calopogon barbatus, bearded grass-pink
North Carolina-R, South Carolina-R, Georgia-R, Alabama-E, Mississippi-R, Louisiana-E
Calopogon multiflorus, many-flowered grass-pink
North Carolina-E, Georgia-H, Alabama-E, Mississippi-U, Louisiana-E
Calopogon pallidus, pale grass-pink
Virginia-H, North Carolina, South Carolina, Georgia, Alabama, Mississippi, Louisiana-E
Calopogon tuberosus, common grass-pink
Virginia, North Carolina, South Carolina, Georgia, Alabama, Mississippi, Louisiana, Texas
Cleistes bifaria, upland spreading pogonia
(Virginia-E), North Carolina-T, South Carolina-R, Georgia-T, Alabama-R, Mississippi-R, eastern Louisiana-E

Cleistes divaricata, large spreading pogonia
Virginia-E, North Carolina, South Carolina-T, Georgia
Corallorhiza odontorhiza, autumn coralroot
Virginia, North Carolina, South Carolina, Georgia, Alabama, Mississippi, (Louisiana-E)
Corallorhiza wisteriana, Wister's coralroot
Virginia, North Carolina-T, South Carolina, Georgia, Alabama-T, Mississippi, Louisiana, Texas
Epidendrum magnoliae var. *magnoliae,* green-fly orchis
North Carolina-T, South Carolina-U, Georgia-R, Alabama-T, Mississippi, Louisiana
Eulophia alta, wild coco
Georgia-R
Goodyera pubescens, downy rattlesnake orchis
Virginia, North Carolina, South Carolina, Georgia, Alabama, Mississippi, Louisiana
Habenaria quinqueseta, Michaux's orchis
South Carolina-U, Georgia-E, Alabama, Louisiana-E, Texas-H
Habenaria repens, water-spider orchis
North Carolina-T, South Carolina, Georgia, Alabama, Mississippi, Louisiana, Texas
Hexalectris spicata, crested coralroot
Virginia, North Carolina-T, South Carolina, Georgia, Alabama, Mississippi, Louisiana, Texas
Isotria verticillata, large whorled pogonia
Virginia, North Carolina, South Carolina, Georgia, Alabama-T, Mississippi, Louisiana-T, Texas
Listera australis, southern twayblade
Virginia, North Carolina-R, South Carolina-U, Georgia-T, Alabama-T, Mississippi, Louisiana, Texas
Malaxis spicata, Florida adder's-mouth
Virginia-R, South Carolina, Georgia-E
Malaxis unifolia, green adder's-mouth
Virginia, North Carolina, South Carolina, Georgia, Alabama, Mississippi, Louisiana, Texas
Platanthera blephariglottis var. *conspicua,* southern white fringed orchis
North Carolina, South Carolina, Georgia, Alabama-E, Mississippi, Louisiana-E, Texas

Platanthera chapmanii, Chapman's fringed orchis
Georgia-R, Texas-R
Platanthera ciliaris, orange fringed orchis
Virginia, North Carolina, South Carolina, Georgia, Alabama, Mississippi, Louisiana, Texas
Platanthera clavellata, little club-spur orchis
Virginia, North Carolina, South Carolina, Georgia, Alabama, Mississippi, Louisiana, Texas
Platanthera cristata, orange crested orchis
Virginia, North Carolina, South Carolina, Georgia, Alabama, Mississippi, Louisiana, Texas
Platanthera flava var. *flava,* southern tubercled orchis
Virginia, North Carolina, South Carolina, Georgia, Alabama-T, Mississippi, Louisiana, Texas
Platanthera integra, yellow fringeless orchis
North Carolina-E, South Carolina-T, Georgia-T, Alabama-E, Mississippi, Louisiana-T, Texas
Platanthera nivea, snowy orchis
North Carolina-E, South Carolina, Georgia-R, Alabama-T, Mississippi, Louisiana, Texas
Platythelys querceticola, low ground orchid
Louisiana-E
Pogonia ophioglossoides, rose pogonia
Virginia, North Carolina, South Carolina, Georgia, Alabama, Mississippi, Louisiana, Texas
Ponthieva racemosa, shadow-witch
Virginia, North Carolina-T, South Carolina-U, Georgia-T, Alabama-T, Mississippi, Louisiana, Texas
Pteroglossaspis ecristata, crestless plume orchid
North Carolina-E, South Carolina-T, Georgia-E, Alabama-E, Louisiana-T
Spiranthes brevilabris, short-lipped ladies'-tresses
South Carolina, Georgia-E, Alabama, Mississippi, Louisiana, Texas
Spiranthes cernua, nodding ladies'-tresses
Virginia, North Carolina, South Carolina, Georgia, Alabama, Mississippi, Louisiana, Texas
Spiranthes eatonii, Eaton's ladies'-tresses
Virginia, North Carolina, South Carolina, Georgia, Alabama, Mississippi, Louisiana, Texas (new taxon, status undetermined)

Spiranthes floridana, Florida ladies'-tresses

North Carolina-U, South Carolina, Georgia, Alabama, Mississippi, Louisiana, Texas

Spiranthes lacera var. *gracilis,* southern slender ladies'-tresses

Virginia, North Carolina, South Carolina, (Georgia), (Alabama), (Mississippi), (Louisiana), (Texas)

Spiranthes laciniata, lace-lipped ladies'-tresses

North Carolina-E, South Carolina-E, Georgia, Alabama, Mississippi, Louisiana, Texas

Spiranthes longilabris, long-lipped ladies'-tresses

North Carolina-E, South Carolina-U, Georgia-E, Alabama-E, Mississippi, Louisiana, Texas

Spiranthes odorata, fragrant ladies'-tresses

Virginia, North Carolina, South Carolina, Georgia, Alabama, Mississippi, Louisiana, Texas

Spiranthes ovalis var. *ovalis,* southern oval ladies'-tresses

Mississippi, Louisiana, Texas

Spiranthes ovalis var. *erostellata,* northern oval ladies'-tresses

Virginia, North Carolina, South Carolina, Georgia-R, Alabama, Mississippi, Louisiana

Spiranthes praecox, giant ladies'-tresses

Virginia, North Carolina, South Carolina, Georgia, Alabama, Mississippi, Louisiana, Texas

Spiranthes sylvatica, woodland ladies'-tresses

Virginia, North Carolina, South Carolina, Georgia, Alabama, Louisiana, Texas (new taxon, status undetermined)

Spiranthes tuberosa, little ladies'-tresses

Virginia, North Carolina, South Carolina, Georgia, Alabama, Mississippi, Louisiana, Texas

Spiranthes vernalis, grass-leaved ladies'-tresses

Virginia, North Carolina, South Carolina, Georgia, Alabama, Mississippi, Louisiana, Texas

Tipularia discolor, crane-fly orchid

Virginia, North Carolina, South Carolina, Georgia, Alabama, Mississippi, Louisiana, Texas

Triphora trianthophora, three birds orchis

Virginia-E, North Carolina-T, South Carolina-T, Georgia, Alabama, Mississippi, Louisiana-E, Texas

Zeuxine strateumatica, lawn orchid*

Georgia, Alabama, Mississippi, Louisiana, Texas

Using Luer's Native Orchids of Florida (1972) in the New Century

Additions, Corrections, and Comments

For those fortunate enough to own or have access to a copy of Carlyle Luer's original 1972 work on the orchids of Florida, some additions, corrections, and comments may be helpful. These should in no way detract from the usefulness of the book but simply allow one to accommodate the results of more than 25 years of research and changes in nomenclature and to include several species that had not been found in Florida as of Luer's date of publication. (Names of authors for the species added are given in the species accounts and checklist in the present volume.)

Preface

pp. 8–9 pl. 1:4 for *Cypripedium calceolus* var. *pubescens* read *Cypripedium parviflorum* var. *pubescens*

Introduction

pp. 22, 23 pl. 4:8 for *Oncidium luridum* read *Trichocentrum maculatum*

Key

pp. 24–25 pl. 5:8 *Calopogon tuberosus* var. *simpsonii* forma *niveus*
p. 28 couplet 14 for *Centrogenium* read *Eltroplectris*
p. 29 couplet 31 contains all of the *Spiranthes* segregate genera
p. 30 couplet 41a add to *Eulophia, Pteroglossaspis*
p. 31 couplet 52 for *Erythrodes* read *Platythelys*
p. 31 couplet 57a for *Polyrrhiza* read *Dendrophylax*
p. 31 couplet 61a for *Encyclia* read *Encyclia* and *Prosthechea*

p. 32 couplet 65a for *Oncidium* read *Trichocentrum*

p. 34 couplet 69a for *Oncidium* read *Oncidium* and *Tolumnia*

Text

pp. 38, 39 pl. 6:5 forma *albiflora*

pp. 42, 43 pl. 8:6 forma *leucantha*

pp. 50, 51 for *Triphora latifolia* read *Triphora amazonica*

pp. 58, 59 pl. 15:8 *albiflora*

pp. 62, 63 pl. 16:1, 6 forma *albiflorus*

pp. 66, 67 pl. 17:6 forma *viridis*

pp. 73, 74 pl. 19:3, 4 for *Vanilla inodora* read *Vanilla mexicana*

pp. 82, 86, 87 pl. 22:1, 2 for *Ponthieva racemosa* var. *brittonae* read *Ponthieva brittoniae*

p. 90 couplet 6a for *Spiranthes tortilis* read *Spiranthes torta*

p. 90 couplet 8a for *Spiranthes grayi* read *Spiranthes tuberosa*

p. 90 couplet 10 for *Spiranthes brevilabris* var. *brevilabris* read *Spiranthes brevilabris*

p. 90 couplet 10a for *Spiranthes brevilabris* var. *floridana* read *Spiranthes floridana*

p. 90 couplet 12a for *Spiranthes cernua* var. *odorata* read *Spiranthes odorata*

p. 91 couplet 15a for *S. polyantha* read *Mesadenus lucayanus*

p. 91 couplet 16 for *S. costaricensis* read *Beloglottis costaricensis*

p. 91 couplet 17 for *S. cranichoides* read *Cyclopogon cranichoides*

p. 91 couplet 17a for *S. elata* read *Cyclopogon elatus*

p. 91 couplet 18a for *S. lanceolata* var. *paludicola* read *Sacoila lanceolata* var. *paludicola*

p. 91 couplet 19 for *S. lanceolata* var. *lanceolata* read *Sacoila lanceolata* var. *lanceolata*

p. 91 couplet 19a for *S. lanceolata* var. *luteoalba* read *Sacoila lanceolata* forma *albidaviridis*

pp. 99, 100, 101 pl. 26:1–5 for *Spiranthes tortilis* read *Spiranthes torta*

pp. 100, 101 pl. 26:6–9 for *Spiranthes gracilis* read *Spiranthes lacera* var. *gracilis* none of the examples are from Florida; this species is not present in Florida

pp. 102, 103 pl. 27:1–6 for *Spiranthes brevilabris* var. *brevilabris* read *Spiranthes brevilabris*

pp. 102, 104, pl. 28:7–9 for *Spiranthes brevilabris* var. *floridana* read *Spiranthes floridana*

pp. 105, 106 pl. 28:1–5 for *Spiranthes grayi* read *Spiranthes tuberosa*

pp. 108, 109 pl. 29:1 *Spiranthes cernua* is not in Florida

p. 109 pl. 29:2–5 are *Spiranthes odorata;* 6–8 for *Spiranthes cernua* var. *odorata* read *Spiranthes odorata*

p. 110 *Spiranthes cernua* var. *odorata* read *Spiranthes odorata*

p. 111 *Spiranthes cranichoides* read *Cyclopogon cranichoides*

pp. 112, 113 pl. 30:1–5 read *Cyclopogon cranichoides;* 6–8 read *Cyclopogon elatus*

pp. 114, 115 pl. 31:1–4 for *Spiranthes costaricensis* read *Beloglottis costaricensis*

pp. 115, 116, pl. 31:5–8 for *Spiranthes polyantha* read *Mesadenus lucayanus*

pp. 117, 118, 119 pl. 32 for *Spiranthes lanceolata* var. *lanceolata* read *Sacoila lanceolata* var. *lanceolata*

pp. 120, 121 pl. 33 for *Spiranthes lanceolata* var. *luteoalba* read *Sacoila lanceolata* forma *albidaviridis;* for *Spiranthes lanceolata* var. *paludicola* read *Sacoila lanceolata* var. *paludicola*

p. 121 pl. 33:1–3 read *Sacoila lanceolata;* pl. 33:4–6 read *Sacoila lanceolata* forma *albidaviridis;* pl. 33:7–9 read *Sacoila lanceolata* var. *paludicola*

pp. 123, 124 pl. 34 *Centrogenium setaceum* read *Eltroplectris calcarata*

p. 126 pl. 35:1, 2, 4, 6 for *Erythrodes querceticola* read *Platythelys querceticola;* pl. 35:3, 5 read *Platythelys sagreana* (no description of *P. sagreana,* but a reference on p. 128 to var. *sagreana*)

pp. 142, 143 pl. 40:3 for *P.* ×*chapmanii* read *P. chapmanii;* pl. 40:7 for *P.* ×*canbyi* read *P.* ×*channellii*

p. 151 for *Platanthera* ×*chapmanii* read *Platanthera chapmanii* and delete the hybrid combination of *P. ciliaris* × *P. cristata*

pp. 153, 156, 157, pl. 45:3, 4, 5, p. 158 for *Habenaria quinqueseta* var. *macroceratitis* read *Habenaria macroceratitis*

pp. 174, 175 pl. 51 read forma *albolabia*

pp. 184, 186–187 pl. 54:5–7 *Restrepiella* is not found in Florida

pp. 191, 192, 193 pl. 56:2–5 *Tetramicra* is not found in Florida

p. 195 couplets 2a, 3, 3a for *Encyclia* read *Prosthechea*

pp. 198, 199 pl. 55:5 read forma *albolabia*

pp. 200, 202, for *Encyclia* read *Prosthechea*

pp. 203 pl. 60:8 *Prosthechea cochleata* var. *triandra* forma *albidoflava*

p. 204 for *Encyclia* read *Prosthechea*

p. 208 for *Epidendrum conopseum* read *Epidendrum magnoliae*

p. 210 for *Epidendrum anceps* read *Epidendrum amphistomum*

P. 210–11 pl. 63:1 forma *rubrifolium*

p. 212 for *Epidendrum difforme* read *Epidendrum floridense*

pp. 221, 222 pl. 68 for *Polystachya flavescens* read *Polystachya concreta*

pp. 232, 233 pl. 71:1, 2, p. 234 for *Cyrtopodium andersonii* read *Cyrtopodium polyphyllum*

p. 236 couplet 1a for *Eulophia ecristata* read *Pteroglossaspis ecristata*

p. 238 pl. 72:6 for albino form read forma *pallida*

p. 240 for *Eulophia ecristata* read *Pteroglossaspis ecristata*

p. 243 for *Govenia utriculata* read *Govenia floridana*

p. 244 for *Galeandra beyrichii* read *Galeandra bicarinata*

p. 244 captions for p. 245 pl. 74:1, 2 *Govenia floridana;* pl. 74:3, 4 *Govenia utriculata;* pl. 74:5–8 *Galeandra bicarinata*

pp. 255, 256, 257 pl. 77 for *Oncidium bahamense* read *Tolumnia bahamensis*

p. 255 couplet 3 for *Oncidium luridum* read *Trichocentrum maculatum*

p. 255 couplet 3a for *Oncidium carthagenense* read *Trichocentrum carthagenense*

pp. 258, 259 pl. 78:6, 7 for *Oncidium carthagenense* read *Trichocentrum carthagenense*

p. 260 for *Oncidium luridum* read *Trichocentrum maculatum;* pl. 78:6 forma *flavovirens;* pl. 78:7 *Trichocentrum luridum*

p. 262 for *Oncidium carthagenense* read *Trichocentrum carthagenense*

pp. 263–64 pl. 80:1, 2 *Leochilus* is not found in Florida

p. 277, 278 pl. 84 for *Polyrrhiza* read *Dendrophylax*

For *Spathoglottis plicata,* see "Native Orchids of the United States and Canada Excluding Florida," pp. 280, 281, 286, pl. 78:5, 6.

No attempt has been made to adjust Luer's index.

Species not found in Luer but given full treatment in the present volume are:

Encyclia rufa

Maxillaria parviflora

Oeceoclades maculata

Pelexia adnata

Platythelys sagreana

Sacoila squamulosa

Spiranthes amesiana

Spiranthes ovalis var. *erostellata*

Spiranthes sylvatica

and the following escapes or waifs:

Bletia florida

Bletilla striata

Epidendrum radicans

Laelia rubescens

Vanilla pompona

Glossary

Note: Many terms are self-defining the first time they occur in the text. Those terms applied to leaf shape often overlap and can be difficult to precisely define; they are often used in combining forms such as oblanceolate: oblong and lanceolate—for a shape that is neither one nor the other but falls in between. Those for degrees of hairiness often have diminutives such as pubescent: downy and puberulent with shorter downy hairs, glabrous: smooth, or glabrescent: nearly smooth.

anterior: front or upper
apiculate: with a short, sharp tip
apomictic: fertilized within the embryo without pollination; an asexual means of reproduction
appressed: placed tightly against; opposite of divergent
auricle: ear-like appendages
bract: a modified leaf
callus: a thickened area usually at the base of the lip
capitate: like a head; with capitate hairs refers to hairs with ball-like tips
carnivorous: insect eating
cauline: on the stem
chasmogomous: with fully open, sexual flowers
cleistogamous: with closed flowers that are usually self-pollinating
column: the structure in an orchid that has both the anthers and the pistil
conduplicate: folded lengthwise
coralloid: coral-like
cordate: heart shaped
coriaceous: leathery
cornucopioid: funnel-form
crest: a series of ridges or a group of hairs; usually yellow or a color contrasting with the lip

cyme: a determinate inflorescence with central flowers opening first

cypress dome: a clonal group of bald cypress trees usually isolated in an open area

doubly resupinate: twisted around twice

emarginate: with a short projection at the tip

ephemeral: short-lived

epiphytic: living in the air

erose: with an irregular margin

fusiform: spindle shaped

glabrous: smooth

glaucous: with a whitish cast

habit: the way a plant grows

habitat: where a plant grows

isthmus: a narrowed portion between the apex and base of the lip

lip: the modified third petal of an orchid

lithophytic: growing on rocks

marcescent: withering but not falling off

mesic: of medium conditions

mucronate: a short sharp, point

mycotrophic: refers to plants that obtain their food through mycorrhizal fungi; these plants often lack chlorophyll

neotropical: of the New World tropics

nominate: the pure species, exclusive of subspecies, variety, or form

oblanceolate: narrowly oblong

panicle: a branching inflorescence similar to a raceme; the flowers stalked

pantropical: throughout the tropics

pedicellate flowers: those flowers held on pedicels or stalks

pedicellate ovary: typically the ovary of an orchid flower where the ovary and the flower stalk merge into one structure

perianth: collective term for the petals and sepals

petals: the inner part of the floral envelope

petiole: the stem portion of the leaf

pleurothallid: a species of *Pleurothallis* or closely related genera

plicate: soft and with many longitudinal ribs, often folded

posterior: lower or rear

pseudobulb: a swollen storage organ that is prominent in many epiphytic orchids and occasionally in a few genera of terrestrial orchids

pubescent: downy with short, soft hairs

raceme: an unbranched, indeterminate inflorescence with stalked flowers; branched racemes are technically panicles

reniform: kidney shaped

rhizome: an elongated basal stem, typically underground in terrestrials and along the strata (tree trunks or branches, etc.) in epiphytes

rostellum: the part of the column, usually beak shaped, that contains the stigmatic surface and to which the pollen adheres

saccate: sack shaped

saprophytes: living off decaying vegetable matter

scandent: somewhat climbing

scape: a leafless stem that arises from the base of the plant

secund: all to one side

segregate genus: a genus that has been separated from another larger genus; see *Spiranthes* for examples

sepals: the outer floral envelope

spatulate: oblong with a narrowed base

sphagnous: an area with sphagnum moss

spike: an unbranched inflorescence with sessile or unstalked flowers

spiranthoid: a member of a genus closely allied to *Spiranthes*

spur: a slender tubular or sac-like structure usually formed at the base of the lip, and often containing nectar

sympatric: growing together in the same habitat

sympodial: where each shoot has a determinate growth and arises from the base of another shoot

taxa (plural of taxon): subspecies, variety, species, form

terete: rounded

terrestrial: living in the ground

twig epiphyte: living on slender twigs, often at the periphery of the host

umbel: an inflorescence where the flower stems all arise from the same point like the spokes of an umbrella

undulate: wavy

waif: applied to a random individual occurrence

whorl: all coming from the same point on the axis in a circular pattern

Selected Bibliography

For new works on taxonomy and on additions to the orchid flora of Florida, see listings given by species in Recent Literature References for New Taxa, Combinations, and Additions to the Orchid Flora of Florida (in part 3).

Ackerman, J. D. 1995. *The Orchid Flora of Puerto Rico and the Virgin Islands.* Memoirs of the New York Botanical Garden 73.

Ames, Blanche. 1947. *Drawings of Florida Orchids.* 2nd ed. Cambridge, Mass.: Botanical Museum.

Ames, Oakes. 1904. *A Contribution to Our Knowledge of the Orchid Flora of Southern Florida.* Cambridge, Mass.: Botanical Museum.

———. 1937. *Zeuxine strateumatica* in Florida. *Botanical Museum Leaflet of Harvard University* 6:37–45.

Buswell, W. M. 1937. Orchids of the Big Cypress. *American Botanist* 43:147–53.

———. 1945. *Native Orchids of South Florida.* Bulletin of the University of Miami (Coral Gables, Fla.) 19(3).

Correll, D. S. 1946. The American species of leafless vanillas. *American Orchid Society Bulletin* 15:328–33, figs. 1–2.

———. 1950. *Native Orchids of North America North of Mexico.* Waltham, Mass.: Chronica Botanica.

Craighead, F. C. 1963. *Orchids and Other Air Plants of the Everglades National Park.*

Garay, L. A. 1980. A generic revision of the Spiranthinae. *Botanical Museum Leaflet of Harvard University* 28(4):278–425.

Goldman, D. H., and S. L. Orzell. 2000. Morphological, geographical and ecological re-evaluation of Calopogon multiflorus (Orchidaceae). *Lindleyana* 15(4):237–51.

Hamer, F. 1982. Orchids of Nicaragua. *Icones Plantarum Tropicarum,* fascicles 7–9. Sarasota, Fla.: Marie Selby Botanical Gardens.

Hammer, R. 2001. The orchids of south Florida. *NANOJ* 7(1):3–84.

International Code of Botanical Nomenclature (Tokyo Code). 1994. W. Greuter, F. R. Barrie, H. M. Burdet, W. G. Chaloner, V. Demoulin, D. L. Hawksworth, P. M. Jørgensen, D. H. Nicolson, P. C. Silva, P. Trehane, and J. McNeill. Regnum Vegetabile.

131. Yokohama, Japan. Available in full at *http://www.bgbm.fu-berlin.de/iapt/nomen-clature/code/tokyo.htm*

Luer, C. A. 1972. *The Native Orchids of Florida.* New York: New York Botanical Garden.

Nir, M. 2000. *Orchidaceae Antillanae.* New York: DAG Media.

Small, J. K. 1933. *Manual of the Southeastern Flora.* New York: published by the author. Pp. 363–99.

Wunderlin, R. P. 1998. *A Guide to the Vascular Plants of Florida.* Gainesville: University Press of Florida.

Wunderlin, R. P., and B. F. Hansen. 2000. *Atlas of Florida Vascular Plants.* Tampa: Institute for Systematic Botany, University of South Florida. CD or online. *http://www.plantatlas.usf.edu*

Three journals offer many articles of interest.

American Orchid Society Bulletin/Orchids
American Orchid Society
16700 AOS Lane
Delray Beach, FL 33446–4351
www.orchidweb.org

Florida Orchidist
South Florida Orchid Society
10801 S.W. 124 Street
Miami, FL 33176
http://members.tripod.com/~SoFlOrchidSociety/sfos1.html

North American Native Orchid Journal
North American Native Orchid Alliance
P.O. Box 772121
Ocala, FL 34477
www.naorchid.org

Photo Credits

With the following exceptions, all of the photographs in this book were taken by Paul Martin Brown. The author is especially grateful to those who so generously lent photographs. Position of photos on the page are indicated by tl= top left, tc=top center, tr= top right, c= center, t=top, b=bottom, lc=left center, rc=right center, bl=bottom left, bc=bottom center, br=bottom right, l=left; r=right.

Jim Ackerman, p. 65 bl, cr; p. 71 tr, tl, bl; p. 173 tr; p. 219 br
Stefan Ambs, p. 303 b, t
Loren Anderson p. 181 tr, cl
Sonny Bass, p. 35 t, br; p. 93 tl
Russ Clusman, p. 205 tl; p. 265 br
Frank Craighead (lent anonymously), p. 117
Kerry Dressler, p. 163 b
Roger Hammer, 27 bc; p. 75 tl; p. 163 tl; p. 173 tl; p. 215 tl; p. 219 tr, l
Hal Horwitz, p. 183
Wes Higgins, p. 293 tl, r
Jim & Rita Lassiter, p. 229 bc
Carlyle A. Luer, p. 37; p. 93 bl, r; p. 69 br; p. 215 tr, bl, br; p. 219 tc; p. 305
Miramar Orchids, p. 87 cl, tr
Cliff Pelchat, p. 109 br; p. 131 tr; p. 309
Dick Riemus, p. 27 tr
Ruben Sauleda, p. 173 bl, br; p. 303 c
George Schudel, p. 181 tl, bl; p. 303c
Miguel Soto-Arenas, p. 33 bl
John Tobe, p. 177 tl; p. 181 br
Roy Woodbury, p. 71 br; p. 97 tr

Index

Primary entries are in bold. Page numbers for species descriptions are in bold and page numbers for photographs are in italics.

Paul Martin Brown is a research associate at the University of Florida Herbarium at the Florida Museum of Natural History in Gainesville. He is founder of the North American Native Orchid Alliance and editor of the *North American Native Orchid Journal.* Brown and his partner Stan Folsom published *Wild Orchids of the Northeastern United States* in 1997.

Stan Folsom is a retired art teacher whose primary medium is watercolor. His work is represented in several permanent collections, including at the Federal Reserve Bank of Boston.